Edu-renaissance
Notes from a Globetrotting Higher Educator

Edu-renaissance
Notes from a Globetrotting Higher Educator

FENG Da Hsuan

Edited by **HO Yi Kai**

World Scientific

NEW JERSEY · LONDON · SINGAPORE · BEIJING · SHANGHAI · HONG KONG · TAIPEI · CHENNAI · TOKYO

Published by

World Scientific Publishing Co. Pte. Ltd.
5 Toh Tuck Link, Singapore 596224
USA office: 27 Warren Street, Suite 401-402, Hackensack, NJ 07601
UK office: 57 Shelton Street, Covent Garden, London WC2H 9HE

Library of Congress Cataloging-in-Publication Data
Names: Feng, Da Hsuan, 1945–   author.
Title: Edu-renaissance : notes from a globetrotting higher educator / Da Hsuan Feng.
Description: New Jersey : World Scientific, [2015] | Includes bibliographical references and index.
Identifiers: LCCN 2015038532 | ISBN 9789814632706 (alk. paper)
Subjects: LCSH: Education, Higher--Asia. | Educational change--Asia. |
    Education and globalization--Asia.
Classification: LCC LA1058 .F56 2015 | DDC 378.5--dc23
LC record available at http://lccn.loc.gov/2015038532

British Library Cataloguing-in-Publication Data
A catalogue record for this book is available from the British Library.

Copyright © 2016 by World Scientific Publishing Co. Pte. Ltd.

All rights reserved. This book, or parts thereof, may not be reproduced in any form or by any means, electronic or mechanical, including photocopying, recording or any information storage and retrieval system now known or to be invented, without written permission from the publisher.

For photocopying of material in this volume, please pay a copying fee through the Copyright Clearance Center, Inc., 222 Rosewood Drive, Danvers, MA 01923, USA. In this case permission to photocopy is not required from the publisher.

In-house Editor: Shreya Gopi

Typeset by Stallion Press
Email: enquiries@stallionpress.com

Contents

Foreword I C. David Naylor	xi
Foreword II Fu-Jia Yang	xv
Foreword III Sung-Mo Steve Kang	xix
Foreword IV Shih Choon Fong	xxi
Foreword V Carter Tseng	xxiii
Foreword VI Yitzhak Apeloig	xxvii
Preface	xxxi
Editor's Note	xxxix

On the Nobel Prize   1

    1. What Does it Take to Become a Nobel Laureate?   3
    2. Why can Two Israeli Scientists Win the Nobel Prize?   9

On University Ranking   17

    3. Global University Ranking:
       How to Understand such a Measurement?   19
    4. University Ranking: Albatross or Incentive?   27

5. Beyond 2011 QS Asia Universities Ranking:
   Lesson Learned from Association of American Universities
   (AAU) for Association of East Asia Research Universities
   (AEARU 东亚研究型大学协会)   31
6. In Search of Humanistic Excellence:
   The Morehouse Experience   37

Public Policy and Education   43

7. Autonomy, Accountability and Governance:
   Challenges of East Asian Public Universities
   in the 21st Century   45
8. Some Thoughts on the Bayh-Dole Act of 1980   53

IT and Education   55

9. A Lecture Across 10,000 Miles:
   The 1993 Nobel Laureate's Physics Lecture Delivered
   from Dallas to Singapore   57
10. Khan Academy:
    Could this be the Onset of Global Undergraduate Education's
    Metamorphic Transformation in the 21st Century?   61

The Budding Universities   67

11. Shantou University:
    An Example of Dynamical Transformation in 21st Century
    Asia Pacific Higher Education   69
    Annex: Impressions of Shantou University — My Seven-Year
    Summary   81
12. University of Macau:
    The Creation of a New Asian University   93
13. A $2 Billion New Campus:
    The Unthinkable Transformation of the
    University of Macau in the 21st Century!   103
14. Korea Advanced Institute of Science and Technology
    (KAIST): Ascension of Asia's Rise in Higher Education   109

15. An Unusual Perspective on Higher Education
    Value-Adding to a Young Asian University:
    Comments Delivered at the Universiti Teknologi PETRONAS   117
16. BINUS UNIVERSITY:
    My First Trip to Indonesia!   131

The New Era   **145**

17. "One Belt One Road", Supercontinent and Neo-Renaissance:
    The Development of Universities in the 21st Century
    and Beyond   147
18. "Basic" and "Practical":
    The Dilemma of Modern Research Universities
    in the 21st Century   161
19. Challenges Faced by Asia Pacific Universities
    in the 21st Century   167
20. Why Canadian Universities should Collaborate with Asia   173
21. A Tale of Three Speeds:
    Challenges for Southeast and South Asia and Taiwan
    Universities (SATU) in the 21st Century   177
22. "Google my late father?":
    What Could or may Happen to India, China
    and United States in the 21st Century   185

New Ideas   **195**

23. A Game-Changing Model for Higher Education?:
    On the University of Nottingham Ningbo China (UNNC)   197
24. Private Universities:
    A Future Force in Global Leadership in Asia Pacific   205
25. Residential College and Asia Today   219
26. New Angle on Obama's Recent Speech on
    "Affordable Higher Education"   225
27. Mindset of the Soul:
    The Meaning of Liberal Arts Education   229

28. California Institute and Technology (Caltech) and National
    Southwest Union University (NSWUU 国立西南联合大学):
    An Unexpected and Extraordinary Similarity
    in Different Space-Time   239
29. Is Nobel Laureate Shuji Nakamura a Scientific Genius?   245
30. Intellectual Bandwidth:
    Holy Grail of Education in the 21st Century   249

On India   253

31. A Practical Example of the Five Dictums of President
    Ma Ying-Jeou:
    National Tsing Hua University in India   255
32. India and I   261

On China   271

33. Challenges for Higher Education:
    A Reflection of My 100 Trips to China   273
34. "Ladies and Gentlemen, there is an Eight Hundred-Pound
    Gorilla in the Room!"   289
35. Stealing Books is not Stealing   297
36. China's "The Great Accelerator": A Decision of Science
    and Politics?   307

On Israel   313

37. "Because We Have Seven World Class Universities!"   315
38. On Aaron Ciechanover   327

On Russia   337

39. "If He is the Best, Give it to Him" (Nikita Kruschedov):
    On Why the Russians are so Good at Science   339
40. An Action-Packed and Intellectually Stimulating Visit
    to Moscow's Scientific and Technological Communities   355

Noteworthy People   365

41. The Two Nobel Laureates Overlapped in the McDermott
    Suite of UTD   367
42. On Nobel Laureate Vitaly Ginzburg   371
43. On Paul Barbara   375
44. Impressions of NCKU and Zheng Cheng-Gong (郑成功)   379
    Annex: My Departure from NCKU   381
45. A Global Intentional Effort: The Lifetime Contribution
    to Tsing Hua by Mei Yiqi (梅贻琦)   387
46. On S. S. Chern (陈省身)   393
47. On Chen Ning Yang (杨振宁)   399
48. "What Physics Have You Done Lately?":
    On Sam C. C. Ting (丁肇中)   405
49. The Supreme Courage of a Chinese Intellectual:
    Preface to a Memorial Volume Dedicated
    to Prof Jin-Quan Chen (陈金全)   409
50. A "Thank You" Note to Iris Chang (张纯如)   413
51. Lee Kuan Yew (李光耀) and Education   415

Appendix

Where it all Begins…   421
Congressional Delegation (CODEL) Weldon and Asia:
    A Personal Account

Foreword I

On the Globalization of Higher Education, Rosetta Stones, and the Improbable Feng Da Hsuan

C. David Naylor

President Emeritus, The University of Toronto

The volume in your hands is a fascinating collection of essays written by Professor Feng Da Hsuan, an award-winning nuclear physicist who has held varied leadership roles in higher education and advanced research in the US and east Asia. The essays are selected from scores of reports and reflections generated by Feng over the last decade in his travel as an emissary for four universities — one in the US, two in Taiwan, and now the University of Macau, where he is Director of Global Affairs and Special Advisor to Rector.

While his academic focus was in basic science, Feng Da Hsuan defies categorization. He is both an effective multi-lingual communicator and a tireless connector of people and institutions. Somewhat improbably, Feng also has a diplomat's grasp of nuance, a lawyer's eye for detail, and a journalist's gift for synthesis and story-telling.

Readers will find out more about Professor Feng's unique background as they read this book, and I will provide only a few snippets here. Feng was born in India in 1945. His father, Paul, had graduated from New York University's law school in 1937, but worked as a journalist in New Delhi. His mother was a Juilliard-educated pianist and music teacher. From India, the family moved to Singapore, where Feng spent most of his childhood. He was a Malaysian citizen when Singapore joined Malaysia, and then a Singaporean citizen when Singapore and Malaysia parted ways. After a spell in civil engineering at Singapore Polytechnic, Feng moved to the US, where he earned undergraduate and doctoral degrees in physics, before undertaking postdoctoral studies in both the US and UK.

Feng then embarked on a highly successful academic career — teaching, publishing ground-breaking research, holding a professorial chair at Drexel University, directing a US National Science Foundation program in theoretical physics, taking time out to serve as vice president of a multi-national high-tech company, and eventually finding his way to the University of Texas at Dallas, where he served as Vice President of Research and Economic Development from 2001 to 2007.

Feng followed his heart and moved to Taiwan in 2007, becoming a Senior Executive Vice President at National Cheng Kung University, and later, Vice President of Global Strategy, Development, and Evaluation at National Tsing Hua University. In the fall of 2014, Feng crossed the South China Sea to join the University of Macau and his former Texas colleague, Rector Wei Zhao.

A skeptical reader at this point might nonetheless say: "Fair enough. But why are Professor Feng's insights worth reading?" Answering that question requires a brief examination of the context of modern higher education.

It is trite to observe that the late 20th and early 21st centuries have been a period of accelerating 'globalization'. I use that term neutrally, to signify simply the movement, variously physical or virtual, of goods, services, ideas, and people across national borders. But sadly, at a point in human history when international ties and cross-cultural understanding should be deeper and stronger than ever, we have also witnessed the emergence of counter-forces in the form of renewed tribalism, fundamentalism, and sectarian violence.

In this troubled context, it is arguable that universities have become the world's institutional Rosetta Stones. By the nature of their teachings, the best universities have long transported domestic students across time and space, challenging their assumptions and beliefs, and opening their minds in ways that promote an empathetic understanding of our common humanity. And it is also true that for centuries, the best and brightest students from around the world have travelled abroad for higher education.

This latter phenomenon has been massively intensified, however, due to the fact that some hundreds of thousands of students travel abroad each year to be educated at a foreign university or college, often in another language, always in another cultural context. Origins and destinations have also been transformed in the last 25 years, with a dramatic widening of the number of countries and institutions that are part of this international traffic.

The above-noted changes in the geography of higher education are most startling in the Asia-Pacific Region. As more universities in Asia rise to global prominence, they are profoundly changing student traffic patterns and transforming the collaborative landscape in higher education and advanced research. These patterns and partnerships both reflect and reinforce emerging global alliances, such as the strong ties being forged between China and much of the African continent. Also notable is the repatriation of faculty talent by Asia-Pacific universities — a phenomenon that has helped to change the culture of many of those institutions.

These dramatic shifts in the landscape of higher education are what led Professor Da Hsuan Feng to call this an era of 'Edu-Renaissance'. The essays he shares in this book provide keen insights into these trends and events. They chronicle the development of universities, regions, and nations, with particular attention to the challenges and opportunities that have arisen as Asian universities gain — or regain — strength and influence. But Feng's short papers do more than that. An inveterate globetrotter with an extraordinary ability to forge relationships among people and institutions, Feng has an eagle eye for cultural differences and strategic strengths and weaknesses in institutions and systems. His findings are set out with his characteristic charm and enthusiasm — but these travelogues are leavened with important lessons in governance, administration, strategy, and geopolitics.

As the relentless social and technological forces of globalization continue to shape higher education across the world, it would be folly to overstate the impact that one individual such as Feng might have.

However, if universities are indeed the institutional Rosetta Stones of our time, then Feng is arguably the sector's Jean-Francois Champollion. Champollion drew on a unique set of linguistic gifts in using the Rosetta Stone to decipher hieroglyphics. And Feng in turn has drawn on a truly unique set of life experiences that help him to decipher and explain the universities of one region or nation to colleagues in other countries or continents. His perceptive writings and peripatetic career illuminate the rise of Asian universities and the growth of a pan-Asian and globalized outlook in those institutions, even as they sharply delineate the universality of challenges facing universities all over our fast-changing world.

Note: Carved in 196 BC and discovered in Egypt in 1799, the Rosetta Stone carries identical messages in two languages and three scripts. Until its discovery, scores of interpreters and linguists had struggled to decipher Egyptian hieroglyphs. Since then, the Rosetta Stone has been both a priceless treasure of the ancient world, housed in the British Museum, and a metaphor for anything that helps to decode languages and facilitate cross-cultural understanding and communication.

Foreword II

Fu-Jia Yang

Academician, Chinese Academy of Sciences
Former President, Fudan University
Former Chancellor, University of Nottingham

If there is absolute joy in writing a foreword for a book, it would be for this one, authored by my friend of 36 years, Da Hsuan Feng!

I first met Da Hsuan in person in 1979 at the Niels Bohr Institute of the University of Copenhagen when he was just at his fledgling stage as a physicist. However, I had known of him a few years before that because he was one of the Chinese American scientists who immediately made contact with Chinese colleagues after China opened to the world in 1977. Since that time, we have become close friends.

Ever since I became an Internet user, probably sometime in the mid- to late-nineties, I started to receive emails from Da Hsuan. This was roughly the period when Da Hsuan made the transition from being a "pure" research physicist to his new career in the corporate world and later as a senior university administrator in Texas, Taiwan and now Macau. Mind you, these are not your everyday emails about mundane events. They are always well-constructed and well-crafted articles about Da Hsuan's professional encounters.

There are three aspects about Da Hsuan which make him a unique individual in the intellectual world.

First, Da Hsuan is a successful physicist. His research in nuclear physics, quantum optics and quantum chaos is well recognized. Only a very small percentage of physicists in the United States, and for that matter, the world, can become a Fellow of the American Physical Society. He is one such physicist. During his tenure at Drexel University, he also held the M. Russell Wehr Chair Professor of Physics. Such recognitions are very rare for most academics.

Second, with a successful career as a physicist, most people would go all the way until retirement. This is where Da Hsuan is unusual. In 1997, he made the jump into the corporate world. Going from the academic to the corporate world per se is not unusual. I can think of and know some outstanding academics taking sabbaticals from universities to carry out research in corporate labs such as Bell Laboratories. But few, in fact, I know of none like Da Hsuan, would enter the corporate world as a Vice President to accumulate under his belt what Da Hsuan refers to as P&L (profit and loss) experience.

Finally, Da Hsuan is unusual because he was able to learn from his corporate experience, in which he managed to put people of different expertise together for a common goal to work in universities, as senior administrator. This I believe allowed him to bring a perspective into research universities which is at best uncommon and very much needed in the 21st century. Here, I would like to underscore that many universities' faculty members in the world would go from being pure scientists to higher education administrators. That is hardly unusual. I for one did just that. But Da Hsuan seems to have the knack of leaving his comfort zone. He went from the corporate world to become a university administrator in Texas. Then he left his acquired comfort zone in Texas and went to Taiwan's two top universities as senior administrator. Again, I know of a number of people who would return to Asia from America, but usually they would be returning to the part of Asia they grew up in. But Da Hsuan, who grew up in Singapore, went to Taiwan and now Macau. Both were totally alien to him prior to his arrival. Of course, by doing so, he said that "it greatly broadens my intellectual bandwidth!" Fusing West (especially the United States) and East (Taiwan and Macau,) he has enriched himself utterly!

There is no doubt that if Da Hsuan only had rich and robust professional and life experiences, but not the profound passion to write, this book would have been an impossibility. In the past twenty years, I have seen his relentless outstanding writings. This is one aspect in which he truly excels. Da Hsuan is one of the rare individuals who is able to observe with hawkish eyes, noticing events which most people do not or cannot, and linking seemingly unrelated events in an utterly natural manner. With such skills and leveraging his flair for the English language, he is able to portray his rich experiences in the most elegant, succinct, and mind you, convincing manner.

In chapter after chapter of this book, I think the reader will detect transparently this style of writing. It is a book which takes the readers on a rich excursion of global higher education. Few can do this like Da Hsuan can, with seeming ease. Indeed, I would say that in personifying himself with such writings, the world is able to see the enormous global transformation and challenges higher education faces.

This is a must-read book for all!

Foreword III

Sung-Mo Steve Kang

President, KAIST
Chancellor Emeritus, University of California, Merced

I have known Professor Da Hsuan Feng for a long time as a close colleague in higher education administration in the United States and Asia. We have much in common. We both attended universities in Asia and the US for undergraduate and graduate studies, and became faculty members and high level administrators after significant industry experience. More interestingly, we both have served administration in Asian institutions following the US institutions.

Professor Feng is a rare authority in linking higher educations of North America and Asia, especially Greater China and Southeast Asia. He is an outstanding scientist, teacher and expert in high education administration, and an impeccable writer and global networker. As such, he has delved into matters of globalizing higher education with keen insight and enviable experience in industry as a researcher, and in academia as a professor and high-level administrator.

This book will be a valuable guide and a must-read for educators, especially for academic leaders seeking globalization. It covers a broad range of interesting topics which are rarely covered in other books on higher education.

Foreword IV

Shih Choon Fong

*Professor and Former President, National University of Singapore
Founding President, King Abdullah University of Science and Technology*

When Da Hsuan invited me to write a foreword to his book, I agreed without hesitation. Never before have I written a foreword for someone I have known less than four months. But I could not resist something so different and unusual.

Da Hsuan and I met for the first time in July 2015 when we served together on the Academic Advisory Council of Malaysia's Universiti Teknologi Petronas. In the course of the Council's meetings in Kuala Lumpur and Ipoh, what I discovered about Da Hsuan stunned me. I wondered to myself how it was that our paths had not intersected earlier. It was later that he told me the same thought had crossed his mind.

Both of us grew up in Singapore. He was educated in the Chinese stream and I in the English stream. After completing Secondary Four (Senior Cambridge in my case), we both decided against the conventional path of going to the university. Instead, we went to the Singapore Polytechnic — I to study civil and mechanical engineering and Da Hsuan to study building and civil engineering. Singapore Polytechnic was and still is a tertiary technical institution with a mission to train mid-level technical personnel. This was not the path most of the more academic-minded youngsters of Singapore would take. Indeed, it was unthinkable in our time.

After Singapore Poly, we yet again went in the same direction, going to the United States for advanced degrees. I completed a PhD in engineering science at Harvard while he received a PhD in theoretical physics from the University of Minnesota. I joined the corporate R&D Lab of General Electric in upstate New York and subsequently found my way into an academic career. This eventually led me to serve as President of the National University of Singapore and Founding President of King Abdullah University of Science and Technology in Saudi Arabia. Da Hsuan also embarked on an academic career and rose to become Vice President of the University of Texas at Dallas, of National Cheng Kung University and of National Tsing Hua University. In between these, he took on the role of vice president in a Fortune 500 company where on a day-to-day basis, he worried about his company's profit and loss, an experience I daresay would be alien to the typical faculty member.

A globetrotter in every sense of the word, Da Hsuan has traveled widely, encountered a broad spectrum of people, taught in universities as well as served in various capacities in organizations on both sides of the Pacific. Through his collection of speeches and essays, Da Hsuan shares his thoughts and insights on higher education and its humanistic dimension with enthusiasm, passion and perceptiveness. His anecdotes and personal experiences in higher education across the globe make compelling reading, more so when one needs to chew on his message in each chapter.

Perhaps an important but perhaps not immediately evident message in this remarkable book is that the outcome of education is UNPREDICTABLE. A youngster's growth path can have multiple "bifurcation" points, and each point can take one to a new level of understanding of oneself and of humanity.

On hindsight, had Da Hsuan and I not pursued our early studies at the Singapore Polytechnic, our lives would likely have turned out very differently. We took a path less traveled and it has made all the difference. There is a time-honored maxim: "fortune favors the prepared mind". Da Hsuan was prepared for change. I am most impressed by how he has reaped the utmost out of each of his life's changes, and leveraged it for the betterment of higher education, and by extension for humanity, both in the United States and now in Asia Pacific.

A good book will leave a good taste in one's mind. This is such a book. Savor it!

Foreword V

Carter Tseng

Founder and CEO, Little Dragon Foundation
Board of Directors, USA Committee of 100
Board of Trustees, USA Give2Asia Foundation

It is my great privilege to have been invited to write the Foreword for Professor Feng Da Hsuan's book *Edu-renaissance: Notes from a Globetrotting Higher Educator*, which addresses a topic most relevant to our contemporaries in higher education and innovation. This book is a diverse collection of writings by a scholar and scientist who has made a very successful career in bridging science, technology and education, working for the past 20 years in the United States and in Asia. I am fascinated by how the author transitioned from being an already very well-respected and tenured Physics professor to becoming a global champion of education with a broad impact on society, all triggered by a talk he attended in 1995, regarding the potential impact of the fledging Internet. The content of the book is extraordinary, embodying decades of Professor Feng's work and expressed in a language that is in itself a masterpiece of artwork.

Professor Feng is a longtime friend. He was born in India, grew up in Singapore and went to the United States for higher education and his subsequent professional career. Then, after 2007, he relocated to Taiwan and Macau, where he transformed himself into a truly well-traveled educator. The multicultural Professor Feng is uniquely qualified to share his insight on higher education due to his rare set of well-rounded, cross-border experiences accumulated over the decades at prestigious higher education institutions. Professor Feng's visionary approach can be seen from his insightful discussions ranging from Chinese and Jewish Nobel Laureates to Mei Yiqi, a great Chinese humanist and educator; from Lee Kuan Yew to Zheng Cheng-gong who came six centuries before him; from India and China on the one hand to Russia and USA on the other; from lofty ideals of a supercontinent and "One belt, One road" to practical concerns of university ranking and budding universities in Asia.

After reading the book, I was enthralled by the originality and eloquence of Professor Feng and the width and depth of the many aspects he covered. Professor Feng discusses a series of diversified, but higher education-centric topics. His perspective is well informed, based on a collection of his own firsthand globetrotting experience as well as conversations with other well-known associates.

Professor Feng spends several chapters of the book convincingly addressing the central question of "What does it take to win a Nobel Prize?" What attributes constitute an effective education ecosystem and culture? This book could not have appeared at a more opportune time, since in October this year (2015) a mainland Chinese scientist, Dr. Tu You-you, became China's first natively born and bred Nobel Laureate. It is perhaps with some irony and even sarcasm that she is being referred to by media as the Professor of "three noes": no post-graduate degree, no study or research experience abroad, and no membership with any Chinese national academy.

I'm also particularly interested in the topic of the "Global Ranking of Asian Universities". How important and how valid is this really? This controversial topic is handled in an analytic, fair, and convincing manner. As a well-traveled educator, Professor Feng gives in-depth reports on universities as diverse as Shantou University and University of Macau of China, KAIST of South Korea, NTU of Singapore, UTD of the US and Technion of Israel.

Another interesting topic is "Challenges of the Asian Universities in the 21st Century", as Professor Feng poses the question: "On what must we focus to evolve Asian universities to become globally first class"? Also, what can we learn from the low SAT average of the highly effective Morehouse College (which produced the Nobel Laureate Martin Luther King Jr.), that transforms students into humanistic leaders because its curriculum teaches "social responsibility, integrity and honesty"? What role do global connectivity and cross-pollination of ideas play in higher education? How do we produce graduates who are bilingual and bi-cultural, and prepared to become the next generation of professionals who will strengthen cross-border interaction and together solve global social challenges? Some striking examples are introduced throughout the book to help illustrate the lessons, including numerous Nobel Laureates with whom Professor Feng has interacted, and many model universities, such as Morehouse College. Professor Feng believes the fundamental purpose of higher education is to create a critical mass of educated people who serve as the basis for human and social transformation.

"The creation of a Neo-Renaissance in the supercontinent", a brand new concept proposed by Professor Feng, resonates with my Little Dragon Foundation's vision of creating a Global Innovation Ecosystem (GIE) that links together all innovation hubs to create cross-pollination, diversity and to boost innovation and bring about benefits on a global level.

Professor Feng provides deep insight into all of the above questions and sheds light on some of the emerging trends of Asia's higher education and the people who will inevitably shape and propel Asia into becoming a global education force in the 21st century. It is fitting that Professor Feng has recently relocated to the University of Macau, which has been charged to lead Macau in crossing over a critical threshold in the major transformation from the super Asian Las Vegas to a fully developed modern city on the China coast.

Finally, the name of the book is most appropriate in describing Professor Feng, who is known for his impressive, multi-faceted resume. Professor Feng is a person equally comfortable in the East and the West, in corporate management and in college administration, and in nuclear physics as well as art, literature and philosophy. As the title suggests, Professor Feng has truly been a globetrotting advocate for education. I salute Professor Feng and congratulate him on the publication of this vital and incomparable book, written by a true modern Renaissance Man!

This "Edu-renaissance" masterpiece is indeed valuable to the entire education community. But at the same time, it should not be overlooked by anyone interested in the future of technology and modernity. I strongly recommend this as food for thought to aspiring young leaders, professionals, entrepreneurs and philanthropists.

Foreword VI

Yitzhak Apeloig

Technion President Emeritus
Distinguished University Professor,
Nahum Guzik Distinguished Academic Chair,
Schulich Faculty of Chemistry,
Technion-Israel Institute of Technology

The World's university academic system has undergone a dramatic revolution in the last two decades, a revolution which still continues. Two important ingredients in this revolution are: (1) the fast rise of the universities in Mainland China, as well as in other Asia Pacific countries such as Taiwan, Singapore and South Korea; and (2) the appearance on the academic scene of terms such as ranking of universities, departments and individual researchers, citations, impact factors and other "quantitative" measures of research productivity and quality. The book of Da Hsuan Feng is an excellent and enjoyable vehicle to gain important insights into this ongoing academic revolution.

A short time after I was nominated to be the President of the Technion — Israel Institute of Technology in 2001, I visited the University of Texas in Dallas (UTD) and met for the first time Professor Da Hsuan Feng who was then the Vice-President for Research at UTD. After this enjoyable first meeting I was added to Da Hsuan's mailing list and began to receive his frequent e-mails in which he discussed various issues which were on the international academic agenda and shared his impressions of visits to various universities around the world, his meetings with Nobel Laureates, and more. As a recently-nominated university president, I found Feng's articles inspiring and illuminating. From each article, I have learned something new! In particular, Feng's articles about the vast changes that were taking place in the universities in China opened for me a window into a world that I had little knowledge about. Many of these insightful observations are now collected in this book.

Da Hsuan Feng's personal history places him in the unique position to write a book about 21st century higher education institutions. He has academic and university leadership experience both in the United States and in the Far East (Taiwan and China). In addition, he has traveled extensively, becoming acquainted with the academic traditions, strengths and weaknesses of many other countries such as India, Russia and Israel. For 20 years, Feng was a "regular" faculty member, a chaired professor of Physics at Drexel University in Philadelphia, USA. In 1997, he changed his career path dramatically and joined the high-tech industry as a Senior Vice President. In 2000, he moved into the world of university leadership, becoming the Vice-President for Research of the University of Texas at Dallas (UTD). In 2007, he made another monumental change in his career and moved to Asia, where he already has held senior administrative positions at three elite universities. Between 2007 and 2011, he was Senior Executive Vice President of National Cheng Kung University, and then became Senior Vice President of National Tsing Hua University, both in Taiwan. In 2012, he moved to China becoming Special Advisor to the Rector (President) and Director of Global Affairs of the University of Macau, one of the fastest-growing universities in Asia Pacific today.

The book is divided into several sections, each with its own deep insights into various aspects of the modern academic world. It starts with some reflections on the Nobel Prize, the most important scientific prize and (regrettably) almost the only scientific prize which draws attention of the general public. Feng chooses to draw attention to two Israeli scientists, Aaron Ciechanover and Avram Hersko from the Technion, who won the Nobel Prize in Chemistry in 2004. His insights into the reasons that allowed scientists from this small, relatively young country with only eight million people to win the Nobel Prize are fascinating and teach an important lesson about how to achieve academic excellence. The next four chapters deal with "university ranking" which has become an important factor in the way that politicians, policy making, students, faculty members and the general public judge universities. In other chapters Feng discusses highly important policy issues to any university leader, such as: public policy and education, IT and education, "basic" vs. "practical" research, the role of Interdisciplinary Disciplines in university education, and shares his interesting thoughts about what may happen to higher education in the 21st century. Several chapters are devoted to Feng's impressions and the lessons which he gained from his visits to leading universities in the US, Canada, China, India, Russia, Israel and other countries. These chapters have important insights into the special unique features of each of these academic systems. As an Israeli, I can state that Feng's articles dealing with Israel's universities and Israeli Nobel Laureates are enlightening, grasping the essence of the "Israeli spirit".

This "Edu-renaissance" book by Da Hsuan Feng is a "tour de force" of the 21st century fast-changing global academic world. It highlights some of the most important issues facing university leaders and provides important insights into the fast-developing universities in China and the Asia Pacific region. Each of the chapters has a "personal touch" with interesting impressions from great scientists and academic leaders, making the book a pleasure to read. I learned much and enjoyed very much reading this book!

Preface

This book is about my experience of higher education!

Prior to 1995, I was a "cocooned" professor of physics, leading a tranquil and what I thought to be an intellectually satisfying life. My professional activities ever since I became a physicist revolved entirely around teaching undergraduates and graduate students, mentoring postgraduate students and postdoctoral fellows, carrying out an active theoretical physics research program and organizing physics conferences with global colleagues. In addition, because we have to "publish or perish," nearly all my writings were of a technical nature, for publications. Last but not least, as the old saying goes, "a vision without funding is hallucination." I was also deeply involved in writing proposals to funding agencies for the aim of executing a robust research program!

While my life was exciting for me as a professional academician, it was essentially identical to the thousands of other colleagues across the United States and the world. If that was all I had, this book could not and should not have been written.

As the old cliché says, "Life is unpredictable!" On a spring day in 1995, a serendipitous event took place and changed my professional life for good. The result was that I wrote my first non-technical article.

This article described how profoundly impressed I was at a talk I heard at the neighboring university, the University of Pennsylvania. The talk was by the congressman representing the district of my home then. His name is the Honorable Curt Weldon. The essence of his talk was about how the fledgling internet (in 1995, it was surely fledgling) could become a vital driving force in the intellectual and economic development of a region. Such a talk by a politician, a Republican no less (since I am Democrat-leaning) was for me indeed mind-opening and provoking. For the first time, it made me realize that true and meaningful political actions are de facto public policy–making ones. I suddenly come to the realization that they indeed could have real consequences for everyone's everyday life!

Thinking back, attending that talk was truly transformational for me. Virtually immediately afterwards, I began thinking about my professional life in an intellectually broader sense. I also began to appreciate, understand and collaborate with people who are entirely on terra incognita to me. Indeed, that event and that single writing exercise in 1995 became my subconscious launching pad for the subsequent two decades of re-born professional life and a habit of writing about my day-to-day new experiences. The result of this habit is this book!

In the last two decades, I ceased to be a cocooned physics professor.

After a mental incubation period of 1995–1997, in September of 1997, I plunged into a different professional career and left my secured position as a chaired-professor of physics. In retrospect, it was the first time I had realized I could not resist challenges, even those unknown ones. I could tell from the looks of many of my colleagues when I mentioned to them that I am pursuing a new life, that they were somewhat, or even very, aghast as to how I could leave such a secured life.

Indeed, in 1997, my professional life took a big change when I became a Senior Manager, and later, a Vice President of a for-profit high-tech company. This lasted for four years. Then I became Vice President of a research university (the University of Texas at Dallas) for seven years. This was followed by the next seven years in which I made an even bigger change: I left the United States, where I had lived for four decades, and became a Senior Vice President of two top research universities in Taiwan, National Cheng Kung University (国立成功大学) and National Tsing Hua University (国立清华大学). Finally, in September of 2014, I assumed the position of Director of Global Affairs and Special Advisor of the Rector of the fledgling University of Macau.

There is no doubt that my professional experiences in the past two decades bestowed on me unprecedented and multidimensional intellectual growth. Before 1997, my wife called me "an absolute physicist," who had virtually no side interests. After 1997, I literally became like a little kid walking into "Toys R Us!" Prior to 1997, I could only be fascinated by the next technical paper I read. After that, I became fascinated by nearly everything surrounding me.

Working for a for-profit company from 1997–2000 with P&L (profit and loss) issues, my day-to-day concern switched from "how to tackle that physics problem" to how to ensure what we do results in "P" and not "L"! Every decision we made in the company depended on developing sensible business models.

In addition, by securing large-scale technical projects, I had to assemble people of multitude backgrounds to work as a cohesive team with a common goal. Even more importantly, I learned to pay less attention to academic qualifications and focused more on what one can do for the project! In fact, I became cognizant that a Ph.D. was not the gateway to "ability," a culture which academic institutions seemed to absolutely adhere to!

Perhaps the most important lesson I took away from this experience was to recognize the importance of the broad and deep government-academic relationship (GAR) developed since World War II. Although in the early 80s I spent two marvelous years as program manager for theoretical physics at the National Science Foundation, it was not until I worked for a high-tech corporation that I became fully aware of the multi-dimensional GAR. During this period, I had to have professional interactions with vast number of U.S. Federal Government Agencies. Not only did I work with funding agencies such as the Department of Defense and Department of Education and so on in the Federal Government of the United States, I also had to learn to work closely with legislators and their staff members, and most importantly, I learned how to collaborate with the lobbyists, the so-called "K-Street" folks. These experiences which I could not possibly have acquired as a cocooned professor enormously benefited my next several academic positions, both in the United States and Asia.

The secret of success, as Congressman Weldon once told me, is "not how big your roller-deck is, but how many people will return your call when you call them!" To do so, one must possess a wide intellectual bandwidth. Therefore, the most invaluable lesson I learned in my years in the corporate world is the profound importance of EQ and connectivity. I learned to be comfortable with people and allow people to be comfortable with me, independent of disciplines and indeed, walks of life.

Armed with knowledge which as an academician I would not have had, in 2000, I began my next position as the Vice President responsible for developing the research strategy of a solo research university in a technological advanced area known as Dallas-Fort Worth (DFW) in the United States. This position presented to me new and exciting challenges.

It was truly remarkable that while DFW was then one of the major centers of telecommunication and defense industries, it lacked higher education institutions that could serve as DFW's intellectual source and providers. For example, in the year 2000, the northern suburb of Dallas known as Richardson was called "the telecom corridor." Global telecom corporations such as Texas Instruments, Nortel, Ericsson, Alcatel and so on either have or had their corporate or North American headquarters in DFW. The same was also true for aerospace and defense giants. Corporations such as Raytheon, Lockheed-Martins, Bell Helicopters and so on also have a massive and palpable manufacturing presence in the region. I think no one would dispute that industries and academic institutions must go hand-in-hand. One without the other is de facto "one hand clapping"! However, unlike Boston Route-128 and Silicon Valley, where outstanding universities first existed before industry flourished, the reverse would be true for DFW. This made raising the research ambience of the solo research university in DFW not only necessary, but a must. Building a meaningful and seamless relationship with industry in the region was a critical step for any research oriented university. It was to this drumbeat that I arrived at DFW!

As Vice President of a research university, I had the opportunity to reach out to my counterparts in many universities in Texas and beyond the border of United States. During my tenure, I took the opportunity to visit many universities from coast to coast in the United States, India, Asia Pacific and Europe. At every visit, because of my portfolio, I was able to probe deeper into the various aspects of different universities. It was during this period that I began to realize the generic complexities of running and organizing universities and the fundamental importance of consistent and continuous leadership, strategy and courage. With these three ingredients, a university strives. Without them, it can, and generally will, falter.

Perhaps the most important lesson I took away from my seven years at DFW was how complex and how fundamentally important it was to create multi-university research collaborations. For as long as I can remember, universities have tended to work in isolation from one another. This was partly because of inter-university competition and partly because of the inherent culture of academic activities. Yet, by the time I arrived at DFW, which was at the beginning of the 21st century, the world had, as Thomas Friedman would say, "become flat!" This flatness made academic institutions genuinely recognize that inter-university collaborations, both nationally and internationally, were not only vital, but a must. With this attitude, a university is relevant. Without it, it can easily become irrelevant!

In my seven years at DFW, I was given the responsibility with my counterparts in several top universities across Texas to develop a consortium specifically for the science and technology research of nanotechnology. To get this consortium off the ground, apart from the university I worked for needing to enhance intellectual strength by recruiting additional faculty members from all corners of the globe as well as creating seamless relationships with existing strengths within the university, the universities involved in the consortium also needed to develop a working relationship to promote the "common good." Last but not least, we needed to also work closely with various Federal Government agencies as well as Local and Federal legislators to ensure funding was forthcoming and continuous.

In reflection, had I not acquired the corporate experiences which I could not possibly have acquired in a university, before coming to DFW, I am convinced that it would have been next to impossible for me to carry out my day-to-day job as well as the development of the consortium. This experience, subtle or transparent, has now made me a firm believer that every position one holds in one's life is in fact a preparation for the next job!

In 2007, my professional life took a monumental turn. I packed up and came to Asia. Very fortunately, despite vigorously protesting, my wife came with me.

Many people I met since I moved to Asia would inevitably ask me the perennial question: "Why?" I presume my move was especially perplexing because my background simply did not fit the places I relocated to: Taiwan and Macau. After all, I was born in India, grew up in Singapore and went to the United States for higher education and my subsequent professional career. Until I arrived in Taiwan, I had never had real experiences, cultural or otherwise, with these two places.

Perhaps the best answer I can give is the old Chinese saying, "Fallen leaves return to their roots!" (落叶归根). Despite the fact that, as my American friends would say, "I am as Yankee as can be," the fact that I had essentially undergone all my advanced education in the United States, and the fact that before I came to Taiwan in 2007, I could not comfortably give a talk or write an article, technically or otherwise, in Chinese, my cultural heritage which I acquired in my fourteen formative years in Singapore was always sub-consciously a part of my DNA. Therefore, when President Michael Ming-Chiao Lai (赖明诏), the new President of National Cheng Kung University in 2007, and three years later, President Lih-J. Chen (陈力俊), the then-President of National Tsing Hua University, recruited me to be their Senior Executive Vice President and Senior Vice President, respectively, I simply followed my heart and could not resist the challenge. I accepted these two positions without any hesitation.

As far as Asian research universities are concerned, there was a rude awakening in the 21st century. In the 20th century, Asian research universities, with the exception of Japan, essentially were in their dormant state. While calling themselves "research" in nature, these universities were primarily "teaching" in nature, and most teaching was at the undergraduate level. It was not an exaggeration that many outstanding products of these universities tended to, and inevitably would, pursue advanced degrees in the Western world and eventually create their professional careers there.

It was quite remarkable that almost as soon as the 21st century came around, higher education in Asia seemed to alter fundamentally. I presume this was partly due to the fact that the economic ascension of many Asian Pacific nations had reached the threshold to be able to "afford" the pouring of financial resources into higher education, for prestige if not for nation building. Higher education financial projects such as "985" and "211" in the Mainland and the 5Y50B (or five-year 50 billion new Taiwan dollars) in Taiwan began to mushroom all across Asia. Also, I am convinced that it was partly because in 2003, the first ranking of global universities, now called the Academic Ranking of World Universities (ARWU), carried out by Professor Nian-Cai Liu (刘念才) of Shanghai Jiaotong University, emerged. Professor Liu's work literally opened up the floodgates for many different rankings. Almost instantly, these rankings not only forced Asian universities to recognize the importance of embedding themselves into the global landscape, but they also fundamentally altered the mindset of universities at all levels as well as how nations and societies-at-large viewed them.

It was not by design but it certainly was to this drumbeat that I arrived in Asia!

In my seven years in Taiwan, I made extensive and in-depth visits to a vast number of higher educational institutions in Taiwan and beyond. Once I arrived in Taiwan, except for North Korea, all corners of Asia were within my reach. I could easily go to northern Asia (Japan and South Korea,) Mainland China, Southeast Asia (Vietnam, Thailand, Malaysia, Singapore and Indonesia) and South Asia (India) without any or much time lag!

Prior to my arrival in Asia in 2007, I had made well over 200 visits to the region. Only after I arrived, however, did I begin to realize that my understanding of how Asian higher education operates was at best superficial. In the seven years in Taiwan, I climbed one of the steepest and truly satisfying learning curves I have ever experienced. I also participated in and organized many Asian higher education policies conferences where I could listen to and learn what education leaders in Asia thought! In my seven years in Asia, I must have had at least several thousands of hours where I could have one-on-one conversations with educational leaders! Without a doubt, these activities made my Asian connectivity, as well as my appreciation and understanding of Asian higher education, grow exponentially. It is no surprise that with this as the background, the volume of my writings also grew exponentially!

These changes in the 21st century for higher education in Asia made it both exciting and frightening. For example, in Taiwan, after a decade and $100 billion New Taiwan Dollars (nearly US$3.2 billion) of public funds being poured into about a dozen universities, societies at large were wondering, if not questioning, how the universities had transformed. Also, with ranking becoming an integral part of a university's administration, one had to constantly ensure that the ways of ranking did not become the "sand-box" of running a university. Having these as underpinnings made having strategies, leadership and courage even more important than ever before. Much of what I have written since coming to Asia, I hope, reflect these challenges and concerns as I see them.

I would like to take this opportunity to thank several people without whose support and mentorship I would not have become what I am now. The first is Academician Fu-Jia Yang, a friend and mentor for more than three decades. His love for China and his insight into the fundamental importance of education were truly inspirational. Professor Kok Khoo (more known in the world as K. K.) Phua initiated the idea of this book. I have seen in the past four decades how K. K. rose and flourished in the world of academics as well as publishing. His profound interest in science, culture, and most of all, education, is also so inspiring. I would say without him this book would not have been a possibility.

I also want to thank Dr Ho Yi Kai, the editor of this book. He made me truly understand that a book is unfinished until the editor is done with it! His mastery in editing, not merely the language but also knowing how to string together ideas which are seemingly unrelated, is truly amazing.

On a personal note, putting this book together would have been an impossibility had I not received complete support and love from my family, my daughter Singyi and my son Yiheng, and of course, my wife Evelyn. In the past forty years, she supported me totally, often sacrificing her own aspirations in life. I know that coming to Asia was not her first choice, and probably not even the second, but she knew it was what I wanted to do and supported me unconditionally. For this, words escape me in expressing my love and gratefulness to her.

Feng Da Hsuan
October 2015

Editor's Note

November 2011 was when I first met Prof Feng Da Hsuan, and also when I first got to witness his insight into higher education. All thanks to Prof Phua Kok Khoo for appointing me to coordinate this talk by Prof Feng, where he shared on "The Challenges of Asia Pacific Higher Institutes in the 21st Century".

I had the privilege of being included in Prof Feng's mailing list and had since been reading his writings, exchanging views occasionally. In late 2013, when Prof Phua invited Prof Feng to publish his educational writings, I had the honor of being chosen by the latter to do the selection and editing for his new book. Two years later, we are glad that the book is able to make its way into your hands!

The products of a globetrotting educator with both foresight and insight enabled us to categorise the selected articles into sections on the new era, new ideas, young budding institutions, and also to feature countries around the world. The author has met many people over the years, having established a vast network, and so we dedicated one section of the book to prominent figures worth noting. Of course, the collection would not be complete without the coverage of hot topics like the Nobel Prize and university rankings.

It is exceptionally meaningful to publish this collection this year, as it marks the 20th anniversary of Prof Feng's educational writing journey! It is also a birthday gift to him, on his 70th birthday! I would also like to thank both Prof Phua and Prof Feng for giving me the opportunity to take part in this wonderful project, and sincerely hope this book will offer all educators and readers concerned with education a fulfilling experience!

Ho Yi Kai
Nanyang Technological University
October 2015

On the Nobel Prize

1

What Does it Take to Become a Nobel Laureate?

These are the introductory comments to the public lecture by Dr Douglas D. Osheroff, Nobel Laureate, 1996, held on January 24, 2011, at Tainan. The author was Senior Executive Vice President, National Cheng Kung University (NCKU).

Douglas D. Osheroff
Nobel Laureate of 1996 for his discovery of superfluidity in helium-3

Dr. Osheroff, colleagues and fellow students:

It is indeed a great honor and pleasure for me to make a few introductory comments on behalf of President Michael Lai to introduce a great intellect, Professor Osheroff.

Ever since I came to Asia Pacific three and a half years ago, whatever country I visited, from Korea to Singapore (with the exception of Japan,) I would hear people asking the perennial question: "when will *my* country have a Nobel Laureate?"

As Professor Osheroff is the first Nobel Laureate I am introducing since coming to NCKU, I thought I would read carefully the biography he wrote for the Nobel website after he won the Nobel Prize, in order to find out:

"*What does it take to become a Nobel Laureate?*"

First, his father was Jewish and his mother was not. That of course does not make him Jewish. (Jewish people are very clever. *You can be Jewish only if your mother is Jewish.*) His parents are nice, but probably no nicer than many average good parents in the U.S.

Second, he said as a young boy, he was curious about how things work. So he experimented with many different things, including gunpowder. That too is interesting, but I can imagine many American youngsters have similar propensity.

Third, for his high school career, he said the following:

> "....*While I liked Physics much more than Chemistry, the Chemistry teacher, William Hock, had spent quite a bit of time telling us what physical research was all about (as opposed to my experimentation), and that effort made a deep impression on my young mind. ......I was intellectually rather lazy, and in high school I would always take one free class period so that I could get my homework out of the way, freeing the evenings for my many projects.*"

So that tells me that he did not spend an inordinate amount of time in high school reading difficult advanced physics or differential equations texts. However, he did have a teacher who made it clear that ideas count. I did not get the impression that his high school career was filled with book work, or attending additional classes in the evenings (补习班) so that he could learn skills to solve more difficult problems. This is clearly different from the definition of "*good students*" in Taiwan.

Fourth, he was good enough to study Physics as an undergraduate at Caltech. More important, in Caltech, he was "baptized" by Physics' maestro of maestros, Richard Feynman, by attending Feynman's introductory physics course. That course, as we know, was the genesis of the now world-renowned three volumes of "Feynman Lectures." It must have been an incredible experience. After all, what Physics textbook would tell the reader that (I paraphrase) "*I cannot tell you the deeper meaning of quantum mechanics. I can only give you more examples on how it works!*"

Fifth, he went to Cornell not because of its reputation as a great university, but because it was "far from Pasadena's smog!" Since serendipity in life is more important than planning, he met his mentor David Lee, his co-Nobel recipient and of course his future wife, Dr. Phyllis Liu. Since Phyllis came from Taiwan, Dr. Osheroff is actually a "Taiwan son-in-law" or 台湾女婿.

David Lee is known to be a great teacher and surrounds himself with many truly exceptional students. I should mention that at Cornell, besides Dr. Lee, there was also the great late Hans Bethe. Although Dr. Osheroff did not mention Dr. Bethe in his biography, I cannot imagine he was not inspired by such an individual, even just by osmosis!

Sixth, after Cornell, Dr. Osheroff went to Bell Labs. Not surprisingly, there he met other greats such as Phil Anderson and Bill Brinkman (who later wrote the famous Brinkman report, which had a profound impact on scientific developments in the U.S.). Submerged in this incredible intellectual landscape, he made additional quantum leaps in his career.

Seventh, after 15 years at Bell Labs, Dr. Osheroff became a professor at Stanford University, where he not only continued his illustrious scientific career, but also became an incredible teacher, despite what a comical Stanford student said: "*Osheroff is a typical example of some lunkhead from industry whom Stanford University hired for his expertise in some random field.*" Dr. Osheroff is obviously a man of great humor and humility!

So, did I learn what the secret to becoming a Nobel Laureate is by reading Dr. Osheroff's biography? Unfortunately, not really! Nothing Dr. Osheroff did at any point, according to him, was totally out of the ordinary so to speak. I did not detect throughout his illustrious career any eureka moment or a series of eureka moments that would have turned him into a Nobel Laureate.

So how did Dr. Osheroff win the Nobel Prize?

Well, I think this may be a wrong question. Indeed, it is not Dr. Osheroff *per se* who matters. Ultimately, it is the profound, ubiquitous, open and truth-seeking intellectual system of the U.S. at all levels, from K-100[1], in processing many many outstanding individuals such as Dr. Osheroff in their developments, that matters.

It should be obvious to all that it is the entire intellectual system which Dr. Osheroff went through, starting from his family education in his fledgling days to high school to Caltech to Cornell to Bell Labs to Stanford, which crafted him to become such a powerful intellectual. I need to point out that while details may be different, the system in which Dr. Osheroff was processed and still is processing through is really quite typical for many people like him in the U.S. The system allows Osheroff-likes to have the necessary freedom and support to have the courage to seek answers to difficult and profound questions, to realize that ideas count. The system also allows Osheroff-likes to leverage creativity to unlock the mystery of our universe. Once you have a large cadre of such people produced over many many decades, then it is natural that some of them will receive the highest scientific accolades humanity can bestow.

So, the question for Asia Pacific is not:

*"When can **my** country produce Nobel Laureates?"*

The question really should be:

"How can we construct educational systems at all levels in order to produce many many individuals who can probe the universe's deep mysteries?"

---

[1] Education from Kindergarten to Grade 12 is usually referred to as "K-12", so now we use "K-100" for lifelong learning!

Ladies and gentlemen, once we can do that, and I am absolutely confident that we in Asia Pacific will do so in this century, then winning Nobel Prizes for Asia Pacific shall never be a question again.

I now introduce to you Dr. Osheroff.

(2011)

2

Why can Two Israeli Scientists Win the Nobel Prize?

These are the opening comments to the 2007–2009 Taiwan–Israel Joint Final Report Workshop, held on October 13, 2009, at National Cheng Kung University (NCKU). The author was Senior Executive Vice President at the University at the time.

Dear participants from Israel and Taiwan:

I am so happy and truly honored to have been asked by the organizer, Professor Shulan Hsieh (谢淑兰老师) of the 2007–2009 Taiwan–Israel Joint Final Report Workshop, to come say a few words of welcome to all the participants from Israel and Taiwan. It is so exciting to see that there is now robust and sustainable scientific collaboration between Taiwan and Israel; both have small populations (23 million and 6 million respectively) and both nations rank education as supreme! I see that the Workshop will cover exciting areas in Biomedical Science (生物医学), Neuroscience (神经科学) and Biomedical Engineering (医学工程).

To our Israeli friends, may I say "Shalom!"

Ladies and Gentlemen, if you asked me what world civilizations have affected me personally the most, I would, without hesitation, say that it is first Chinese, then Jewish! I am confident that as a scientist, my experience is by no means unique.

Indeed, well before I became fully cognizant of who a Jew is, or what it means to be Jewish, the first political leader I encountered was David Marshall, the first Chief Minister of Singapore in 1955. David Marshall was an orthodox Jew of Iraqi origin!

Of course, even as a very young boy, I had heard about Albert Einstein. But I did not know he was Jewish until much later in life.

I began my career as a physicist, in fact, as a nuclear physicist, by learning from my thesis advisor, Ben Bayman and by reading the group theory book by the late Mort Hamermesh. Both were faculty members of the University of Minnesota. They were Jewish and grew up in New York City.

Later on, I had to read the papers by an Israeli physicist, Gino Racah (thus Racah algebra, and the Racah Institute of Physics at Hebrew University is named after him), followed by having to read the monumental book on Nuclear Shell Models by two other Israeli physicists from the Weizmann Institute, Igal Talmi and Amos de Shalit. As it turns out, nearly all the technologies one needed in doing nuclear structure computations at the time when I was still a graduate student were contained in this book. These three physicists were all at one point household names in the world of nuclear physics, and incredibly, all three had come from this little country of a few million people in the Middle East.

I never met the late Racah and the late de Shalit, but I did become a good friend of Igal Talmi. It was he who invited me to visit Israel (and so far it is still my only visit to Israel) in 1979 to attend the International Conference on Group Theoretical Methods in Physics in Kiryat Anavim, a *kibbutz* (a well-known Israeli cooperative) near Jerusalem.

Since those days, I do not believe there was a single day that went by in my nuclear physics career without some intellectual dealings with either Israeli physicists or American physicists of Jewish decent. Something remarkable happened to me in 2004. During the month of October, 2004, as the Vice President for Research and Economic Development of the University of Texas at Dallas, I led a Senior Research Executive delegation from research universities in southwestern United States and Mexico to visit Seoul and Daejeon in South Korea and Beijing and Shanghai in China. Also, earlier that year, I visited the Malaysian Academy of Sciences.

As you all know, in the past several decades, we in the Pacific Rim have had enormous enthusiasm and energy, as well as significant public resources to put towards accelerating the research capabilities of our academic institutions, especially our research universities.

"How to produce Nobel Laureates", fortunately or unfortunately, was a theme that was quite prevalent.

Right in the midst of my 2004 October visit, the Swedish Academy announced that two of that year's Nobel Prizes in Chemistry would be awarded to Israeli scientists, Avram Hershko and Aaron J. Ciechanover. Both were home-grown scientists from the Technion in Haifa. For Israel, this was the first time that two of its scientists were recipients of the highest scientific accolade.

In the past week, Nobel Prizes were announced one after another so I sense that it is very much on everybody's radar screen. Remarkably, one of the awardees this year was Ada Yonath of the Weizmann Institute, who became the latest Chemistry Nobel Laureate.

Indeed, we all know that the moment a Nobel Prize is announced, the perception is that the recipient is instantly catapulted into intellectual immortality. Even to the non-scientific world, a Nobel Prize is equivalent to supreme greatness. Here, I must recall my good friend Aaron Ciechanover's immortal words:

> *"Doing absolutely the best science should be the incentive and sufficient award. Nearly all great scientists do not win Nobel Prizes. So one must keep in perspective that winning a Nobel Prize simply means you are really good in that area. No more, no less!"*

It was therefore not surprising that at nearly every stop on my Pacific Rim tour in October 2004, conversations with colleagues, students and media turned to what makes "scientific excellence" and why Israel was so fortunate. So, the question of why Asia does not have home-grown Nobel Laureates was asked at every stop I made in South Korea and China.

The fact that two Israeli scientists won the Nobel Prize based on work done in Israel gave me an opportunity to examine the success of Israel's scientific community and how those lessons may be used to guide the development of scientific excellence around the world. While I am sure that this is a topic I will investigate in more depth in the future, what I have discovered so far leads me to the conclusion that Israel has a strategy for developing a strong research community.

Scientific Landscape of Israel

It is easy to read the bios of Hershko and Ciechanover and see that they are outstanding scientists. However scientific excellence cannot be achieved in isolation. These two scientists could not have achieved their well-deserved scientific supremacy if Technion and Israel had not supported them wholeheartedly in an environment where reaching world-class scientific prominence would create work worthy of a Nobel. Since an Israeli scientist is usually listed among the leaders in nearly every research field one can think of, that environment surely must exist. For example, in my narrow field of nuclear structure physics, pioneers such as the late Amos de-Shalit and Igal Talmi of the Weizmann Institute are certainly household names. With just slightly over six million people, Israel has seven primary research universities:

- Bar-Ilan University in Ramat Gan
- Ben-Gurion University of the Negev
- Haifa University in Haifa
- Hebrew University of Jerusalem
- Technion, Israel Institute of Technology in Haifa
- Tel Aviv University
- Weizmann Institute of Science in Rehovot

With six million people, the Israeli Government decided to put their research resources to roughly one million population per outstanding research university. To see if I could find how this environment was created, and perhaps more importantly, maintained, I decided to surf the websites of Israeli research institutions and find an example which illustrates the strengths. I picked the active Department of Chemistry at Weizmann.

The faculty members of this department are:

1. *Lia Addadi*, the Dorothy and Patrick Gorman Professor
2. *Jacob Anglister*, the Joseph & Ruth Owades Professor of Chemistry
3. *Deborah Fass*, Associate Professor
4. *Amnon Horovitz*, the Carl & Dorothy Bennet Professor of Biochemistry
5. *Mark Safro*, the Lee & William Abramowitz Professor of Molecular Biophysics
6. *Irit Sagi*, Associate Professor and Incumbent of the Maurizio Pontecorvo Chair
7. *Zippora Shakked*, the Helena Rubinstein Professor of Structural Biology

8. *Joel L. Sussman*, the Dr Walter and Dr Trude Borchardt Professorial Chair in Structural Biology
9. *Stephen Weiner*, the I.W. Abel Professor of Structural Biology
10. *Ada E. Yonath*, the Martin S. and Helen Kimmel Professor of Structural Biology; Director, The Helen & Milton A. Kimmelman Center for Biomolecular Structure & Assembly; Director, The Joseph & Ceil Mazer Center for Structural Biology

Note that all 10 faculty members of this department, except for one Associate Professor, are "endowed chair professors." Even the other Associate Professor holds a chair. Imagine the pressure felt by the Associate Professor who does not have an endowed chair!

One of the faculty of this department, Ada Yonath, as we all know, became world-renowned last week by becoming the latest Nobel Laureate in Chemistry.

Please allow me to quote the press release from Weizmann about her prize.

The statement was indeed inspirational:

"Solving the ribosome's structure would give scientists unprecedented insight into how the genetic code is translated into proteins; by the late 1970s, however, top scientific teams around the world had already tried and failed to get these complex structures of protein and RNA to take on a crystalline form that could be studied. Dreamer or not, it was hard work that brought results: Yonath and colleagues made a staggering 25,000 attempts before they succeeded in creating the first ribosome crystals, in 1980."

25,000 attempts! This is a tour-de-force! There is also no mention of Science Citation Index (SCI) publications! This is science at its best and its purest!

I checked a few other departments and this is usual for the Weizmann. It is very telling about the department. After all, establishing endowed chairs is not trivial, because every chair requires significant and sometime years of effort from the University administration to convince an individual or philanthropic organization (and usually they are American or European well-to-do Jews) to donate the necessary financial resource as endowment for it.

Nearly every department I looked at in the seven Israeli universities has at least one endowed chair in any department. Thus a conclusion I have drawn is that Israeli research universities are not waiting for the government to totally fund these positions, but have been proactively seeking private donors to create such positions. I often say that

"Vision without funding is hallucination."

If, as it would appear, it was a major goal of Israeli universities' administration to find and nurture funding sources for outstanding researchers to power the intellectual efforts, having endowed chair professorships would certainly go a long way in creating a culture in which researchers could have the tools and funding required to achieve supreme excellence.

Getting funding for endowed chairs is a marriage of two parties: The university and the philanthropist. The fact that Israel has so many endowed chairs tells me that that Jewish community worldwide recognizes the fundamental importance of "people!"

In 2005, I became good friends with the former President of the Technion, Yitzhak Apeloig, and its Nobel Laureate Aaron Ciechanover. And I saw the level of energy these two individuals put into raising funds worldwide, especially in the U.S. I also learned about the pro-active fundraising effort of the Technion in the U.S. through an organization called the ATS, the American Technion Society!

Ladies and gentlemen, success takes vision and hardwork! It is not an accident!

During a trip in October of 2004, I was asked by a Chinese reporter what I thought the weakest link in U.S. research universities was. My answer was that while there are many weak links — one is the performance evaluation of full professors — for outstanding universities, such a weakness is mitigated by external (especially global) and internal peer pressures. Unfortunately, for lesser-placed universities, such pressures are often absent and the quality of research of a full professor must rely on self-generated pressure.

This does not appear to be a problem in Israeli universities!

Epilogue

I quote a favorite phrase of another good friend of mine, Nobel Laureate the late Alan MacDiarmid of the University of Texas at Dallas, and that is "*Science is people.*" For Israel, home growing outstanding scientists as well as attracting world renowned scientists from abroad (primarily from the U.S. and former Soviet Union), appears to be strategies of building its national scientific prowess.

Israel recognizes that scientific excellence must come from truly outstanding scientists who are intellectually global and NOT local. Utilizing private funds to fund endowed chairs is one of the many ways to attract them. Israeli universities certainly seem to be masters of this process.

It is therefore not surprising that in the landscape of many outstanding scientists in a variety of fields, two in 2004 and one in 2009 won Nobel Prizes. Their accolades may be interpreted not just as their personal successes but as the result of a land which places intellectual par excellence, second to none in priority!

When you have many, I am sure "quantum fluctuation" will allow a few to be recognized by the Nobel committee.

I said in October of 2004 that "*if there are even more additional Nobel laureates emerging from Israel in the (near) future, I would not be surprised!*"

I rest my case in 2009!

Thank you so much for your attention.

(2009)

On University Ranking

3

Global University Ranking: How to Understand such a Measurement?

The author was Special Advisor to the Rector and Director of Global Affairs, University of Macau, when he rewrote this piece from a series of articles he had written in the past few years on the similar topic.

Preamble

A good friend of mine who is a Vice President for Research at one of U.S.' top research universities once made a famous comment regarding global universities ranking:

> "In general, I trust no rankings, except those that made my university look good!"

However humorous such a comment may be, it points to the fundamental issue of how higher education institutions should comprehend the meaning of global universities ranking.

Global universities ranking is unquestionably a 21st century phenomena. The "pioneer" of this higher educational phenomena is Professor Nian-Cai Liu (刘念才) of Shanghai Jiaotong University (上海交通大学). I had the pleasure of meeting Professor Liu in Dallas in 2003 where he mentioned to me that he was in the process of proposing a scheme to "rank" universities globally. Being naive nor understand what "unintended consequences" of such an action may cause, I was quite intrigued by such a suggestion.

Professor Liu inaugurated the now world famous Academic Ranking of World Universities (ARWU) of Shanghai Jiaotong University in 2004. Soon after many others followed. Today, with the dust somewhat settled, I think most people in higher education worldwide would consider three specific rankings to be most visible and perhaps credible. They are ARWU, Times Higher Education (THE) Ranking and the QS World University Ranking.

It is certainly not an exaggeration that these rankings had, and continue to inexplicably transform the global higher education landscape, not just superficially, but fundamentally! This is especially so in Asia Pacific in which all relevant paper and electronic news media would go haywire every time one of the three rankings announces its annual rankings.

One can hear such discussions in the corridors of nearly all, if not all of Asia Pacific universities administration buildings. It can, and will, directly or indirectly impact how students, especially at the undergraduate level, select universities to attend. It could also become the "murmur" of the town about the "quality of a university" measured by the rankings. The impact, I am afraid, is wide and deep.

In a recent forty minute speech by one of the presidents of a top Asian university, the entire theme was concentrated on how under his watch, the university was able to inch into the "top 100" of a particular ranking system, with no mention of how new and innovative schemes in "education" were instituted to enhance the students ability to face challenges in the 21st century! This unfortunate situation tells us that ranking could even significantly distort the thinking of education leaderships.

This article is not about how good or how bad a particular ranking system is. It is also not about whether a ranking enhances or diminishes the quality of education. I am not discussing whether University A has a high rank means that its educational process is outstanding. I leave that to another paper. In fact, whether any ranking has anything to do with the fundamental reason for the existence of universities, namely, to produce products (*a la* students) to be ready and able to face the challenges in the 21st century, is highly debatable! It is about how as academics and leaders of education policies makers should understand the "obvious statistical" meaning of rankings as so-called "measurement" processes.

Global Universities Ranking is a Measurement

In the eight years since I came to Asia, I noticed that there was a crescendo of conferences, forums, group meetings and what have you surrounding the theme of "world class universities" and/or "top ranked universities." These conferences were organized by either the "rankers" such as the QS World University Ranking or by individual universities. As a senior university administrator, I had the opportunity of attending some of them.

In general, if I may be so bold, I found that in many such gatherings, the speakers tend to discuss narrowly the achievements of their individual universities in raising their rankings, or how they enhance certain efforts which clearly would increase their rankings respectively, and less or none on "why are we doing this and how does this benefit our understanding of what is a world class university."

Let us ascertain what **is** ranking first. Ranking, supposedly, is a measurement of the quality of the university. I think anyone who has engaged in any kind of measurement exercise, albeit scientific, social or what have you, is familiar with the concept of **"error bar."** When a measurement is made for a particular action X, to have meaning, it must be accompanied by an error bar of + or −Y, where Y is the error.

To understand this concept, let us take the well-known example of polling in a political election. In fact, with Taiwan's election now in full swing, the polling of how voters will vote, even on a daily basis, is a tidal wave hitting the news media. For example, if the poll of a particular candidate is say 45 percent, it must be accompanied by an error of say + or −3 percent! That is the necessary but not sufficient condition to render the poll meaningful.

Global universities ranking, just like polling, is also a measurement. When a ranking system mentions that university A is ranked X, in principle, it is a measurement of the "quality" of the university, compares to university B or C. But without an error associated with a ranking, comparing A with B or with C universities is at best ambiguous.

Amalgamating ARWU-THE-QS as a measurement of global universities ranking with error bar attached to it.

As far as I could surmise, no ranking, albeit Academic Ranking of World Universities (ARWU) of Shanghai Jiaotong University, Times Higher Education (THE) or QS World University Ranking provide the error bar information.

I will now propose a new way of establishing the error by combining the results of all three rankings. I would not say this is a unique way of establishing the error bar of a global universities ranking, but it nevertheless is one which is plausible.

Let me give you a rationale why I think the following is a reasonable method.

I will illustrate this by examining the cases of Harvard University, Tokyo University and Nanyang Technological University rankings in 2015, 2013 and 2011 for ARWU, THE and QS ranking. I have taken these three years, span over five years because I believe ranking has real meaning only if it spans over a sufficiently longer period. The progress, or the lack of it, of a university cannot and probably should not be measured year to year, but over time.

The data is as follows:

Harvard University	ARWU	THE	QS
2015	1	2	X
2013	1	4	2
2011	1	1	3

Tokyo University	ARWU	THE	QS
2015	21	23	X
2013	21	27	32
2011	21	26	30

Nanyang Technological University	ARWU	THE	QS
2015	151–200	61	X
2013	201–300	86	41
2011	201–300	174	47

What information can one deduce from the above data?

Clearly Harvard being in one of the top 3 positions, according to all three rankings, is stable and unquestionable.

Interestingly, the University of Tokyo being in the top 20-30 region is also stable and unquestionable in all three rankings.

Nanyang Technological University, however, varies widely in all three rankings. In QS, NTU is relatively stable in the 40 or so region, in THE, it changes (improves) enormously from 2011 to 2015 from 174 to 61. Interestingly, in ARWU, it is also stable but in the well above 150 region. It is interesting to note that in ARWU, NTU's improvement appears to be marginal whereas in both THE and QS, the improvement is exceptional, if not spectacular.

By combining all three rankings together, then from the point of view of measurement and error bar, Harvard University overall ranking from 2011 to 2015 should be around 2 with an error of + or −1. Tokyo University's overall ranking in the same time span should be around 25 with an error of + or −5. NTU's overall ranking is the trickiest to ascertain. I would say roughly it is 100 with an error of +or-80.

With this as out underpinning, I would say that according to the combined ARWU-THE-QS ranking, in the years between 2011 and 2015, Harvard is ahead of the University of Tokyo. It is also true that Harvard and University of Tokyo are unquestionably ahead of Nanyang Technological University based on the combined ARWU-THE-QS ranking.

Let me also take the data of another top Asian university, Tsinghua University, as example.

Tsinghua University	ARWU	THE	QS
2015	101–150	49	X
2013	151–200	52	48
2011	151–200	58	48

Once again, Tsinghua University ranking with this scheme is just as tricky and confusing, yet unavoidable as that of NTU. The only difference between Tsinghua and NTU is that for the former, the THE and QS rankings are fairly stable whereas for the latter it has great changes (or improvements.) What is true however, as far as ranking is concerned, is that it is very difficult to make definitive statement as to whether Tsinghua University is higher ranked than NTU, or vice versa!

The fundamental point is when the rankings of NTU and Tsinghua in the joint ARWU-THE-QS ranking system have such enormous error associated with it, the results of the rankings are certainly open to debate.

So why should this be the case?

Let me propose a possible way to understand this issue. Think of it as throwing darts on a piece of paper. If the paper on the wall has no holes, then every dart you throw at it will hit the paper. If the paper has a small number of holes, then every dart you throw at it may hit paper. Therefore the chances of you hitting the paper may not be as high as a blank piece of paper. If the paper has many holes, then depending how you throw the dart, it sometimes will hit the holes, and sometimes not. Surely the possibility of hitting the holes will greatly diminished.

Ironically, a university could be thought of as a piece of paper. If it has very very few weaknesses (*a la* holes,) then whatever ranking system you "throw" at it, it will come out smelling like a rose. If it has more weaknesses, then it will drop in ranking. If it has even more weaknesses, then if the ranking methodology somehow accentuated the weaknesses, then its ranking will reflect that fact, as in the case of ARWU for NTU. If on the other hand the ranking methodology somehow accentuated the strengths, then its ranking will be much better.

Epilogue

I think no one would dispute that the tidal wave, namely global universities rankings, initiated by Professor Liu Nian-Cai is going to be around for the foreseeable future. The so-called big-three rankings, ARWU, THE and QS have already make their indelible footprints on the social landscape, for sure in Asia Pacific. It can also be easily argued that they have impacted the operations of the higher education processes globally as well as regionally in a palpable manner.

It is clear that no single ranking system, whether it be ARWU, or THE, or QS could give definitive answer as to how well a university is ranked. The reason is that each ranking system, although there are overlapping conditions for ranking, seems to probe different parts of what they consider as their meaning of "quality spaces." With that, it is therefore not at all a surprise that they would, and did, produce different, if not vastly different results.

What I have shown in this exercise is that one probably can have far more confidence in the rankings of Harvard University and the University of Tokyo then you could in the rankings of NTU and Tsinghua University. Ultimately, I think it is most important, if not critical, for any university who wants to improve its ranking is to seek "stability of results" in the ranking of universities.

I think whether the rankings, ARWU, THE or QS, or altogether, have made universities, for sure the new and emerging universities in Asia Pacific, better institutions in the 21st century has a great deal of room to argue. Be that as it may, at the end of the day, what is even more important for education decision makers to bear in mind is that in doing so, one should not and must not forget the basic reason of the existence of universities in the first place: to educate young minds to be ready for the challenges of the 21st century!

4

University Ranking: Albatross or Incentive?

The author was Senior Executive Vice President, National Cheng Kung University, when he wrote this piece of reflection.

Recently, a globally-recognized top university president visited an Asian university. The president of this Asian university asked the visitor why for a particular ranking, this university's position in the past year had dropped a few places. The answer of the top university president was short and blunt: "I do not know, but we are still what we are!"

A few days ago, I received an email from the president of a well-known university. His comment was
  "…rankings tend to distort behavior of those not at the very top…."

In the 21st century, higher education operation is an expensive endeavor. For any university, whether the financial resource supporting the effort comes from tax-payers or private sources, it is "somebody else's money." For this reason, program evaluation to ensure quality control becomes a universal theme. A natural "spinoff" from this theme is global university ranking.

I am not here to critique or defend the methodologies of various rankings. I do want to reflect on the above two comments.

Undoubtedly, the two comments are closely linked.

The first comment is an expected "kneejerk" reaction for any world recognized top university. As the old saying goes, "perception is reality."

After all, the perception that, for example, Cambridge is regarded as the top university in the world needs NO ranking to affirm its leading position. For such universities, their administrative and academic challenges lie much deeper and ranking is the least of their concern, if at all. While the top university president who made the first comment may sound "arrogant," it surely came from his heart! As the old saying goes, "truth hurts." This is the truth.

The second comment needs serious reflection. The two key words here are "distort behavior." What does that mean? There is a Chinese saying: 人往高处走，水往低处流 (Men move upward, water flows downward). It is an irresistible and to a certain extent a good human nature to want to improve. An "index" that a university is improving is how its ranking improves. What is important to recognize here is that the time scale of the change in ranking is usually of the order of one year. The fact of the matter is that financial resources for public institutions come from tax-payers, thus making annual evaluation of the quality a bureaucratic necessity. As I mentioned earlier, for those perceived in the top, they are above this form of evaluation. Only for those in the second-tier does this becomes an important index, if not the only one!

The one year time scale of ranking presents a dichotomy with the construction of quality education. As the old Chinese saying goes: 百年树人 (It takes a hundred years to cultivate people). An educational institution takes time much longer than a one year to show improvement. Faced with this dichotomy, it is conceivable that there are educators who would look for short cuts to improve the ranking of their institutions, such as finding "quick and easy" ways to improve numerical rankings. In effect, ranking may be relegated to an exercise of number manipulation. Such short cuts could deviate, and sometimes significantly, from the mission of education. That would constitute the meaning of the phrase "distort behavior".

There is almost a cliché now, stating that the 21st century is an Asian century. Just as 19th century and 20th century were the European and North American century, respectively, and higher education played a critical if not fundamental role, Asian universities must play the same role if the cliché is to become reality in the 21st century. Higher education should and must be the driving force. To this end, establishing a fundamental, sound and inherently deep-rooted strength for Asian higher education should be the mission. I am sure that it was with this in mind that the president who mentioned "distort behavior" in the process of improving ranking of our higher education institutions must be minimized or mitigated.

(2010)

5

Beyond 2011 QS Asia Universities Ranking: Lesson Learned from Association of American Universities (AAU) for Association of East Asia Research Universities (AEARU 东亚研究型大学协会)

The author was Vice President (Global Strategy, Planning and Evaluation), National Tsing Hua University, Hsinchu, Taiwan, ROC, when he wrote this report.

At AEARU meeting on April 1st, 2011
From left: Feng Da Hsuan, President Tony Chan of HKUST, President Lih J. Chen of NTHU and Vice President M. C. Yip of NTHU

Preamble

Global and/or regional universities ranking is a modern day academic Olympics. Within a short decade in the 21st century, it has already deeply penetrated the social fabric. This is particularly true in Asia Pacific. Indeed, it is both remarkable and expected that whenever any university ranking system announces its results, the media in Asia, and Taiwan is not an exception, goes haywire. Yesterday (May 23, 2011), QS announced its 2011 rankings of Asia universities (which only included universities from East Asia, Southeast Asia and South Asia. Middle-East universities are excluded.)

It is also understood that one should always take such rankings with a grain of salt. Often, media tends to examine a particular ranking in isolation, and does not try to reveal correlations with other rankings to ascertain whether there are "self-consistencies," or more importantly, whether there is new or hidden information embedded.

To this end, for the 2011 QS Asia Ranking (QSAR), I found that by placing this ranking side-by-side with the other two highly visible ranking systems: the 2010 Shanghai Jiao Tong University ranking (better known as the Academic Ranking of World Universities ARWU) and the 2010 Times Higher Education (THE) World University Rankings (I took the 2010 data because the respective 2011 data is not yet available), I was able to ascertain some my former suspicions.

Association of East Asia Research Universities (AEARU) and Association of American Universities (AAU)

A month ago, I reported that I attended the executive committee meeting of AEARU (东亚研究型大学协会) in Hsinchu. The current chair of the committee is Dr. Tony Chan (陈繁昌), President of Hong Kong University of Science and Technology (HKUST 香港科技大学). Also, after 2011, Academician Lih J. Chen (陈力俊), President of National Tsing Hua University, shall assume the chairmanship.

For the above reasons, when I realized that HKUST was the "valedictorian" of the 2011 QSAR, I naturally became curious as to what that would mean to AEARU. In particular, since members of AEARU were supposed to be many of the best research universities from Japan, South Korea,

China, Taiwan and Hong Kong, I wanted to see whether the 2011 QSAR would support this perception. If indeed it were true, I further wondered whether the other two ranking systems, ARWU and THE, could corroborate such a conclusion. Finally, I also wondered what AEARU could learn from its "senior," the Association of American Universities (AAU).

I found the answers to the above questions embedded in the rankings, if they were taken collectively. The following two Tables contain the information I was looking for.

Table I. Global standing of AEARU members.

AEARU University Name	2011 QSAR*/ National ranking	2010 SJTU world ranking/National ranking	2010 THE/National ranking
Hong Kong			
HKUST	1/1	201-300/2-4	41/2
South Korea			
Seoul National University	6/1	101-150/1	109/3
KAIST	11/2	201-300/2	79/2
Pohang U of Science and Tech	12/3	301-400/5-7	26/1
Japan			
University of Tokyo	4/1	20/1	28/1
Kyoto University	7/2	24/2	57/2
Osaka University	8/3	75/3	130/4
Tohoku University	9/4	84/5	132/5
Tokyo Institute of Tech	9/4	101-150/6	112/3
University of Tsukuba	23/8	151-200/7-9	Not in top 200
China			
Peking University	13/1	151-200/1-2	37/1
Tsinghua University	16/2	151-200/1-2	58/3
Fudan University	21/3	201-300/3-7	Not in top 200

(*Continued*)

Table I. (Continued)

USTC	24/4	201-300/3-7	49/2
Nanjing University	28/6	201-300/3-7	120/4
Taiwan			
National Taiwan University	21/1	101-150/1	115/2
National Tsing Hua University	31/2	301-400/3-4	107/1

*QSAR = QS Asia Ranking.

By putting all three ranking systems side-by-side, it is quite transparent that the AEARU members are indeed some of the best universities in their respective country.

Take the case of South Korea, for example, the three universities in AEARU (Seoul National University, KAIST and Pohang University of Science and Technology) are nearly always the first, second the third ranked universities, although their positions could be "reversed." Also, in Pohang's case, one of the three ranking systems places it in the 5–7 position. Perhaps this indicates to us that for each ranking system, there must be inherent "error" (which is not always easy to enumerate) incurred. However, taken as a whole, we can be reasonably confident that these three universities are certainly three of the best in South Korea.

The situation is also true for China's members in AEARU. However, there is one anomaly — for the THE ranking, Fudan University, a well known university, is not listed in the top 200. With that as caveat, the five AEARU members do represent the best China has to offer. Likewise, in all three rankings, the Japanese AEARU members do represent the best from Japan.

With the above information, what can one learn from AAU?

AAU was organized one hundred and eleven years ago by fourteen universities in the U.S. The following information is the founding members current rankings by the three ranking systems.

Table II. American Associated Universities (AAU) founding members' current World standing.

Name	2011 QS	2010 SJTU	2010 THE
University of California Berkeley	28	2	8
University of Michigan	15	22	15
University of Wisconsin-Madison	48	17	43
University of Chicago	8	9	12
Columbia University	11	8	18
Cornell University	16	12	14
Harvard University	2	1	1
Johns Hopkins University	17	18	13
University of Pennsylvania	12	15	19
Princeton University	10	7	5
Stanford University	13	3	4
Yale University	3	11	10
Clark University		Withdrew in 1999	
Catholic University of America		Withdrew in 2002	

From Table II, I was able to extract the following information.

First, while there was no such thing as ranking of universities in 1900, it is reasonably true that these were already some of the very best universities at the time. Indeed, after a century of development, 12 of the 14 are certainly some of the most recognized and thus powerful universities on Earth today. Among the 12, apart from the University of Wisconsin at Madison which has been placed in the 40s by two of the three rankings and University of California Berkeley which has been placed at 28 by QS, all could be designated as "highly ranked" (or <20). The two founding members, Catholic University of America and Clark University, after a century of evolution, found that they no longer belong to this league of universities. So, just as with AEARU, AAU founding members are all outstanding universities at their genesis period.

Second, despite having 111 years of history, AAU today still has only 62 members. For example, it took the three outstanding universities in Texas, The University of Texas at Austin, Rice University and Texas A and

M University 29, 85 and 101 years respectively before they were admitted. This is an indication of how difficult it is to become a member. Also, for the first time since its founding 111 years ago, a member, the University of Nebraska, was asked to "leave the club". Interestingly, seeing the writings on the wall, Syracuse University voluntarily resigned its membership. Since asking a member to leave the Association requires 2/3 majority of the members agreeing, which in normal circumstances would be nearly impossible to achieve, this volatility may be an indication that AAU members have decided that it needs to shed its "old-boys" posture and maintain its "research excellence (elite)" status as its fundamental characteristic. By doing so, it could also become a more powerful voice representing research universities in the U.S. (and to a lesser extent Canada as well, since two of Canadian top universities, the University of Toronto and McGill University, are also members.) This evolution of AAU for the past century could very well give AEARU an indication as to how it may evolve in the 21st century.

Third, there is one fundamental difference between AAU and AEARU. With AAU, except for the two Canadian universities, all members are within the U.S.

With AEARU, members are from Japan, China, Taiwan, Hong Kong and South Korea. Thus the cultural differences between the universities of AEARU from different countries are more than those in AAU. Hence, to find a "collective voice" representing research intensive universities in East Asia in AEARU may be more arduous than it is for AAU members in the U.S. After all, the relationships between Japan, China, Taiwan, Hong Kong and South Korea are politically complex and convoluted. Of course, if a collective voice could indeed be found in this landscape in the 21st century, AEARU as an international organization may become even more important than AAU, which is a uni-national organization.

Epilogue

I am pleased that the 2011 QSAR has sparked one to look at East Asia universities in a different light. By reflecting on the evolution of AAU in the 20th century, I am confident that one will see an equally exciting evolution of AEARU in the 21st century.

(2011)

6

In Search of Humanistic Excellence: The Morehouse Experience

This was an after-banquet speech for the EITC (Emerging Information and Technology conference), held on August 8, 2007, at Princeton University. It touches on the quality and achievement of universities, fairly in line with the contemplation of university standards and ranking. The author was with the University of Texas at Dallas and (soon to be) Senior Executive Vice President of National Cheng Kung University, Taiwan, when he delivered the speech.

From right: T. P. Ma from Yale, Len Feldman from Rutgers, Dean Wei of Princeton, Feng Da Hsuan, Ruby Lee from Princeton, Fu-Jia Yang of Nottingham, Michael Lai of NTHU, and two others organizers.

Distinguished guests, Ladies and Gentlemen:

I am humbled by this heavy responsibility and great honor bestowed on me by Michael Wang to say a few words to this august group. In fact, I am a little embarrassed because there are so many people in the audience who could and should be standing where I am standing now. In particular, I would like to recognize two individuals. They are Academician **Fu-Jia Yang**, Chancellor of Nottingham University and former President of Fudan University and my life time mentor, and my soon-to-be boss, Academician **Michael Lai**, President of **National Cheng Kung University** (NCKU).

As I was preparing this speech, I could not help but recognize that this may be the last talk I will present in public where my by-line is an American institution. Indeed, for the past 35 years, ever since I received my doctorate from the University of Minnesota, I have always had US institutions as by-lines (except for the two years as a postdoc in the UK). Using today's U.S. presidential campaign verbiage, this is a "change!"

So, what should I talk about that will have some interest to you, and me? To seek guidance, I plowed through many speeches of notable individuals. The two that impacted me most were by President Richard Levin of **Yale University** who recently gave, in my opinion, a definitive speech in Hong Kong's Asia Society entitled "Confronting China's Challenges," and President Shih Choon Fong of the **National University of Singapore** who delivered the 2006 State of the University Address entitled "A Good University Teaches, A Great University Transforms."

Ladies and gentlemen, when I knew that I would be taking on a heavy responsibility as the Senior Executive Vice President of NCKU, I read carefully Academician Lai's Presidential Inauguration speech. It was indeed an inspiring speech. He outlined his vision for the university, eloquently and succinctly. Yet, of the many words and phrases he uttered, of the many ideas he proposed, one word stood out, and it was "humanistic".

Quite by serendipity, around the same time I was reading Lai's speech, Chancellor Fu-Jia Yang was kind enough to send me a speech he will be delivering in the Annual Conference of Chinese Science and Technology Association on September 8 this year. In his usual eloquence, he too talked about many educational issues of fundamental importance.

Yet, the central theme was also about "humanistic" education, namely that as educators, especially as higher education administrators, we must aim to produce citizens of the 21st century with a healthy if not strong dosage of humanistic characteristics.

It is therefore very interesting that while President Levin and President Shih did not specifically talk about "humanistic education," in fact if you read carefully in between the lines, that too seems to be their underlying theme.

It is remarkable that all four higher education leaders seem to come to the same conclusion. In the 21st century, with the world the way it is, with so many dark and menacing challenges confronting Mankind, some of them if not mitigated soon, may or could cause the demise of humanity; the world must have more citizens who possess a humanistic outlook, who can emerge from universities with a sense of responsibility on their shoulders and with a fearless can-do attitude to confront and solve global problems.

When a friend of mine from Morehouse College of Atlanta heard that I will soon be going to Taiwan, he was kind enough to send me a warm congratulatory note. Little did he know that his note opened up a "Pandora's box" for me! It sparked me to learn more about his university, from which I came to the realization that in fact, Morehouse's sole educational aim is to produce citizens with strength, courage and the characters which I have outlined above.

The first thing about Morehouse which hit me "in between my eyes" was its alumni. As someone once told me, "alumni are the souls of an institution". If that were the case, Morehouse is indeed endowed with tremendous souls! Just think that among the many highly successful alumni of Morehouse, you have nationally and internationally notable individuals such as:

- **Martin Luther King Jr**, a Nobel Laureate and civil rights leader, who is unquestionably the soul of this nation;
- **Julian Bond**, chairman of the National Association for the Advancement of Colored People (NAACP) and also a great civil rights leader;
- **Samuel Jackson**, a great actor of all times;
- **Maynard Jackson**, the first African American Mayor of Atlanta, Georgia;

- **David Satcher**, Surgeon General of the United States;
- **Spike Lee**, an Academy-nominated film director and producer;
- **Walter E. Massey**, an outstanding theoretical physicist, Director of the National Science Foundation under President George H. W. Bush, former Provost of the University of California System and most recently President of Morehouse;
- **Edwin Moses**, an Olympic gold medalist, sports administrator, and innovative reformer in the areas of Olympic eligibility and drug testing;
- **Louis W. Sullivan**, former U.S. Secretary of Health and Human Services; and
- **Nathaniel Bronner**, Founder of Bronner Bros, a cosmetics empire.

Ladies and gentlemen, these are but a small sample of the great alumni of Morehouse College. These individuals are not great, they are giants! Everyone had done and continues to do something that enhances quality of life of people on earth, and uphold the dignity of humanity. So, with this as background, I made an extra effort to learn more about Morehouse College.

I must admit that what I learned about Morehouse truly dumbfounded me. I found out:

(a) how "**small**" it is, it has only 3,000 students;
(b) how "**poor**" it is, it has an endowment of around $50 million; and
(c) how "**low**" its entering class' average SAT score is; around 1070 (1600 of a maximum 1600.

Compare this with other "well-known" liberal arts colleges, such as Swarthmore College, which is just around the corner from Princeton. The difference cannot be more startling.

Swarthmore is even smaller then Morehouse College, with only about 1,500 students. Yet, Swarthmore has an endowment well over a billion dollars and its incoming class SAT average is around 1400. Swarthmore is known around the country to be a superb institution.

So, if you compare Morehouse with Swarthmore, you would think that Morehouse College cannot possibly produce leaders for the U.S., surely it is not supposed to produce icons of our national soul, such as Martin Luther King Jr., it is not supposed to produce some of the greatest artists, some of the greatest scientists, some of the greatest entrepreneurs and so on!

Yet, Morehouse is incredibly successful in producing true leaders. All of these leaders have something in common, and that is that what they have done, or are achieving, will enhance the quality of life and dignity of human race. Indeed, few colleges in the U.S., or anywhere else on earth for that matter, can claim to have alumni who have had so profound and deep an impact on our globe in the 20th and 21st centuries.

Hence, what renders Morehouse so successful? This question truly intrigues me.

Quite remarkably, founded 140 years ago with a mission to teach freed slaves to read and write and be productive citizens in the society, Morehouse College had to battle against segregation and human indignity. Yet, despite all this, it has evolved and emerged to become the personification of searching for humanistic excellence in education.

The answer was succinctly given by Otis Moss III, a second-generation Morehouse Man. According to Morehouse's Wikipedia webpage, Moss had been accepted by Harvard and Yale divinity schools, and "was attracted to Morehouse by the mystique."

"What impressed me," Moss says, *"was that brothers who went to Morehouse went through a molding, a transformation process. I won't say they were indoctrinated, but they were presented with the ideals of social responsibility, integrity and honesty. There was a spirituality that emanated from the school and its graduates that was not found anywhere else."*

Yes indeed, what Moss said about Morehouse, making sure that students who emerge from Morehouse possess *"social responsibility, integrity and honesty,"* is in fact the essence of humanistic excellence. Morehouse is not slowed by low endowment and not slowed by relatively low SAT scores from its incoming class. It immerses its students in a thick atmosphere of self-confidence and creativity, while ensuring that they think of themselves as integral parts of the human race.

I think the best summary I can find about Morehouse came from President Leroy Keith, who presided over Morehouse some 15 years ago. Keith said that *"through a series of evolutionary and intellectual adjustments, (Morehouse) has become more than what we started out to be. And although we are not perfect, we are striving, continuously striving, for that level of perfection that everybody wants as a goal — and we think we are better at what we do than anyone else. And when you can say that, I think you have just about said it all."*

Ladies and gentlemen, the more I learn about Morehouse College, the more I am convinced of the importance of "humanistic excellence"! In Morehouse, I found that excellence.

In the 21st century, humanity needs more Morehouse Colleges.

As I embark on my new journey in Taiwan, I am excited by the fact that everyone I have encountered, here and in National Cheng Kung University, are interested in promoting this aspect of education with all their might. I hope you will all give me your helping hand so that together we may be able to render NCKU as an example of a lighthouse in this world in the 21st century. The world needs more illumination, not less.

Thank you so much for your attention.

(2007)

Public Policy and Education

7

Autonomy, Accountability and Governance: Challenges of East Asian Public Universities in the 21st Century

This was a speech for the "Futures of Chinese Higher Education" conference, held on May 14–15, 2013, at the Harvard Center in Shanghai. At the time, the author was Senior Vice President, Global Strategy, Planning and Evaluation, National Tsing Hua University, Hsinchu.

"Clearly, direct government control of research universities is absolutely not conducive to the intellectual, cultural and economic contributions which the research universities can and are expected to make to societies, to nations, and to humanities."

I am indeed pleased to have the honor of presenting to this group of distinguished educators some of what I believe to be the critical issues challenging Asian higher education today. Of course, I should make it clear from the start that these issues are highly complex and multi-layered.

In this talk, I neither have the ability nor the time to touch on all aspects. Therefore I thought it is best for me to simply discuss briefly what I consider to be the "source," i.e. the upstream of upstream, of challenges for Taiwan's outstanding public research universities. Some of the generic aspects, I believe, would have relevance to all universities in Taiwan and in Asia Pacific. To this end, I look forward to the Q&A time where I can have the pleasure of your feedback. I think without the slightest exaggeration that higher education in Asia Pacific in the past several decades has seen spectacular transformation. With economic growth, extra resources were pumped into higher education. For example, Mainland China initiated the so-called 211 project in 1990 and 985 project in 1998, while in Taiwan, the 5Y50B project was initiated in 2006. Similar projects were initiated all across Asia Pacific, especially in the 21st century. These projects all have the primary mission of greatly lifting the quality of research (public) universities. I believe that these initiatives contributed significantly to the fact that many universities on both shores (a politically correct term for Mainland China and Taiwan) are now blinking brightly on the global radar screen.

There is a common wisdom which states that "vision without funding is merely hallucination." The 985, 211 and 5Y50B projects merely ensure that educators are not hallucinating. However, there is a follow up statement (of mine) which states that "funding without strategy and careful execution will inevitably lead to chaos". Hence, I think one should be cautious and regard the extra funding initiatives as constituting merely Phase I of a long process of uplifting public research universities in Asia Pacific. While nations in the region should and must continue the strong and robust financial support of its top national universities (those who do not would do so at their own peril), in Phase II and beyond, to further move it intellectually would require more than just monetary resources. As human organizations operating with large amount of public funds, public universities in Asia Pacific must not only be well funded, but also well lubricated. To lubricate, I believe there are three fundamental components. They are:

(1) Autonomy (in Chinese, it is 自治,)
(2) Accountability (问责或课责) and
(3) Governance (治理).

These three terms will be used throughout this talk so I will refer to them collectively as AAG.

For those in the audience who understand Chinese, you may have already noticed that the most confusing Chinese translation of AAG is the middle A, namely, Accountability. In the past five years since coming to the Asia Pacific region, I have asked many people what the translation for "accountability" would be. Most gave me either the wrong translation, or the one I have quoted. It is worth noting that the meaning of 问责 or 课责 is not immediately obvious to anyone who understands Chinese. This may be an indication that the whole concept of accountability which is so fundamental in our discussion here is either not well understood or not a practice within our culture. I will come back to this point later.

In a defining speech on the subject delivered at the Asia Development Bank Conference on University Governance in Denpasar, Indonesia on April 26, 2004, former President and Vice Chancellor of Simon Fraser University, Dr. Michael Stevenson, made the following fundamental, succinct and generic observation of AAG for public universities:

"I believe in all universities around the world we are all dealing with very important issues of how to strike the proper balance between universities and governments, how to strike the proper balance between the autonomy of universities and the reasonable accountability of universities for the public funds that sustain much of their activity."

In the 21st century, maybe because public universities are now gaining global recognition, Asians have ubiquitously discussed and debated furiously about AAG in higher education. Why? I believe there are at least three fundamental reasons.

First, East Asia's political improvements, accompanied by economic and social transformations, have propelled the number of public universities to increase with breathtaking speed. In Taiwan, it went from few tens in the 90s to more than 60 today. As a physicist, I would call such an expansion "non-adiabatic!" With varying degrees of non-adiabaticity, the same is also true in Mainland China, the Republic of Korea, Malaysia, Indonesia and Singapore.

Second, many universities in this period either made the decision, or could not resist the temptation or withstand the social and political pressures, to transform from primarily teaching centric to teaching and research centric. Due to the unwritten understanding that "public universities must also become societies' economic engines", many also included "technology transfer" as one of their major missions.

Third, in the past several decades, the world became, as Thomas Friedman would say, "flat". This flatness, which is a euphemism for globalization, impacts profoundly and at times, distorts the higher education enterprise.

These aforementioned changes in Asia Pacific place new demands and new mindsets are required in operating this terra-incognita for many decision makers. According to the Oxford Dictionary, autonomy means "having the freedom to act independently", accountability means "required or expected to justify actions or decisions", and governance means "the action or manner of governing a state, organization, etc.". From these definitions, clearly the three needs to be viewed as a "trinity" (三位一体) and not a "tripartite" (三方.)

Autonomy

It is probably no surprise that countries which highly value autonomy generally have better universities. Yet, many Asian universities, certainly those in the two shores, still lack autonomy, although it seems that Mainland China now is making great progress in this direction.

In Taiwan, the lack of autonomy is profound. Issues such as tuition, the number of faculty members, students and staff members are tightly regulated by MoE (Ministry of Education). The same is true for all academic issues, which include the final approval of any tenure decision. After spending more than five years in Taiwan's higher education system, I found that the most frightening two Chinese characters within the higher education landscape are Bao (报) Bu (部.) Bao Bu literally means "report to the Ministry of Education". For Taiwan's national universities, no actions, albeit large or small, are executable unless MoE bestows approval.

In addition, national universities also lack human resource and financial autonomies.

It is inconceivable to have a 21st century modern university whose directors of human resource and finance do not completely report to the president. In fact, I would say that these directors report to the president only in name, but in reality, the Human Resource Director also reports to the Ministry of Personnel (人事处) while the Finance Director also reports to the Ministry of Accounting (主计处) and the Ministry of Audit

(审计处.) These ministries are under the large umbrella of the Executive Yuan and each has a Minister on par with the Minister of Education! Such a public institutional organizational structure is known as a "one whip" (一条鞭,) a system which according to my non-historian perspective can trace its origin to as early as the Ming (明) Dynasty, around the 14th century!

It is no wonder that this profound lack of autonomy has rendered Taiwan universities sluggish, especially when compared to its neighbors, in understanding Asia Pacific's fast pace culture, and intellectual and political transformation. In my opinion, it faces the imminent danger of profoundly hindering Taiwanese students' competitiveness as well as universities being creative in their operations, locally and globally, in the 21st century. Indeed, being creative regionally and globally for any aspiring universities in the 21st century is no longer a luxury but a fundamental necessity!

Accountability

It is structurally fundamental that accountability must be inherently understood and practised at all levels of a 21st century university. Here I will give one example of this lack of accountability in Taiwan national universities. To a certain extent, this lack of accountability is due to the lack of autonomy. As the quality of a university is directly linked to the quality of its leadership, especially the president, the presidential selection committee of the university must be accountable for its actions. Until 2005, national universities' presidents were appointed by the Ministry of Education. This means that MoE was the "Selection Committee," if you want to call it that. In that scenario, I am fairly confident that no one in the MoE was held accountable for their actions. Today, presidents of national universities have well-defined term limits and are selected by a Selection Committee with representation from faculty members, staff members, students, alumni and last but not least, a small number of MoE-appointed individuals.

While this is indeed a significant step towards a more open system of selection, the Selection Committee unfortunately is still not accountable for its action, i.e., the selection of the president, since it is immediately disbanded once the selection is made. The Selection Committee does not have the jurisdiction to oversee the performance of the president. Of course, as experience would tell us, even the best possible accountable system could result in bad presidents. The point I would like to make here is that with accountability imposed on the Selection Committee, this could greatly diminish such possibilities. If nothing else, it will render the process of selection by the Committee that much more stringent and arduous, both of which to me could be viewed as positive!

Governance

The structure of Taiwan's national universities' governance has not changed very much, if at all, in the past five or six decades, even though Taiwan's societies have made fundamental transformations. The source of the rigidity of the governance structure, just as the accountability challenge, is due to the lack of autonomy. Currently, there are many layers of challenges facing the governance structure which I would not have time to talk about here. I will only discuss the one I consider to be the most fundamental challenge facing all national universities in Taiwan.

As I have mentioned before, it is inconceivable that a human organization such as a university in the 21st century would not have complete human resource and financial autonomy. To render these operations under the direct control of the president of the national university should and must be the highest priority in designing a modern governing structure of national universities. As I have mentioned in my discussion of autonomy, this would require relaxation of not only the Ministry of Education, but also the Ministry of Human Resource. In fact, since audit should be an independent organization, there should be a separate audit office within the university which reports directly to the Ministry of Audit.

East Asian public universities were, and many still are, regarded as the tight responsibilities of government agencies, be it educational (as in the Department of Education) or research (as in funding agencies such as the National Science Council (NSC) in Taiwan.) Hence, in the 21st century, the question of how to develop a new AAG operational mode for Asian public universities became one of utmost urgency. In this new decade of the 21st century, it received intense discussions and in some countries, became prototype implementations (such as with Seoul National University in the Republic of Korea).

In 2009, when I was a Senior Executive Vice President of National Cheng Kung University, my boss President Michael Lai asked me to look into the issue of Fai-Ren-Hua (法人化), FRH or Corporatization of the university, an issue that was receiving quite a bit of discussion as well as controversy at the time in Taiwan. It was then that I discovered by reading the speech of President Michael Stevenson that the FRH for national universities is in fact AAG. From my analysis I presented here, one would not have proper accountability or governance if one did not have autonomy. Indeed, I have come to the conclusion that autonomy ranks supreme! To truly understand the issue of FRH, I assembled an NCKU Presidential Blue Ribbon Panel (of which Michael Stevenson was an important member of course and how I was able to convince him to join the Panel would have to be discussed another time). After one year of extensive and intensive discussion with emails, telephone calls, and finally a two day in-depth meeting – one day in MoE and one in NCKU in Tainan – the Panel issued an unprecedented and historical white paper. In this white paper, the Panel without any hesitation outlined the fundamental challenges of Taiwan national universities and made the following recommendation:

> "*Rigid government control and protection by the Ministry of Education. In Taiwan, higher education is regulated as a governmental affair, limiting its innovative potential and hence competitiveness locally and internationally. In particular, the control on tuition, enrolment and faculty salary needs to be reviewed and reformed in a way to make higher education in Taiwan be able to swiftly respond to changing international and regional academic landscapes to keep its capacity to fulfill its educational, academic, economical, industrial, and humanitarian missions.*"

The whitepaper went on to make the most important suggestion:

> "*NCKU's governance restructuring such as piloting a role model governing Board that can help establish a trustworthy autonomy of NCKU and help the President. There should be a clear timetable and organization charter that can address issues such as accountability, resilience to interest groups and dedication to serve NCKU towards its educational missions.*"

As I have mentioned, Taiwan's 5Y50B project initiated in 2006 has and will allow its research universities to reach a new level of excellence from a few decades ago. However, that should be considered only as "Phase I" of a long-term project. In "Phase II" and beyond, the next level or levels of excellence require the universities' operations to be well-lubricated. These golden words from the 2009 NCKU Presidential Blue Ribbon Panel are precisely what "the doctors have prescribed" for Taiwan's research universities to move to the next plateau or plateaus of excellence.

In view of what I have discussed, coupled with what the Blue Ribbon Panel had succinctly stated, there are two imminent needs which one must re-examine.

First, one needs to laser-focus on how to develop in the educational landscape a mindset of excellence and a strategic attitude through inherent self-confidence.

Second, one needs to re-examine the intricate and complex relationship between research universities and the government.

Indeed, in Taiwan's situation, it is no longer confined to re-examining the relationship between universities and MoE, but relationships among universities and the Ministry of Personnel (人事处,) Ministry of Accounting (主计处) and Ministry of Audit (审计处.) I think it would be naïve if one thinks that this is easy. After all, if such a system is a legacy from the Ming Dynasty, the arduousness of reforming it cannot be underestimated. However, I believe that the alternative, i.e., not making any reform, would simply be disastrous. I am convinced that if the current structure is not transformed significantly and quickly, by the establishment of governing Boards, suggested so succinctly by the Blue-Ribbon Panel, national universities in Taiwan will continue to suffocate, and there is the real possibility that they will decline!

Clearly, direct government control of research universities is absolutely not conducive to the intellectual, cultural and economic contributions which the research universities can and are expected to make to societies, to nations, and to humanities.

Thank you very much for your attention.

(2013)

8

Some Thoughts on the Bayh-Dole Act of 1980

This was written to the National Tsing Hua University communities when the author was Senior Vice President, Global Strategy, Planning and Evaluation, at the university.

Members of NTHU Communities:

My presentation yesterday at the E+ conference in National Tsing Hua University, in which I mentioned the fundamental impact of the Bayh-Dole Act of 1980, made a fundamental change, almost in the form of a tsunami, to universities worldwide. In the past 33 years since its inception, the Bayh-Dole Act has been under great discussion, debate, even scrutiny.

Bayh-Dole Act as the basis of industry-academy collaboration

Enacted in the U.S. in 1980

(Before Bayh-Dole) : The patent of Government-funded research developments belongs to the government -> Commercialization is difficult

(After Bayh-Dole): The patent as the research result belongs to the university
- University researches funded by government
- Patent holder university act for the research result introduction to the society

Enacted in Japan in 1999(20 years later than the U.S.)
(After Bayh-Dole): Patents funded by competitive government fund belong to universities

One of the participants, Dr Terri Chen, a patent engineer of Rhodes Attorneys at Law, P.C. sent me this article, the theme of which is to challenge the wisdom of the Bayh-Dole Act, especially the fundamental impact of life science patents (but not exclusively) on humanity. A poignant sentence made by the author Dr. Howard Markel in an article[1] is as follows:

> *"It's time for Congress to recalibrate Bayh–Dole. Profits and patents can be powerful incentives for scientists, businesspeople, and universities, but new and ongoing risks — including high prices that limit access to lifesaving technologies, reduced sharing of scientific data, marked shifts of focus from basic to applied research, and conflicts of interests for doctors and academic medical centers – should be mitigated or averted through revisions of the law."*

I believe that as a leading research university, not just in Taiwan but the world, we in National Tsing Hua University have the solemn obligation to engage proactively in this important conversation within the campus communities. Indeed, the Bayh-Dole Act is a "public policy" and with it can have, and does have, profound impact on humanity. A great university cannot and must not shrug off such responsibilities.

(2013)

---

[1] http://www.nejm.org/doi/full/10.1056/NEJMp1306553#t=article

IT and Education

9

A Lecture Across 10,000 Miles: The 1993 Nobel Laureate's Physics Lecture Delivered from Dallas to Singapore

This was written when the author was Vice President for Research and Economic Development of the University of Texas at Dallas.

On a warm morning at about 7:30 am, August 23, 2007, in a small conference room on campus in the University of Texas at Dallas (UTDallas), U.S., and at that very same moment, at 8:30 pm the same day, on a usual sultry evening in a large lecture theatre on the campus of the National Institute of Education of Nanyang Technological University (NTU), Singapore, something truly remarkable and memorable was about to happen simultaneously:

— At UTDallas, with blurry eyes, the 1993 Nobel Laureate in Physics and now Regental Professor at UTDallas, Russell Hulse, was getting ready to deliver a lecture entitled "From Nobel to Community," not to a huge audience in front of him, as would normally be the case, but a "lonely" videoconferencing camera;
— At NTU, 10,000 miles away from Dallas, some 300 science teachers from Singapore's K-12 communities, together with the leadership from the National Institute of Education, were ready and eager to listen to Russell's lecture.

This lecture, which took nearly six months of careful coordination from organizers at both ends of the Pacific, would be as fascinating as it was remarkable. It was about how the celestial system of a binary pulsar, a pair of closely-dancing (roughly 250,000 miles apart) neutron stars with 1.4 times the mass of the sun, was discovered and how it then was recognized that the system was a perfect laboratory to test Einstein's theory of gravity as well as gravitational radiation.

And how remarkably accurate Einstein's theory withstood this very severe test of nature!

The scientist in me told me that this must have been one of the great, if not the greatest, 20th century astronomical "accidental" (an adjective which Russell always modestly used) discoveries.

Indeed, this discovery was so spectacular and its physics implications so profound that it was always assumed by the global scientific community that it was a matter of when, not if, the ultimate accolade would be bestowed to these scientists, Russell Hulse and Joe Taylor, who made the discovery and subsequently understood its implications.

Indeed, in 1993, 18 years after the discovery was made, it finally happened. Hulse and Taylor received the truly well-deserved Nobel Prize!

Still, the lecture the audience in NTU was about to receive would not just end with scientific discussion. Russell would also be telling the audience how he, a deep intellectual (this is my description of Russell, he would never say that about himself), made the decision after receiving the most esteemed scientific accolade to devote his professional life to promote science among young minds of the world as a cultural experience.

As usual, Russell peppered the lecture with his usual elegance and humility. Yet, to me, I saw another dimension that may be even more profound, at least at the humanistic angle. After all, except for the "small" quirk that Russell was physically 10,000 miles from the audience, a lecture by a distinguished scholar to such an audience should be nothing more then a normal occurrence in any university.

The vast distance, which would make such an occurrence unthinkable a few decades ago, was shrunk to zero by modern technology, the technology of videoconferencing. This had to be one of the most palpable manifestations of Thomas Friedman's "flat world." In the following hour after Russell began to speak, I could actually see how attentive the audience was at Singapore's end, and how meaningful human interactions would take place "in real time" (except for the minute time delay due to another fundamental physical manifestation, the finiteness of the speed of light).

Indeed, in the subsequent hour, the boundaries constructed by humanity, ethnic differences, language differences, and what have you, all seemed to have melted away with "vanishing" distance. I felt that the audience in Singapore was de facto existing in the same physical space with us in Dallas, or us with them in Singapore. What an exciting thought! Indeed, for that hour, we were all in a tiny global village, undergoing normal human discourse.

As I was about to step in front of the camera to introduce my good friend Russell Hulse to 300 science teachers in my hometown Singapore — at least one I found out later was from my alma mater River Valley High School — a moment of 1964 flashed through my mind, when I was a young man, in Singapore's old airport, getting ready to board a Pan Am Boeing 707 for my maiden voyage to the U.S.

In that old airport, I could still "see" many parents sending their children off to this far, far distant land called the U.S. My mother was among them. Most had bewildered and worrying expression on their faces, wondering when they would see their children again, if ever. The U.S. was such a distant land that the difference between it and the moon from Singapore was miniscule at best! Normal human emotions at that moment brought glittering tears down the cheeks of many.

Yet, returning to the present, I realized that the audience in front of me was over 10,000 miles away, and I was about to introduce Russell to them in "real time", except for the half-second delay due to speed of light being finite. Unlike all previous times when I had the honor of introducing Russell, this was the first time the audience would exist in cyberspace. Also, this was the first time I was to speak to 300 virtual individuals from my hometown!

Today, there would be no glittering tears on the cheeks, but anticipation of what the lecture was all about...10,000 miles away.

Just then, I had a moment of "blue-sky thinking". I thought to myself what it would be like, say soon, when videoconferencing is merely a trivial turnkey effort and academic culture so mature and intense that an occurrence such as this would no longer be a rarity, but a commonality. What would be the intellectual landscape be, say, between universities separated by vast distances and great oceans, when there are literally hundreds of such lectures going on daily; just like today on a daily basis, there are hundreds of such lectures going on, but most are confined to physical walls of classrooms or lecture halls. In that new paradigm, what would be the definition of a GREAT university, I wondered. What could happen to a graduate student from Asia who could literally control and maintain sophisticated equipment thousands of miles away, or vice versa? The impact on the intellectual and economic landscapes, and indeed on humanity, would surely be immeasurable!

This blue-sky thinking was especially apt for me personally because this happened to be the last day that I would be associated with UTDallas. Soon, I would be associated with a university 10,000 miles away, across the great Pacific Ocean. How should I, as someone with strong ties to North America and Asia, be building such bridges?

As I was blue-skying, suddenly, reality hit home when the Master of Ceremony on Singapore's side, Professor Riley, proudly mentioned that the audience there had eaten a wonderful buffet dinner before the lecture. Knowing how great food in Singapore can taste, a fantastic fusion of Chinese, Indian and Malay cuisines, I could almost smell and taste, in my mind, a palpable mental "makan" (Malay word for eating), so to speak!

If only videoconferencing could also make food transportation a reality. When will "Beam me up, Scotty" be a reality, I wonder?

(2007)

10

Khan Academy: Could this be the Onset of Global Undergraduate Education's Metamorphic Transformation in the 21st Century?

This was written on March 16, 2011, when the author was Senior Vice President, Global Strategy, Planning and Evaluation, National Tsing Hua University, Hsinchu.

A free world-class education for anyone, anywhere.[2]

...he (Khan) started a revolution...

— *Bill Gates*[3]

Einstein once said that "Everything should be made as simple as possible. Not simpler!"

Preamble

On March 14–15, sitting in the airplane while watching some mindless movies on route from Dallas to Los Angeles to Taipei, I could not resist the temptation of my mind's reverberation on what I had read, heard and watched from Khan Academy's website a few days ago and what I have learned since.

---

[2] http://www.khanacademy.org/about
[3] http://www.youtube.com/watch?v=UuMTSU9DcqQ&feature=player_embedded#at=81

In fact, as an incurable educator, I simply could not stop wondering about the possibility (or possibilities) if this global, free-for-all, one man show (or revolution, as Bill Gates called it) of Sal Khan were to be successful and can globally scale-up to multi-languages as well as multi-disciplines normally covered in undergraduate schools worldwide. I cannot imagine that undergraduate education as we know it today will not undergo a monumental transformation in the 21st century.

So what is Khan Academy and what does it do? What is the big deal?

Simply put, Sal Khan is an obviously smart, maybe even brilliant, young man, who was educated at a number of elite North American universities.

While he was enjoying the lucrative career of being a hedge fund investor, serendipitously he found himself leveraging on the internet to help his cousins who were in need of assistance in (presumably) algebra. He found out that by carefully imposing a time limit of 12 minutes for each teaching session, developing the subject matter step by step, and recording what he "lectured" to his cousins by utilizing the web via YouTube in the form of "blackboard" instructions, his nephew was able to over and over again go back to the lectures and eventually understood the subject matter. According to the client's (in this case, his nephew's) feedback, this was far better than the face-to-face instructions.

With this genesis, Khan began to prepare more and more 12-minute instructions, not only about algebra, which he soon expanded from simple algebra to differential equations, but also about physics, chemistry, biology, economics, finance and so on. To date, there are some 2,100 lectures. Once this was done, thanks to YouTube, these 2,100 lectures are available free and round-the-clock to anyone from all corners on earth, as long as they have internet access!

Once this fever caught his attention, Khan made the decision to quit his hedge fund investment job and devoted himself full time to developing Khan Academy!

Within a year, some 24 million "students" had "attended" Khan Academy's 2,100 lessons. Remarkably, there is only one (yes, ONE) faculty, namely Khan himself!

I Test it Out

I have to admit whenever I heard about anything remotely resembling "distance learning," my skeptical antenna would go up. Having heard about, learned and in some cases even participated in what could be called "distance learning", I find it either unsatisfactory at best, or a dismal failure at worst.

Well, I thought to myself, since Bill Gates thinks it is good, I should at least check out what it is like. I was skeptical even with Bill Gates' endorsement. After all, while Gates is a world-class entrepreneur, I am unsure about his credentials on education, especially teaching.

I naturally was drawn towards the category entitled "Chemistry", among the 2,100 sessions, and the one that caught my attention was a session known as "Entropy Intuition". The reason I picked this one was because when I was an undergraduate, I could not think of anything more aloof and more abstract than the concept of entropy. To me it seemed that that pioneers of thermodynamics simply pulled the concept out from thin air. I remember asking myself over and over again then: "How could this be?" I also asked myself, "How smart do you have to be to notice something as elusive as entropy?"

Well, I watched the video. To say that the lecture "blew me away" is an understatement. Using the simplest language and utilizing totally understandable but nontrivial examples, Khan was able to explain the concept of entropy. Listening to Khan, who spoke slowly, clearly, succinctly, and most of all, confidently, about a subject as abstract as entropy, I am convinced that anyone who intends to learn can and will learn from him. Indeed, maybe not the first time watching this lecture, but by watching it over and over again, one can.

After this experience, I remember saying to myself: "Well, Khan was probably a physical science or engineering major when he was a student. Being a good student, he must have mastered a course on thermodynamics. While it is good that he was able to give such a nice lecture on a subject he learned well, maybe it would be a stretch for him to talk about something that a normal physical science or engineering major would be comfortable with."

Well, how about biology?

Quite by accident, my daughter, who happens to be a medical school faculty, was visiting us the same day I discovered Khan Academy. Sitting next to her, I noticed that she was watching and listening intensely to something on her new toy: an iPad. It was a lecture on the discovery of ATP, or Adenosine Triphosphate. The voice coming out of the iPad sounded like some serious researcher discussing the subject matter. Being curious, I asked my daughter which famous professor was talking about this and why she was listening to it. Her answer startled me: "It's not a famous professor. It's some guy named Khan who puts thousands of lectures on various subjects on YouTube and this is simply a short lesson about this subject. It has been a while since I learned this subject, and it is so fundamental in my business. So I wanted to review it. You know what, Daddy, Khan gave the best review that I could find!"

My jaw dropped when I heard her comment. I quickly opened up the same YouTube link. As an amateur, I was also curious about ATP ever since I learned from my late friend Britton Chance that his development of optical spectroscopy to study living tissues had something to do with this complex molecule. Well, I found that the lecture was really, really good. Step by step, I learned about the meaning and the utilization of ATP. Indeed, I can see how an expert like my daughter or an amateur like me can learn about the subject from watching this session known as "Introduction to ATP or Adenosine Triphosphate".

At this point, imagine having two world-class lessons on entropy and ATP. Then imagine that this is scaled up to 2,100 world-class lessons on mathematics, chemistry, physics, biology, banking and money, cosmology and astronomy, current economics, finance, history, venture capital and capital markets, and more.... This is what you have today in Khan Academy.

Einstein once said that "Everything should be made as simple as possible. Not simpler!" Going through various YouTube lessons, I noticed that Khan adheres to this principle rigorously. He does not "talk down" to students. He does not simplify the subject matter to make it look easy, or worse, trivial. He hits the core meaning of the subject, and asks the student to keep up with him in the development of the subject, in a pace that the student can be comfortable with. Anyone who intends to learn the subject, from any corner of the world, can learn it from these world-class lessons. Suddenly, the world of learning is really flat!

All this is done by one faculty, à la Khan.

I am sold!

My Conjectures about the Education Implications of Khan Academy

The following are my conjectures about the possible impact of Khan Academy on undergraduate education worldwide, if it is scaled up even further.

I specifically confined my conjecture to undergraduate education because graduate education and beyond, in my mind, does require teacher-student interactions. For example, my good friend Aaron Ciechanover and his doctorate mentor Avram Hershko won the Nobel Prize in chemistry by discovering the so-called "ubiquitin", a subject critical to protein degradation. I of course have no knowledge of what their interactions were like, but I am quite sure that it must have been a body-contact sport, and not through the internet. After all, learning at this level is not simply a "transfer of known knowledge" because the research level, which is at the edge of knowledge, is generally about the unknown, and not the known. So from this point of view, it is probably difficult to bring the Khan model to bear.

However, much of the undergraduate body of knowledge is relatively static. It is unlikely that it will change significantly. The only change would be "additional" new lectures. I can imagine that someday, Khan Academy will not have just 2,100 lectures, it will have 10,000, 100,000 or even a million and beyond. If Khan can find other lecturers as good as he is, who speak other languages, then Khan Academy will have parallel lectures in Chinese, Tamil, Japanese, Korean, Vietnamese, Malay, Arabic, Hebrew, French, German, Italian and what have you. After all, as we all know, information growth can be, and is, explosive.

What Khan has done is to leverage his intellectual strength to understand a very large number of disciplines, and then leverage his superb communication skills, sort of what one would call "the old fashioned way", to bring the fundamentals and salient points of each discipline to students anywhere, anytime.

In hindsight, I feel that with the proliferation of the internet in space-time dimensions, coupled with someone who seems to be a naturally outstanding teacher with great showmanship, the creation of an education model like Khan's is waiting to happen. In its present form, a student in the remote back water of central Russia can receive the same excellent education as a student from one of the major metropolitan areas of North America or Asia Pacific.

And it is happening now! I believe this is why Bill Gates refers to this as a "revolution!"

Should universities today pay attention to this very innovative education paradigm? Well, I believe that it would be to the peril of universities if they do not. After all, newer and newer generations of young people will grow up with internet as an integral part of their everyday living and learning.

Does this mean the demise of undergraduate education as we know it today, if Khan Academy begins to penetrate into the psyche of current universities? I do not believe so. This is because the way Khan cleverly makes full use of the internet and its inherent tools, such as YouTube, to deliver ubiquitously this innovative way of teaching, will surely attract the attention of new generations of students. I can also envision that the students can vote with their feet in the utilization of this form of instruction to learn, if not to supplement, the learning process — the standard curricula they receive from their respective universities. At least in its present form, I believe this is how the Khan Academy paradigm could impact undergraduate education in a palpable and profound manner.

Mind you, I do not believe that Khan Academy is a static concept. Nor will Khan be satisfied with the current status, no matter how successful he is already. It will dynamically change. I anxiously await the appearance of "Khan Academy 2" or "Khan Academy 3" or what have you. Surely they will appear. Even more certain is that they will impact global higher education in an unexpected manner.

(2011)

The Budding Universities

11

Shantou University: An Example of Dynamical Transformation in 21st Century Asia Pacific Higher Education

The author was Senior Executive Vice President, National Cheng Kung University, when he did this report and reflection.

Photo of Board of Trustees of Shantou University taken on July of 2010. The person in the middle in red is Mr. Li Ka-Shing (李嘉诚.). Li is the Honorable Chair of the Board. The person on Li's left is the Honorable Li Hai (李海,), Chairman of the Board and Vice Governor of Guangdong Province (广东省). Other notable members of the Board are Fu-Jia Yang (杨福家), Chancellor of UK's Nottingham University, Li Peigen (李培根), President of Huazhong University of Science and Technology and Chen Jiaer (陈佳洱), former President of Peking University.

Preamble

Higher education development is one of the fundamental consequences of economic growth. Without this, sustainable economic growth for the benefit of humanity is not feasible, if not impossible. Its importance was amply manifested in Europe and North America in the 19th and 20th centuries, respectively. Hence, it is no surprise that with the backbreaking speed of Asia Pacific economic growth in the second half of the 20th century and the first decade of the 21st century, one saw in the region an explosion of higher education. For example, the number of universities in Taiwan in the last three to four decades has increased between five to six fold!

I am fortunate to have had the opportunity to observe in detail in the Asia Pacific region, the establishment and/or profound transformation of a number of such institutions. The creation and/or transformation of the following four universities, all of which were created in past three decades with the intention of driving the region to new intellectual and economic heights, serve as exemplaries of how robust this Asia Pacific trend is. They are:

1. Hong Kong University of Science and Technology (HKUST, 香港科技大)
2. National Quemoy University (NQU, 国立金门大学)
3. Macau University (MU, 澳门大学)
4. Shantou University (STU, 汕头大学)

In a nutshell, just as many other universities which had mushroomed in Asia Pacific in past several decades, all four were created/transformed because of "right time (天时,)," "perfect location (地利,)" and "someone had the right idea (人和.)"

For the first three universities, HKUST, NQU and MU, if Hong Kong and Macau were not economically robust and politically ready and/or stable at the time of their creations and/or transformations, and if the intricate cross-straits relationship between Mainland and Taiwan was not much less confrontational, there would be no stable platforms for any of the three to have been created, let alone grow!

The fourth university and the subject of this article, Shantou University, however, had a very different genesis. Even though HKUST and NQU were the brainchildren of two fearlessly driven individuals of significant intellectual strengths and political connections (吴家玮 for HKUST and 李金振 for NQU), and grew rapidly either in the last decade of the 20th century or the first decade of the 21st century, STU was the brainchild of a sole individual of significant personal wealth and deep regional influence.

This person could not resist the love for his hometown and his deep and personal passion regarding the fundamental importance of education for national improvement, and also had an enormous financial muscle in the beginning of the 80s for him to realize his dream. That person is Mr. Li Ka-Shing (李嘉诚), unquestionably one of the, if not the, most powerful Asian mega-entrepreneur in the 20th and 21st centuries. According to Forbes.com, in 2010, Li was the 14th-richest individual in the world with net worth of about USD 21 billion. By creating a university in his hometown, I would assume that Mr. Li must have taken some calculated risk. For one thing, in order for such a new university to be successful (however success is defined) with impact down the road in the region as well as in China in general, leveraging his personal prestige as a world class entrepreneur would be transparently unavoidable.

Thus, leveraging his personal connections with the Chinese central and Guangdong provincial governments, Mr. Li made a bold move in building a university in Shantou. I should say that this is particularly intriguing case study because Mr. Li was and still is one of the world's most successful mega-entrepreneurs who instinctively knew that return-on-investment (ROI) in establishing an education institution is at best tenuous, at worst a financially draining proposition, i.e., NOT a good business venture in either the short or long run.

With this as genesis, STU was born in 1981 (quite by serendipity, that same year, the University of Macau was also born). Nearly 30 years later, it is today a full-fledged comprehensive university, with colleges spanning the entire gamut, from medicine and engineering to law and literature and so on.

Board of Trustees of Shantou University

In fall of 2006, I had the honor of being invited by the Li Ka-Shing Foundation (LKSF, 李嘉诚基金会) to become a member of the Board of Trustees of the university. So in May 2007, I attended my first meeting of the Board and started my personal observation of the growth of this interesting university.

Unlike many virtual "Boards of Trustees" of Chinese universities, which generally serve in peripheral and advisory capacities, STU's Board de facto is the "oversight" of the university at a 10,000-foot level. According to its charter from day one, this Board is one of two bodies which the President, the sole chief executive (and to a certain extent the Executive President as well) of the university, report to. The other presidential line of report is the Guangdong Provincial Education Office. Guangdong Province is one of the economically most powerful provinces of China. With 90 million inhabitants, it geographically sits right next to Hong Kong.

A university is a very complex human organization. As this is the "first" administrative layer of a Chinese university, I noticed that LKSF is very careful (and kind) so as not to overburden the precious professional time distinguished members need to devote to understanding the fundamental and complicated issues of STU. Hence, the Board meets only once a year and during the meeting (which usually lasted for two hours), the senior members of the university would present in detail the progress of the university as well as new initiatives taken during the past year. Each presentation was followed by questions and comments by Board members and answers by university administrators and members of the Li Ka-Shing Foundation (which I will mention about in more detail later.)

It is to be expected that the time constraint prevented ample, in-depth discussion on the mission and operations of STU. Still, I felt that in the past four years, essentials of STU developments were able to be conveyed to the Board, and the Board had enough time to make significant and detailed suggestions. (*In attending the University of California System's Board of Regents meeting in March of this year, I noticed that its Board meets once every other month for two whole days. Between official Board meetings, there were also subcommittee meetings. So each member actually has to commit to something like one meeting every month. For STU's Board, it is not possible under the present conditions to follow the University of California mode.*)

In order to put his fingerprints on the Board, Mr. Li serves as its Honorary Chairperson. The annual Board meeting always dovetails with

STU's graduation ceremony. A number of us also took the opportunity to deliver speeches to students and faculty, which always included extensive Q&A time, thus allowing us to have first-hand knowledge of the aspirations of students and faculty members.

Apparently, Mr. Li never once missed any of the graduation ceremonies in the past quarter of a century, nor any Board meetings. For someone whose one of many day jobs is managing one of the world's largest conglomerates — Mr. Li is Chairman of Hutchison-Whampoa Limited, which operates in 55 countries and has over 220,000 employees and whose financial turnover in 2006, according to its website, is "approximately HKD268 billion (USD34 billion)" — this can only be termed as **true commitment**. For me, this makes being a part of the Board all the more heavy with responsibilities.

Li Ka-Shing Foundation, Li Ka-Shing's "third son"

As I mentioned earlier, Mr. Li established the LKSF. In order "to put resources where his mouth is" and to run the many philanthropic activities globally as efficiently as possible, Li set up LKSF, a not-for-profit organization sitting in Hong Kong. The Foundation, as far as I can tell, is operated efficiently by a relatively small cadre of dedicated, and by nature of the business being global, very hard working staff members. Mr. Li is so passionate about this Foundation, and what it is doing worldwide, especially with respect to STU, that in his recent acceptance speech for his Lifetime Achievement Award from Forbes, he referred to it as his "third son!" I can sense that staff members of LKSF spent a considerable fraction of their time in STU, working hand-in-hand with the administration.

The activities of LKSF are global and numerous. Examples are as follows:

- Funding (with nearly HKD 2 billion donated to date, which at today's exchange rate, is more than USD 250 million) and overseeing the overall operations of STU;
- Funding of USD 66 million of the Lee Kuan Yew (李光耀) School of Public Policy of the National University of Singapore; Funding of USD

40 million of the University of California Berkeley for the Li Ka-Shing Center for Biomedical and Health Sciences;
- Funding of CAD 25 million of the Li Ka-Shing Knowledge Institute of Michael's Hospital in Toronto.

Perhaps the most notable achievement within China is the so-called "Cheung Kong Scholars" program. This program is described as follows[4]:

"In support of the Chinese Government's objective to promote national prosperity through science and education, the Foundation established The Cheung Kong Scholars Program in collaboration with China's Ministry of Education. The Program's two main initiatives — The Cheung Kong Achievement Award and the engagement of specially appointed professors — recognize outstanding Chinese scholars and encourage them to return to China. Donation amount: HK$70 million"

To date, there are more than 1,000 Cheung Kong Scholars (长江学者) dotting China's intellectual landscape. Undoubtedly, just like the 1,000 or so CUPEA Laureates in the 80s and 90s — from a program which educated some of China's best and brightest physics students, and was the brainchild of Professor Tsung Dao Lee (李政道) (Nobel Laureate in Physics in 1957), and who have become the pillars of the science and technology globally today — the Cheung Kong Scholars will surely be the movers and shakers of China's intellectual and economic pillars in the years to come.

Meeting the Shantou University Community

In order to learn more about Shantou University and how it operates, and to explore ways in my capacity as the Board member to assist this new and unusual university in China, the Foundation graciously invited me for a visit on May 28 and 29, 2007. During my visit, I had extensive discussions with STU's senior administrators. Since then, in my four

---

[4] http://hgm2002.hgu.mrc.ac.uk/Sponsors/LKSF.htm

Board meetings, I had more discussions with STU communities, from students to presidents:

- President of the University, Xu Xiaohu (徐小虎). Interestingly, Xiaohu means "little tiger". By training, Xu is a forensic scientist and a former Dean of the Medical School of Shantou University.
- Executive President (执行校长) Gu Peihua (顾佩华). Gu joined Shantou University five years ago. He is on leave-of-absence from his position as a Distinguished Professor of the Department of Mechanical and Manufacturing Engineering of the University of Calgary of Canada and a member of the Canadian Academy of Engineering. He brought a palpable international vision and deep knowledge of western universities' administrative structure to STU.
- Consultant to Shantou University Medical School from LKSF Dr. Frieda Law (罗敏洁). Prior to working with the LKSF, Dr. Law was a medical educator and program director with Project HOPE (USA), based in Shanghai Second Medical University. During this period she established a first-class paediatric and neonatal facility at the Shanghai Children's Hospital. Dr. Law received her medical education from the University of Melbourne in Australia.
- During this past Board meeting, I had one interesting conversation with a young second year interior-design major student who boldly wanted to discuss with me about the cross-straits relationship. This student came from the deep rural area of an interior province, whose family was obviously of very meager means. The only reason she could attend STU was because of the university scholarship. Despite her "humble" beginning, I found her incredibly well-read. She was also able to articulate clearly her view of the cross-straits relationship, and what it meant to generations of young Chinese like her.

Some Personal Perspectives on STU

1. Shantou, which is part of what Chinese refer to collectively as "Chaozhou (潮州)", is a region that has linkages to very powerful overseas Chinese. For example, a significant percentage of Thai-Chinese, many of whom are well-to-do, have this region as their heritage.

In Singapore, where I grew up, although this clan is not the majority, the Chaozhou Association (潮州会馆) is a very economically powerful local entity. Many important and highly successful Singaporeans in banking and education are people one refers to as "Chaozhou Ren (潮州人)", or people of Chaozhou. Of course, Mr. Li is probably one of their most "favorite sons". Since Shantou is a bit far (four to five hours' drive on the superhighway, which translates to approximately 200–250 miles) from the Hong Kong–Shenzhen–Guangzhou (香港-深圳-广州) economic corridor (one notices that the enormous and amazing Asian Games of 2010 was held in Guangzhou, which is a clear manifestation of the corridor's dynamism), its development still has a great deal of room for development. However, since the Overseas Chaozhou clan (潮州帮) is known to be fiercely pro-hometown, I suspect that this region will catch up with the rest of Guangdong, with assistance coming from the Chaozhou clan in the foreseeable future.
2. Another interesting aspect of Chaozhou is that the local language (潮州话) has the same linguistic genesis as the language of Southern Fujian (闽南), even though they are in different provinces. Just as with Chaozhou, many overseas Chinese are also from Southern Fujian. Curiously, any casual visitor to the Southern Fujian district would immediately notice the enormous and robust growth of the region. In recent years, one of the Chinese government's major projects is to develop what is known as the "western ocean region" (海西), which means the Fujian province primarily. In my four years as the Board member of STU, I thought there must be excellent opportunities to link up with that region of China.
3. In many of his speeches, Mr. Li outlined his grand vision and lofty goal for STU, which is for it to become an institution whose products, namely students, will someday mitigate some of humanity's ills. His profound interest in healthcare and life sciences, which became abundantly clear from our repeated visits to the Medical School and affiliated hospitals, the ground breaking news of a massive new medical school infrastructure, and talking extensively to Dr. Law, even in the area of "hospices," is indicative of Mr. Li's profound interest in and respect for human dignity. While this is clearly an incredibly tall order, everyone I talked to in more or less the same language agreed that

Shantou University's experiment is unique, full of challenges, but also rich in opportunities. Of course, how the "experiment" will turn out in the long run, say within a decade or two, or maybe longer, is unclear. Yet, I do detect a significant sense of optimism. I also sense from the discussion that from the perspective of the LKSF as well as from the university, there is some level of anticipation that the Board may be critical in this journey. I find such a challenge exhilarating.

Epilogue

One of the critical and urgent tasks in my mind, when confronting STU, and for that matter to varying degrees, HKUST, NQU or MU, is to define, however vaguely, what image it (or they) should project not just to China but to the world. To this end, careful recruiting of individuals with outstanding ability and ethics, without compromise, may be one of the important and critical steps. As Executive President Gu emphasized to me during the past four years of our interaction, to move rapidly along the pathway outlined by Mr. Li, recruiting better and better people for the university, in faculty and administration, is not a luxury, it is a must.

As I mentioned earlier, this is possible (because of the resources available, which is what I mention often: vision without funding is hallucination) and difficult (because the university is perhaps still far from

Pictures from left to right of Noyes, Hale and Millikan. These were the three gentlemen who transformed a vocational school in dusty-old California in the early 20th century into today a global powerhouse of science and technology.

its projected destiny). To this end, I am reminded of the genesis of Caltech (加州理工学院) in early 20th century. During the era of Noyes, Hale and Millikan, the three giants who left their high positions in East Coast and Midwest intellectual epic centers and went to dusty-old West Coast in the early 20th century, Caltech was set on a pathway of supreme excellence built on powerful intellectual strengths and administrative organization. Thus armed with a vision, with resources, and most importantly, with network (a euphemism for globalization), Noyes *et. al.* made Caltech, Caltech! ***They made the world have a deep perception that Caltech is world-class*** (and perception is reality).

Standing behind STU is not your average, well-to-do individual, but a mega-entrepreneur without peer in Asia Pacific who is armed with a powerful vision. With this as an underpinning, if the likes of Noyes, Hale and Millikan can either be nurtured among those already within STU or recruited from outside, how can STU not achieve the aim as outlined by Mr. Li? I find this possibility intriguing and see no reason not to be optimistic for the long-term development of STU.

Post-comment

Perhaps the most startling fact to me personally is that I discovered that the Director of one of STU's colleges, Cheung-Kong College of Arts and Design, is Professor Kan Tai-Keung (靳埭强). Professor Kan not only is one of the most well-known designers in Asia in particular and the world in general, but he also happens to be the brother of my office-mate Dr. Kan Kit-Keung (靳杰强) at the University of Texas in Austin when we were both aspiring young physicists. Interestingly, Kit-Keung today also has emerged to be one of the most remarkable modern-art artists in the 21st century. The Kan brothers are breathtakingly exciting artists!

But the intriguing story does not end here. I soon discovered from the web that Professor Kan's Deputy Dean is Professor Wang Shouzhi (王受之), one of the most well-known designers and a distinguished professor at the Los Angeles/Pasadena Art Center College of Design. Well, Professor Wang happens to be none other then my cousin-in-law. His wife's father and my father are BROTHERS!

Having Kan and Wang as its leaders, I am sure that Cheung-Kong College of Arts and Design is already highly regarded as one of the best in China!

T. K. Kan

Who says that between any two human beings, there are six degrees of separation!

(2010)

Annex

Impressions of Shantou University — My Seven-Year Summary

Shantou University: An artist's rendition of a new sports center

The Genesis

Seven years ago, before I came to Asia, I was recruited to be a member of the Board of Governors (董事会) of Shantou University (汕头大学). The genesis of Shantou University centers on a very exquisite "Teo Chew Nang (潮州人)," or a person from Chaozhou ("Teo Chew" is the pronunciation of "Chaozhou" in the local dialect). That person is Mr. Li Ka-Shing (李嘉诚). As a young man growing up in Singapore, I have had many schoolmates who were "Teo Chew Nang". Geographically, Chaozhou is the name of a city which is situated in the

Northeast part of Guangzhou province (广东省). This part of China is embedded with rich Chinese culture. For example, one of the famous Tang Dynasty neo-Confucianists and poets, Han Yu (韩愈), made a profound impression to the region when he was here.

Its dialect, 潮州话, or the Chaozhou language, is vastly different from

Han Yu

that of Guangzhou (广州), but while different, it is akin to that of Xiamen (厦门) in the Fujian Province (福建). This interesting feature turns out to have social, cultural and political implications for the region, which I will mention at the end of this report.

Impressions of Shantou University — My Seven-Year Summary

Enclosed map depicts where Chaozhou is located. Adjacent to Chaozhou is a twin city known as Shantou (汕头). Hence, the region is also sometimes referred to as Chao-Shan (潮汕).

Perhaps because they are neither *here* (Guangzhou) nor *there* (Xiamen), the people of Chaozhou are known to be fiercely loyal to each other. Their cuisine is also not just delicious, but is transparently different from that of Guangzhou and Xiamen. In many parts of Asia, such as Hong Kong, Thailand, Malaysia, Indonesia and Singapore, one can easily find such people dotting the intellectual and economic landscapes. In Singapore, for example, where I grew up, Chaozhou Kinsman Center (潮州会馆) is unquestionably one of the most powerful, if not the most powerful, political, economical and cultural organizations in the country. Their intellectual and economic presence is palpable. The same can be said in Hong Kong and Thailand.

If one were to find a "favorite son" of Chao-Shan in the 20th and 21st centuries, that person is unquestionably Mr. Li Ka-Shing, who today is commonly known as the "richest man of Asia (亚洲首富)".

He lives in Hong Kong, but one can easily find Mr. Li's entrepreneurial footprint in all corners of the globe.

Growing up poor, Mr. Li had very limited formal education. Yet, perhaps because of his raw intelligence and his inherent persevering characteristic, Mr. Li had not only been able to self-educate, but was able to deeply understand the fundamental importance of education, for himself, and more importantly, for his fellow human beings. One of his famous quotations amply emphasizes how he deeply values knowledge through education:

"Knowledge cannot be merely a degree or a skill... it demands a broader vision, capabilities in critical thinking and logical deduction without which we cannot have constructive progress."

From left: Li Ka-Shing, Fok Tai-Fai and I in an engaging discussion over lunch on June 27, 2013, about the future of Shantou University. It is remarkable how absorbed is Mr. Li about many of the details of the development of Shantou University.

In the early 80s, as China entered its post-Cultural Revolution era, Mr. Li, who already was an extraordinarily wealthy man then, wanted to do something for his hometown. He noticed that the Chao-Shan region, despite having nearly 10 million inhabitants, had no university *per se*. So, working with Guangdong Province, he single-handedly created Shantou University. For the past three decades, Mr. Li has wrapped his heart and soul into this university. The foundation under his name known as the Li Ka-Shing Foundation (李嘉诚基金会) became and still is a dynamical engine of overseeing the proper yet visionary growth of the university. Indeed, for three decades, Mr. Li bestowed substantial financial resources as well as directional guidance to ensure the fledgling Shantou University (30 years is still young for an institution) may one day be intellectually robust and globally meaningful for humanity.

The Board of Governors

A number of public universities in China had each instituted a rudimentary "Board of Governors (BoG)". Unfortunately, most are nothing more than window dressings, which means that not only do they lack the right compositions, they are also without responsibilities or accountabilities. In fact, they hardly ever meet.

The 2013 BoG meeting in the Shantou University Board Room. The meeting was held on June 28, 2013.

It is in this sense that one needs to commend Mr. Li and Shantou University. The BoG was formed in 1987. Although I have to admit that it still has some distance to go before it can be considered as world-class, it nevertheless has gone some distance in reaching that goal.

Shantou University's BoG has 25 members. Mr. Li is its Honorary Chair. The *ex-officio* chair is the Vice Governor of Guangdong province, in charge of education. There are two advisors in charge of finance and legal issues. The BoG serves in a *pro-bono* capacity. Also, five truly outstanding individuals in the China and Hong Kong landscape are serving as special advisors to the BoG. For example, Academicians Chen Jia'er, a well-known accelerator physicist and former President of Peking University, and Academician Ba Denian, a notable Chinese immunologist, physician and former President of Peking Union Medical University, are serving as advisors. In my past seven years on the BoG, I have seen how seriously they take their advisory role, and comments they made were inevitably noteworthy. Four members of the board (beyond the chair) are Guangdong Provincial government and Chao-Shan municipal government officials, four are Shantou University senior administrators, and five are Li Ka-Shing Foundation officers. The remaining eight members (not including me) are all well-known and powerful academics from China, Hong Kong and the U.S. For example, the list includes Academician Fu-Jia Yang, the former Chancellor of Nottingham University and former President of Fudan University, Academician Li Peigen, President of Huazhong University of Science and Technology, Professor Chew Shew-Ping, Vice President of Hong Kong University, Professor Fok Tai-Fai, Vice President of the Chinese University of Hong Kong, and Professor Lin Haifan, Director of the Yale University Stem Cell Center.

In the past seven years, a tradition was slowly formed where members of the BoG would take the opportunity to give open lectures to Shantou University communities. This was my third time doing it. It was indeed a gratifying experience interacting with students and faculty in this manner. This is another excellent example of how to operate an outstanding BoG meeting.

What I observed in the past seven years is that the BoG is progressively and enthusiastically engaging in multi-dimensional educational and administrative issues. This past meeting was certainly no exception. In this one, there were certainly exciting and spirited discussions of many forefront areas of global educational endeavors which Shantou University is initiating or experimenting with. Issues included how liberal arts education in the form of residential colleges is best instituted throughout the university and how the now global hot-topic of "Massive Open Online Courses (MOOC)" is now being experimented with on campus.

There was a discussion which particularly intrigued me and that was the issue of "Li Ka-Shing Economics". This is obviously a spin-off from Mr. Li's enormously successful global entrepreneurial career. Indeed, in my opinion, what perhaps is of particular interest not only to Shantou University communities, but to Asia in general, is how to translate this success as a manifestation of "Asian inherent self confidence". In a recent speech, I said the following:

> "...Asia must develop a deep sense of inherent self-confidence and without which the 21st century is surely not to be the Asian Century."

Some Interesting Anecdotes

I find it quite curious that somehow my life was linked to Shantou University. When I first joined the BoG in 2007, I immediately noticed that the then Dean of Cheung Kong College of Art and Design was none other than the famous Hong Kong artist Mr. Kan Dai Keung. The world is indeed small. Mr. Kan's younger brother, Kan Kit-Keung, was my office mate when we were BoG postdoctoral fellows in nuclear physics in 1974–1976 at the University of Texas in Austin. But serendipity does not end there! Last year, Mr. Kan Dai-Keung resigned from his position at Shantou University, and the university hired another outstanding design artist, Mr. Wang Shouji from the U.S. Now it gets eerie — Mr. Wang is my cousin Feng Da-Mei's husband!

I have to admit these two recruitments of world class artists, Mr. Kan and Mr. Wang, are a clear manifestation that Shantou University in the past decade has made colossal effort to bring in the best of the best to propel the university's global reputation.

This photo was taken on June 27, 2013. The person standing on my right is Dean Wang Shouji. The gentleman "lurking" in the background who appears blurry is Vice President Chew Shew-Ping from Hong Kong University.

Shantou University Graduation Ceremony

One of the nice spin-offs of the BoG meeting was that it always dovetailed with Shantou University's June graduation ceremony. This was indeed a grandiose ceremony, even as such ceremonies go. I think this is partly because Mr. Li's enormous, colorful and successful life made him take on a "rock star" image as far as many Asians are concerned. This is of course especially true since for every graduate, Mr. Li's effort of creating Shantou University has literally "changed his/her life". Naturally at the graduation ceremony, the graduates simply could not hold back their inner appreciative feelings towards Mr. Li. Maybe because my last name begins with an "F", for the past seven years, I have always had the honor of standing behind Mr. Li as we walked into the auditorium. Therefore, I could observe firsthand the electrifying outpour of gratitude from some 2,500 graduates. Believe me, that was indeed an unforgettable sight.

Having the entire BoG dressed up in graduation gowns and marched first through the mountains of students and then stay the whole time on stage, in my opinion, added much to the already humanly warm ambience of the ceremony. Indeed, as I walked behind Mr. Li, I could see many students smiling at me, and some even extended a hand to shake mine, as if saying "thank you" to me and all my fellow BoG members. Such palpable feelings are priceless!

Finally, the highlight of the ceremony surely goes to the comments made by Mr. Li. For me, the 2013 comment was particularly profound. In his speech, Mr. Li uttered these words to the entire audience:

> "...being called the "richest man in Asia" gave me a taste of enormous complexity. My life is full of challenges. Amidst these challenges, as a human being, I continue to strive to be a Chinese who loves my people; as an entrepreneur, I continue to strive among all contradictions in my responsibilities, to serve my social responsibilities."

These careful words seem to summarize how Mr. Li views the wealth he has amassed!

Shantou University's 2013 graduation ceremony. Graduates, friends and family members gave their thundering roar when Mr. Li entered the Hall!

I am on stage at the extreme right

Shantou University and Chao-Shan

Will Shantou University one day becomes a world-class university, as envisioned by Mr. Li? I think only time will tell. I can say categorically that members of the university as well as the Li Ka-Shing Foundation are doing their utmost to provide the right vector for the university towards this eventuality.

If there is one area where there is significant room for improvement, it lies not within Shantou University, but without. By "without," I mean the Chao-Shan region. I think most people would agree with me that for some reason or reasons, Chao-Shan seems to be missing the boat of robust economic development. Unlike its two neighbors, Guangzhou and Xiamen, Chao-Shan as a region certainly does not appear to command excitement. Indeed, in the past seven years since I became associated with Shantou University, Chao-Shan region remains in a "sleepy posture". Certainly, anyone who is familiar with Xiamen and Guangzhou knows well that in seven years, these two cities could easily have "reinvented" themselves.

So what does that mean? In the modern world, a university is no longer an island. It needs intellectual and economic nourishments from "without". However, as long as Chao-Shan continues not to move forward economically in a robust manner, at some point the growth of Shantou University could hit a ceiling.

That to me is perhaps the greatest challenge for Shantou University in the 21st century. Unfortunately, such a challenge may be beyond the control of the university. If this challenge can be mitigated, I have every confidence that Shantou University will not only could fulfill the dream of Mr. Li Ka-Shing, it could be a shining castle on the hill!

(2013)

12

University of Macau: The Creation of a New Asian University

This was written when the author was Senior Executive Vice President, National Cheng Kung University (NCKU).

Preamble

Undoubtedly, East Asia's robust economic growth and overall political stability prompted higher education in the region to also make metamorphic transformation. A few days ago, together with Professor Yungnian Yang, Associate Vice President for Research and Professor Yi-Yuan Chen (陈益源), Chairman of the Department of Chinese Literature of NCKU, we visited one such university. It is the University of Macau (澳门大学).

There are a few fundamental reasons why we came to the University of Macau.

First, as I often jokingly say, "*good people all come from Texas!*" Well, it so happens that about a decade ago, the new president of University of Macau, President Wei Zhao (赵伟) overlapped with me in Texas. Zhao was then Associate Vice President for Research of Texas A and M University and I was Vice President for Research and Economic Development at the University of Texas at Dallas. That overlap made us become good friends and we have interacted on-and-off in the past decade. So, after Zhao became the new president of University of Macau a year and a half ago, and now that we are both in Asia, I wanted very much to come to visit him.

Second, about two months ago, my boss President Michael Lai attended a "Both Shores and Four Regions Higher Education Summit (两岸四地大学高峰会)" to commemorate the ground breaking ceremony of the

President Wei Zhao

University of Macau's new campus (more later about this). Afterwards, Zhao once again encouraged me to make an extra effort to come to visit the University of Macau. In the past two years, Zhao was informing me of a number of exciting developments at the University of Macau. Having that information in mind, and what I learned about the transformation of Macau as being unquestionably one of the fastest, if not the fastest, growing cities in Asia, certainly whetted my appetite to have an in-depth understanding of how the growth of this university is due to the fact that it is embedded in such a progressive city.

Third, before the trip, I made a phone call to Zhao, trying to understand what the main strengths of his university are so that I could prepare for the trip to ensure that the outcome of my visit would be as fruitful as possible. Since Zhao is a world-renowned computer scientist, I was expecting him to inform me that his university, under his leadership, and with enormous support from Macau's Special Administrative Region (澳门特别行政区政府), is moving full speed ahead in science and technology. Although that is indeed the case, Zhao also startled me by informing me that the University of Macau now has a strong Chinese Literature Department, since it is the university's mission to create a modern

university in Asia with Asian roots! That conversation prompted me to invite Professor Yi-Yuan Chen, Chairman of the Department of Chinese Literature of NCKU, to join me on this trip.

Whom Did we Meet in the University of Macau?

We were indeed gratified to meet the following leaders of the University of Macau:

- Wei Zhao (赵伟), Rector of the University
- Rui Martins (马许愿), Vice Rector for Research
- Annie L. M. Chen (陈丽明), Functional Head of International
- Relations
- Yuefan Hao (郝雨凡), Dean of Faculty of Social Sciences and
- Humanities
- C. L. Philip Chen (陈俊龙), Dean of Faculty of Science and
- Technology
- Timothy A. Simpson, Head of Department of Communications

- Jianguo Shi (侍建国), Associate Professor of Chinese
- Shoutong Zhu (朱寿桐), Professor and Interim Chair of Chinese
- Jin Hua Jia (贾晋华), Associate Professor of Chinese
- Rebecca Mei I. Tai (戴美仪), Administrative Assistant, Global Affairs
- Office

From this list, it is clear that we met a significant portion of the leadership of the university, and a sizable component of the University of Macau's Chinese Department. During the morning session on April 29th, a significant component of our discussion was centered on how NCKU's Chinese Department could collaborate with the University of Macau's Chinese Department. Details about this collaboration will be summarized separately by Professor Chen of NCKU. Suffice here to mention that in his short remark, Professor Chen pointed out a very interesting historical fact, and that is the deep relationship between Macau and Vietnam, with Chinese culture as its conduit!

Speech by President Wei Zhao

The highlight of our official meeting on the morning of April 29th was the comprehensive speech delivered by President Zhao about the University of Macau. Mind you, this was not your everyday speech from a president about his/her university. Rather, it was an in-depth view of the structure of his university, its mission, its changes, and its future. It was clear to me that this speech came from Zhao's "guts". It symbolized his profound excitement as well as his deep sense of the enormous responsibility on his shoulders. Indeed, even though the University of Macau has been in existence since 1981, it is only quite recently that Macau SAR has made the solemn decision to pour massive resource into the university to transform it to a major research university. In this landscape, President Zhao has been given the arduous responsibility of architecturing the university into a relevant Asian university of the 21st century!

The main theme of his talk, if I may be so bold to summarize, is that the development of the university governance and the university education mission form a "two-dimensional space". This means that the development of the University of Macau has to come from a close coupling of these two fundamental aspects. Indeed, the normal cliché of educational excellence must be measured in such a two-dimensional coordinate system.

(a) The University of Macau's governance structure

According to Zhao, the University of Macau, which is a public university, is moving rapidly from the "traditional governance" to a "current governance" structure. The traditional governance is one in which all fundamental affairs of the university, major finances, academic affairs and human resources, are controlled and operated by the Government. The current governance is one in which the government empowers a Board to handle these affairs. It is interesting to note that the Macau SAR Government specifically developed a legal structure, in which the definition of "empowering" was spelled out for the University of Macau in detail. At this stage at least, it is not applicable to Macau's other universities, such as the Macau University of Science and Technology (澳門科技大学)!

It is worth noting that all universities in neighboring Hong Kong are operated by their respective Boards from Day One (all eight universities have their own Boards), which is an inheritance from the British system. I presume that even though before the sovereignty transformation of Macau in 1999 — it was under Portuguese jurisdiction and not British, the fact that Macau and Hong Kong are joined at the hips surely means that a great deal of the lessons learned in Hong Kong can easily be transported to Macau. This may be one example of the transport.

(b) The University of Macau's educational mission

Zhao made it abundantly clear that the University of Macau is moving from the traditional "in-class (课堂内)" education, i.e., giving a student a professional education, to the more "out-of-class (课堂外)" education. Not only is the University of Macau concerned about four to eight years of education of a particular student and turning him/her into a specialist of a certain human intellectual endeavor, it is also concerned about education beyond that, the so-called life-long education in which the student as the eventual citizen of the world can contribute to the well-being of humanity in general. This is a lofty goal indeed.

A very interesting educational development of the University of Macau in the coming years is the development of a "residential college" system, a model that has long been the hallmark of several world-class universities such as Oxford, Cambridge, Yale and Rice. The advantage of such a form of education scenario is obvious: students from Day One of their higher education experience will and must learn to live as cohorts with students with different interests. The advantage of such a life-training is immeasurable. In the University of Macau, the prototype is starting this academic year, and by 2013, according to Zhao, it will be fully implemented!

Expansion of the University of Macau

No discussion of the University of Macau at this stage is complete without talking about its physical expansion.

As I have mentioned earlier, President Michael Lai attended a meeting in the University of Macau to commemorate the expansion of its campus. This is merely the tip of the iceberg. After all, the expansion of the University of Macau is a combination of bold political decisions, involving Macau SAR's Government and Mainland China and educational transformation.

To say that Macau is geographically small is an understatement. There is very little land for any kind of physical expansion in the SAR. However, Macau is literally a stone's throw away from Mainland China, and therefore it is only reasonable and natural to find a creative way in which the university can expand into the Mainland and still be considered an SAR university. That way came recently!

The following is taken from the University of Macau's website, depicting the dizzying speed of transition that took place in 2009.

- 2009 年 4 月 24 日 (2009, April 24)
  特区政府向中央提交报告, 请
  求在珠海横琴岛拨地作为澳门大学建设新校区之用,
  并授权澳门
  特别行政区管辖新校区
  Macau SAR submitted a proposal to the Central Government, requesting the utilization of the land in Zhu-Hai prefecture's Heng Qin island (adjacent to Macau) to be designated as the University of Macau's new campus, and transfer power to Macau SAR to have jurisdiction of the land.
- 2009 年 6 月 27 日 (2009, June 27)
  全国人大常委会正式批准这一请求
  The National People's Congress approved this request.
- 2009 年 12 月 20 日 (2009, December 20)
  澳大新校区奠基典礼圆满举行, 胡锦涛主席亲临现场为新校区纪念牌匾揭幕, 并送赠亲笔八字题辞: "爱国爱澳 博学笃行"
  The University of Macau broke ground for the establishment of the new campus. President Hu Jintau attended this ceremony.

From the above three dates, it is obvious that the transformation of the University of Macau is unprecedented in speed and scope. What is indeed epoch-changing in this expansion is that the Mainland has *de facto* given the sovereignty of nearly one square kilometer, which is a 3 percent increase of Macau's land area, to Macau SAR. With the relinquishing of the sovereignty, the University of Macau can use the land for its expansion and still remain a part of Macau's higher education. In fact, I now understand that the border of the new campus is regarded as the new border between Mainland China and Macau SAR!

Another incredible outcome is that with the expansion, the University of Macau will expand 20 times. Zhao also told me that Macau SAR has already committed over US$1 Billion (over NTD$30 Billion, or 三百亿新台币), to build the physical structures of the new campus. Even with this commitment, Zhao is also engaging in a very proactive fund-raising drive. This I am sure he learned from his days in the U.S. as an administrator in Texas A and M University and RPI! This is indeed breathtaking!

An artist's rendition of the new campus

Some Thoughts About the Visit

In the past two months, President Lai and I, together with a number of colleagues, visited several of our neighboring countries: South Korea, Singapore and now Macau. Also, after my visit to Macau, I will stop by to visit (again) Hong Kong Polytechnic University.

First, it is not difficult to see that in the entire East Asia region, there is robust economic growth. With economic growth comes educational growth. Indeed, we saw proactive transformation of higher educational institutions, such as Seoul National University, Nanyang Technological University, and now the University of Macau. It is worth noting that in every instance, these universities are all rapidly moving towards what Zhao refers to as the "current governance" structure.

Second, the physical expansion of the University of Macau will surely not stop there. It will and must be accompanied (aggressively) by an expansion of quality faculty, which only then will be followed by attracting quality students locally and worldwide. At the moment, the University of Macau has some 1,000 faculty and staff members and 6,000 students. When the new campus 20 times larger in physical size is completed in 2013, these numbers surely must be also expanded significantly. In this regard, I also learned about the proactive recruitment of universities in Hong Kong — by 2011, all its universities will go from the British system of a three-year undergraduate program to the US system of a four-year undergraduate program. This expansion will also require Hong Kong universities to seek new (and outstanding) faculty members. Since Macau and Hong Kong are both very much Chinese societies, it is not difficult to envision that Taiwan higher educational institutions can be one of the targets for their recruitment effort!

Third, I must say that perhaps it is my own inability to think through the ramifications, that I find it a little disconcerting that the growth of Macau SAR and with it, the growth of the University of Macau, depends solely on the "gaming industries". Of course, gaming industries, which are now a part of the economic development plan, have come a long way in the last several decades. Governments such as Macau and now Singapore who bestow "gaming" as an industry have new vistas in its operation in such a way that social fabric does not degrade, at least not significantly. In this sense, it is quite remarkable that even with gaming as the underpinning, there are people in Macau SAR who consider having a world class university down the road of fundamental importance.

Ultimately, building a great higher education, which is one of the fundamental building blocks of a modern society, takes not only resources, but sustained visionary leadership and patience. The Chinese have a perfect phrase for this, and that is 百年树人 (It takes a hundred years to cultivate people).

Today, the University of Macau obviously has the resource and the leadership, in Zhao, in his colleagues, and in Macau SAR. I have no doubt that the current leadership will create the right culture so that there will be patience to withstand future ups and downs, which ALL universities will face in their growth. It will not and must not allow changes in landscape to alter its now well-established goal in the 21st century and beyond.

Fourth, I am a firm believer of cooperation and competition, or "coopetition". As Taiwan is now embedded in Asia Pacific, it must be part of the higher educational coopetition. Our strengths, which are plenty, and our weaknesses, which are equally plenty, are obvious to even the most casual observer. I think that the more we learn from our neighbors, the more we can be cognizant of our weaknesses, and can take the necessary to mitigate them. I hope that these trips are small steps toward this goal.

(2010)

13

A $2 Billion New Campus: The Unthinkable Transformation of the University of Macau in the 21st Century!

This was written when the author was Senior Vice President, Global Strategy, Planning and Evaluation, National Tsing Hua University.

On March 6–8, 2013, the Vice Rector of University of Macau, Professor Haydn Chen (陈海东), graciously invited me to visit the university, and to deliver one of the Liberal Arts Lectures, a series he initiated several months ago since assuming the Position.

In land mass, Macau is tiny. It has roughly 30 square kilometers. This "minuteness" is only matched by its small population of about half a million. Politically, Macau was a Portuguese colony from the 16th century. In 1999, it became a Special Administrative Region (SAR) of the People's Republic of China. It is the second region (the first is Hong Kong) to take on this special feature under the now world famous auspices of the so called "one nation two systems" (一国两制). Since becoming an SAR, Macau has made enormous strides in economic development. Its "gaming" industry, a euphemism for the gambling industry, has grown exponentially. Indeed, today, Macau's gaming revenue is many times larger than its closest competitor, Las Vegas in the U.S.

The higher education history of Macau is a short one. Prior to 1981, there were, for all practical purposes, no tertiary educational institutions. Secondary school graduates of Macau either would go to Hong

Kong, Taiwan, the Mainland or overseas for advanced education. This situation was altered somewhat when the University of Macau (UM, 澳门大学) was founded in 1981 as a private institution. Later, in 1991, some eight years before the "political hand-over," UM's ownership was transferred to Macau's government, thus becoming a public university. I suspect that with the looming hand-over in the horizon, the Portuguese colonial government probably did not have the time or the resources, and maybe even more importantly, the need to seriously considering building UM into a modern university. For these reasons, UM's campus, just as Macau, is minute. It is roughly 1/20th of a square kilometer. It must be one of the smallest, if not the smallest, land area universities in the world. Indeed, there would be no area to expand even if the desire was there, and I suspect there was not!

Hence, just as 20th century ended for Macau rather quietly, so was the University of Macau!

There are a number of regions of the world who have made gaming industry their primary or sole economy. The one I mentioned earlier, Las Vegas, is one. Atlantic City in New Jersey is another. On a much smaller scale, Monte Carlo in Europe is another. Then there is Macau. All the others are situated in North America or Europe. Macau is the only one in Asia and it is the only one that in the 20th century had undergone monumental political transformation.

That transformation would be nothing extraordinary if Macau merely leveraged the opportunity to render itself from a small gaming center in the 20th century to become a mega-sized gaming center in the 21st century. If that were the case, Macau could be considered as merely a larger Las Vegas.

But something in the middle of the first decade of the 21st century made Macau absolutely and stunningly different from all its counterparts in North America and Europe. The leadership of Macau, having now acquired a very deep financial pocket, began to think of how to leverage this "newfound wealth" to transform Macau into something that it was not before.

They realized that what was sorely missing in Macau was a world-class university. The leadership of Macau inherently understood that for

Macau to reach the next level of being a world-class city, it must become a city of "knowledge"! Not having a world-class university could be and was the major stumbling block in having that eventuality occur!

So their attention turns to the only public university in Macau, UM!

Building a world class university needs at least four major components:

(1) **Financial resources;**
(2) **A strategically minded and sustainable leadership team with courage and vision;**
(3) **Land mass to expand;**
(4) **Hiring a world-class faculty and attracting world-class students!**

The first Macau now has. For the second, it launched a worldwide search for a new Rector (Portuguese terminology for a President) of the university.

The third became a major challenge. As I mentioned, Macau, with only 30 square kilometers, had absolutely no land to spare. If UM could not expand land wise, then there was no hope that it could one day become a world-class university. There is a Sung Dynasty poem by the famous poet Lu You, in which two lines read as: 山重水复疑无路 柳暗花明又一村. Essentially, it means that however hopeless the situation may appear to be, there is always a way out. This philosophy, it appears to me, is the underlying reason why Asia Pacific today is one of the most robust regions in the world. People always seem to find a way to mitigate difficulties.

The solution to the problem of land sounded almost like a **miracle**.

Macau is entirely within the jurisdiction of the People's Republic of China. There are two parts to Macau, a Northern part which is a peninsula linking with the Mainland and a Southern island known as Tum-Zai (Cantonese pronunciation 氹仔). Sitting on the Western side of Tum-Zai, just across a narrow water of about 250 meters wide, is a large and totally underdeveloped island of the Mainland known as Hengqin Island (横琴岛).

Apparently someone in Macau's leadership in the fledgling era of the 21st century figured out that perhaps the university could acquire land there for expansion.

There were two problems which needed to be solved.

First, the land is not in Macau.

Second, even if UM could build a campus on Mainland's land, the legal jurisdiction would be Mainland's and not Macau's. In that scenario, the university would be a Mainland university and not Macau's.

Facing these two challenges, the Macau leadership decided to kill two birds with one stone. That is, to negotiate with the Central Government of the People's Republic of China about "renting" one square kilometer of land on Hengqin Island to Macau. The land would then be utilized by the Macau Government to build a new campus of UM. This was a very complex issue because by doing so, Macau and the Mainland *de facto* would have to redraw their border. The laws in this one square kilometer would be that of Macau's. For example, the currency would be Macau's dollars and not Renminbis!

Another interesting feature about Macau as an SAR: it has no water rights. So the surface of the water between Tum Zai and Hengqin is under the Mainland's jurisdiction. This means that if one were to utilize a boat to cross from Tum Zai to Hengqin, then the passenger would have to cross the "Mainland," and presumably obtain whatever travel document is needed to do so. One can easily imagine the bureaucratic nightmare associated with that scenario!

Remarkably, after several years of negotiation, the government of the People's Republic of China accepted these conditions. To ensure that one could overcome the issue that China owns the surface of the water, it was negotiated that a tunnel built under the water would be in the jurisdiction of Macau!

Hence, in 2009, pumping into close to US$2 billion, with a "b", into the construction project, a new campus of more than 80 very large and ultra-modern buildings on the "newly acquired land of Macau" on Hengqin Island broke ground! In the following photos which I took a few days ago standing on the side of Tum Zai, you could see that breathtaking view of the new campus near completion! It is worth pointing out that all the mountains in the background behind the buildings belong to the People's Republic of China!

In the Q&A session of my speech, I made the comment that going suddenly from a 1/20 square kilometer campus to a one square kilometer campus is analogous to what we learn in thermodynamics, and that is the "non-adiabatic expansion of a gaseous system". When expansion of a gaseous system is very fast, faster than the system has time to readjust to the new conditions, chaos is inevitable! But, this is certainly preferred over the alternative in this case, which is no expansion at all. Facing such an immediate and somewhat uncertain future, it is no wonder that everyone I talked to in my two days at UM, from leadership to students, was full of enthusiastic anticipation!

Will UM eventually become a world-class university? I think only time will tell. The fourth challenge I outlined earlier should not be underestimated. In discussing with the leadership and many faculty and staff members, I sensed that all recognized the fundamental challenges UM faces. But I do sense there was a palpable and ubiquitous sense of optimism. With that, I think the battle is half won already!

I have often said lately that it is really incredible, and perhaps purely because of serendipity, that there were many things that were simply "unthinkable" in the 20th century, which are now "thinkable" in the 21st century. For example, building an international high-speed rail in Asia Pacific was unthinkable in the 20th century, be it economically or politically. Yet in the 21st century, it is now thinkable.

No one in the 20th century would have thought that this sleepy town known as Macau would one day "hail Mary" to the front line of higher education. Who would have thought in the 20th century that by the early part of the 21st century, Macau would "rent" land from the Mainland in order to build a world-class university? The fact that this is now a reality within grasp tells us how far Asia Pacific has come along, **POLITICALLY, CULTURALLY AND ECONOMICALLY!**

For me, the University of Macau should be viewed as Asia Pacific's higher education window to the world. If successful, its impact will be global! The world must focus on this development of Macau!

How exciting indeed!

(2013)

14

Korea Advanced Institute of Science and Technology (KAIST): Ascension of Asia's Rise in Higher Education

This was written when the author was Senior Vice President, Global Strategy, Planning and Evaluation, National Tsing Hua University.

A memorable photo with President Steve Kang of KAIST

Preamble

In my six years of working at the ground level of higher education in Asia, I was extraordinarily fortunate that I came at the right moment, namely the 21st century, to observe a palpable ascension of Asian higher education. Besides the two universities I had and have served, namely National Cheng Kung University in Tainan and National Tsing Hua University in Hsinchu, I also have had in-depth interactions with several other universities throughout the Asia Pacific region. I believe these institutions serve well as anecdotes in an ascension landscape. These universities included the following:

1. **Macau University**. This university is reinventing itself in every sense of the word: financially, intellectually, and even "politically"! Currently, the new US$1 billion campus, funded by Macau's SAR, is situated on a new Macau Territory on Mainland China's land.
2. **Shantou University**. This university, situated in Shantou, China, is the baby of one of Asia's wealthiest men, Sir Li Ka-Shing (李嘉诚爵士). Shantou is the home town of Li. For seven years now, I am fortunate to serve on the Board of Directors of this university and observe firsthand its transformation. The latest breathtaking collaboration between Shantou University and Technion of Israel, standing on the underpinning of a US$120 Million donation from the Li Ka-Shing (LKS) Foundation will surely propel both universities to new heights.
3. **Binus University**. This ambitious private university in Jakarta, for which I became an academic advisory board member, is the largest and most comprehensive university in Indonesia. Indonesia is the fastest rising, the largest in land mass and population and politically rapidly maturing country in Southeast Asia. Indeed, anything happening in Indonesia is worth keeping an eye on.
4. **Universiti Teknologi Petronas**. Petronas, Malaysia's national oil corporation, sponsored this university. Situated in Ipoh, some 200 kilometers north of the capital Kuala Lumpur, and of which I am an Academic Advisory Board member, this university is becoming the fastest-growing private technological institution in Malaysia.

While the above-mentioned universities do provide me with a broad sense of how Asian higher education is ascending, it does not include the understanding of how the speed at which Korean universities are progressing is akin to what we Chinese say in the Mahjong lingo, signifying fundamental incompleteness, namely "three and one short" (三缺一).

Founded in 1971, today, the Korea Advanced Institute of Science and Technology (KAIST) has emerged unquestionably to be one of the top research intensive universities in Asia, and is making significant strides in blinking on the global higher education radar screen. Thus it seems to me that a good appreciation of this university greatly value adds to my understanding of Asian universities' ways and means.

Hence, when my good friend Sung-Mo "Steve" Kang, former Chancellor of the University of California Merced, was inaugurated as the new President of KAIST in the Spring of this year and announced that he would be organizing the 2013 International Presidential Forum on Global Research Universities (IPFGRU,) I said to myself that I absolutely must go to observe how this university is doing.

Some information about KAIST

It is very interesting to note that both Korea and Taiwan have one "overpowering city" in the nation. They are Seoul and Taipei respectively. Just like my university, the National Tsing Hua University (NTHU) is in the middle of Taiwan's science city of Hsinchu which is 100 kilometers south of Taipei, KAIST is situated in the science town of Daejeon, which is about 160 kilometers south of Seoul. Not being in the major metropolitan area of the country presented to NTHU and KAIST similar challenges, as far as undergraduate recruitment is concerned. From several sources, I learned that a large percentage of KAIST undergraduates originated from a nationwide set of special science high schools. Students who studied in these high schools were specially chosen for their science and mathematics talents. Since KAIST has a pipeline to such schools, the challenge of recruitment not being in Seoul is probably less severe than that of NTHU not being in Taipei.

KAIST has six colleges. They are:

- College of Natural Sciences
- College of Life Science and Bio Engineering
- College of Engineering
- College of Information Science & Technology
- College of Liberal Arts and Convergence Science
- College of Business

A cursory examination of the academic programs would give one the impression, which is probably not far from reality, that the university is heavily science- and technology-centric.

By any definition, KAIST, just like NTHU, is a small school. Just as with NTHU, KAIST has about 10,000 students, of whom only 4,000 are undergraduates. Also, just like NTHU, the number of faculty members of KAIST is around 600. It is worth underscoring that while the number of students and faculty of KAIST and NTHU (12,000 and 600 respectively) are similar, the annual budget of KAIST is US$750 million, which is a factor of three larger than NTHU. I learned in this trip that KAIST is within the portfolio of the newly-established (by its current and new President Park Geun-hye) Ministry of Science, ICT and Future Planning, and not the Ministry of Education. Clearly, placing this university within a Ministry with "Future Planning of the Nation" must have profound implications for the development of the university.

My interactions with KAIST

My first interaction with KAIST occurred in 2004. That year, I led a delegation of nine Vice Presidents for Research from Texas, Oklahoma, Louisiana and the Republic of Mexico to visit Asia Pacific. KAIST was one of our stops. At that visit, we met with the then KAIST president, Professor Robert B. Laughlin. Professor Laughlin was the 1998 recipient of the Nobel Prize in Physics and that year he was appointed KAIST

President. Since he was both foreign-born and a Nobel Laureate, his appointment as KAIST's President indeed generated quite a bit of stir both in and out of Korea. It was deemed a bold move of Korea. I have to admit that the meeting with Laughlin that day in KAIST has given me a great deal of memorable moments.

I also met Laughlin's successor President Nam-pyo Suh in 2009 when I attended the IPFGRU 2009 in Seoul. President Suh, an MIT-er all his life, served as KAIST President between 2006 and 2013. During his tenure, KAIST made many dramatic transformations. Without any question, Suh moved KAIST further along with his well-known tenacity.

What is the Lesson from KAIST for me?

As an outsider, while both presidents had pushed KAIST into a multitude of intellectual disciplines and administrative changes, my perception of Laughlin and Suh is that both were highly research-oriented leaders. To this end, I thought it would be interesting to find a "scale" to measure its research growth rate.

As we all know, in the 21st century, ranking of universities is prevalent globally, especially in Asia Pacific. There are three rankings which are often quoted and they are the Shanghai Jiao Tong University ARWU (Academic Ranking of World Universities), QS ranking and Times Higher Education (THE) rankings.

While all three ranking systems have significant pros and cons, in my personal opinion, ARWU is probably the one that is best, although not without flaws, to indicate the research propensities and qualities of a university that it is ranking. It is also very transparent with the rules it sets up to carry out the ranking and less dependent on the nebulous concept of "personal impressions". It would therefore be interesting to see how, in the 10 years from 2003 to 2013, during the Laughlin-Suh eras, KAIST fared in the ARWU ranking. The result is given in the following table.

Year:	Range:
2003	301–350
2004	302–403
2005	301–400
2006	201–300
2007	203–304
2008	201–302
2009	201–302
2010	201–300
2011	201–300
2012	201–300
2013	201–300

If one goes by the ARWU ranking, the growth of KAIST in the 10 years was indeed significant. Its ranking has gone from the 300–400 range to the 200–300 range. I would be remiss in my analysis if I did not point out that there is a great deal of discrepancy among the AWRU ranking and the other two commonly mentioned rankings: QS and THE. For KAIST and the two other top Korean institutions in 2013, the difference between the three is as follows:

University	ARWU	QS	THE
KAIST	201–300	60	68
Seoul National University	101–150	35	59
Postech	301–400	107	50

This discrepancy is not confined to Korean universities only and seems to be quite universal for most outstanding Asian universities:

University	ARWU	QS	THE
HKUST	201–300	34	57
Beijing Tsinghua University	151–200	48	68
National Taiwan University	101–150	82	134
National University of Singapore	101–150	24	29

I am not sure how one should understand such a discrepancy between ARWU and the other two ranking systems for Asian top research universities. The fact being that ARWU is such a globally well-known and probably-well regarded ranking system, one probably could not and should not ignore it. After all, if one were to take the top three universities according to ARWU, there is no such discrepancy among the three systems (slight tongue and cheek for UC Berkeley).

University	ARWU	QS	THE
Harvard	1	2	4
Stanford	2	7	2
UC Berkeley	3	25	9
Tokyo University	21	32	27

I have also listed Tokyo University in the above ranking. It is obvious that the discrepancy which existed in the other Asian universities I listed does not exist for Tokyo University.

One should recognize that "ranking" *per se* is a "measurement". As any physical experimentalist would know well, a measurement without the associated "error bar" constitutes only half the story. Granted, to provide a ranking error bar for each measurement is probably a near impossibility. However, perhaps one could boldly say that the discrepancy between the three rankings may be considered an error bar. If this interpretation is reasonable, then the error bar associated with Harvard is something like + or −1, for Tokyo University it is + or −5, whereas for KAIST could be much larger. I suspect the truth about KAIST and other Asian universities is probably somewhere between these extremes. So, perhaps while Asian universities need to take the rankings seriously (after all, their societies and governments certainly do), they should take it with a large grain of salt.

Nevertheless, it seems to me that the interesting question for now for KAIST and other Asian universities is how to seek a blueprint to significantly uplift the quality of universities, in teaching, education and service to the communities, regions, nations and the world. For example, what the National University of Singapore is doing by deeply developing liberal arts education is certainly something one could cheer about.

As Asia becomes more and more important, in fact some may even call it pivotal, in its economic position in the world, Asian universities' responsibilities to make the world a better place for humanity are equally heavy. I am confident that if and when such a path is located, higher rankings of Asian universities will naturally be uplifted to hitherto unachieved heights!

(2013)

15

An Unusual Perspective of Higher Education Value-Adding to a Young Asian University: Comments Delivered at the Universiti Teknologi PETRONAS

These comments were delivered on August 10, 2010, at the Universiti Teknologi PETRONAS (UTP) Academic Advisory Council meeting in the PETRONAS Twin Towers of Kuala Lumpur, Malaysia. The author was Senior Executive Vice President, National Cheng Kung University.

On August 10, 2010, the Universiti Teknologi PETRONAS Academic Advisory Council (AAC) held two meetings. Both meetings took place in the Malaysian icon: the PETRONAS Twin Towers. In the morning, for two and a half hours, the meeting was chaired by the Rector (President) of the university, Datuk Dr. Zainal Abidin bin HJ. Kasim. In the afternoon, for two hours, it was chaired by Chancellor of the university and former Prime Minister of Malaysia, YABhg Tun Dr Mahathir Mohamad. YABhg stands for Yang Amat Bahagia, which means "The Honorable" in the Malay language, and Tun is the highest honor/title bestowed by the king of Malaysia. Datuk is a title given by the Sultan of any State in Malaysia.

Photo of the entire AAC. This was taken on the 86th floor of PETRONAS Tower, in the lobby next to Tun Dr. Mahathir's office.

As members of AAC (the full list is given in Annex,) we were requested to make comments and possible suggestions on improving the quality of the university. The following is a summary of what I said in those two meetings. For convenience, I have fused both comments into one. Prior to the meeting, AAC members were provided with very extensive and candid materials/literature about the university. Careful reading of these documents allowed me to have a good sense of the university walking into the meeting.

The Honorable Tun Mahathir Mohamad, Rector Datuk Kasim, my fellow AAC members, colleagues of UTP, it is indeed a great honor and pleasure, not only for me, but also for my university, National Cheng Kung University in Tainan, for me to sit on this Council. Judging by the biographies of the AAC members, this is indeed an august group of individuals with deep intellectual strengths and vast administration experiences. Personally, I am excited to serve with this group because

I am sure I can learn a great deal from interacting with you in the coming years.

Just like what my fellow Texan Dr. Prior said, as a new member, it would certainly be presumptuous of me to make suggestions on how to improve UTP. In fact, what I have to offer at this moment is based entirely on my personal (and perhaps narrow) professional experiences. Hence, they may or may not be relevant to the future growth of UTP. However, since this is a "long marriage" between UTP and this class of AAC, I am sure that as time goes on, we will learn more about the university, and the quality of the people associated with it, and in return you about us beyond what our bio said about us. I should mention that based on my very short interactions thus far, the derivative of the growth curve of UTP is definitely positive!

When Rector Kasim graciously invited me to serve on AAC, I did soul-search on what I think I could offer this young and aspiring university in Southeast Asia. In the end, I hope my somewhat unusual career as an academician as well as corporate manager, and my life long professional career in North America and, finally, adding three years as the senior administrator of one of the fastest growing universities in Asia Pacific, would allow my unusual perspective of higher education to value-add to this exciting and young institution.

I should mention also that during these few days in KL, besides the Rector of UTP (the person on the left,) I also had the pleasure of meeting the Vice Chancellors of Universiti Tunku Abdul Rahman (UTAR),

Professor Dato' Dr. Chuah Hean Teik (the person in the middle,) and University of Malaya (UM), Professor Datuk Ghauth Jasmon (the person on the right.) Among these three leaders, there is one common trait and that is that they are all highly energetic, full of optimism and bursting with ideas. With educators like them, I can easily imagine that in the next few decades, Malaysia could be Asia's higher education powerhouse.

I would like to begin by quoting Charles Eliot, Harvard University's president in the late 19th and early part of the 20th century. He said that

> "... a university, in any worthy sense of the term, must grow from seed. It cannot be transplanted from England or Germany in full leaf and bearing. ... When the American university appears, it will not be a copy of foreign institutions, or a hot-bed plant, but the slow and natural outgrowth of American social and political habits... The American college is an institution without a parallel; the American university will be equally original."

As an aspiring Asian university in the 21st century, I think it is worth remembering these profound words of Eliot in the 19th century. In fact, if in the above quotation you were to replace "England or Germany" with "Western", and "American" with "Asian," this quotation could easily be UTP's motto.

The Honorable Tun Mahathir Mohamad and Rector Kasim, as a former Malaysian (in fact my first passport was a Malaysian one), this country always occupies a special place in my heart. I witnessed its tremendous progress: from the fledging days of independence to what it is today, a nation of robust economic strength. In parallel, just as most Asian countries, educationally, especially higher education, Malaysia in the last few decades has gone through a metamorphic transformation: from the days of barely having only one university, to what it is today, a nation of having approximately one university per million inhabitants, and quite a few are literally knocking on the door of becoming research universities. Ladies and gentlemen, I can tell you that in this sense, Malaysia is an envy of Taiwan.

With populations of 23 million and 27 million, respectively, Taiwan and Malaysia have about the same population. However, you have some 30 universities, and Taiwan 170!

All universities, especially those in Asia Pacific, professed that they want to be "globalized". In this sense, Malaysia has one advantage that few others possess. While most nations in Asia Pacific are "uni-racial", Malaysia's population with significant representations from Malay, Indian, Chinese, Eurasian and European communities is definitely multi-racial. I should mention also that not only is Malaysia multi-racial, it is also an exemplary country that manifests racial harmony. In fact, walking along the streets in Malaysia, it is not an unusual sight to see people of very different ethnicity walking hand-in-hand together. In this sense, as most universities in Asia Pacific globalized by making an effort to bring in "foreigners", a Malaysian university can very easily "internally globalize!" This is unquestionably your strength and I am sure you will explore it to the maximum. I will talk about three main issues today. They are:

1. Sustainable funding of UTP.
2. Branding and recognition of UTP.
3. Global trends of higher education.

1. Sustainable funding of UTP

Ladies and gentlemen, in these two days, we talked a lot about the "vision" of UTP. However, we all know that "vision without funding is hallucination!" I am sure Rector Kasim knows well that he should not and must not engage in hallucination, at least not too much! Funding, especially proper funding, is the life-line of the vision. Here, I will not talk about some of the usual, such as an endowment (even for public universities now), and hard infrastructure funding. I have heard bits and pieces about these funding, such as what PETRONAS had thus far contributed and the formation of an endowment for UTP. Also, it goes without saying that faculty should be as proactive as possible in raising research funding to build their professional careers. However, since I have not read anything about such funding in details, nor have we had time to discuss them in the meetings, I think it would not be proper for me to make comments. Perhaps one of the future meetings, we could concentrate on this aspect of UTP.

Let me make a few generic comments.

First of all, fund raising should not and must not be amateurish. Except for asking anyone to give you his/her first born, asking for "money" is perhaps the deepest and most profound form of human interaction. In fact, it is clear in Asia Pacific that even public universities, such as my university, a national university, or a private university such as UTP who has a giant (PETRONAS) standing behind it, fund raising is absolutely critical to achieve excellence. So, building a proactive fund raising infrastructure within the university is no longer a luxury, but an absolute necessity. It must be a high priority. The conventional wisdom is that the sooner you recognize that, the better you will be.

Second, in today's media-intensive world, any human organization needs a clear and eloquent voice to tell the world why it should exist. For the corporate, that voice should and must be the CEO's. The recent disastrous example of BP's CEO Tony Haywood is a clear failure of the voice. For a university, that voice must be the president/rector. I think the president of Yale University, Richard Levin, could be the guiding light for all of us. By going to Yale's website, you can read the motivating and intellectually rich speeches of Dr. Levin[5]. Do pay attention to how he so meticulously prepared every single speech in the past decade and a half. I cannot imagine that when the top person of a university demonstrated total seriousness and commitment about the business of education, it would not be a motivating factor for the entire university and not have a positive impact on multi-dimensional university's fund raising effort.

2. Branding and Recognition of UTP

As in any human organization, branding and recognition are vital components of its existence. To brand and be recognized as a corporation, there must be a product. For example, imagine branding Coca Cola without a formula for the drink. Likewise, we need to have products for a university. I remember the famous quotation of my good friend the late Alan MacDiarmid, Nobel Laureate in Chemistry in 2000. He said that "science is people." Indeed, the primary purpose of a university is its intellectual efforts. Such efforts are pursued by people, not the most advanced equipment, or the most impressive buildings on campus. To me, the reputation of a university is its people IN-HOUSE. This is an irreplaceable dictum.

---

[5] http://opa.yale.edu/president/speeches_statements.aspx.

We have heard various talks by my fellow AAC colleagues about what are some of the possible exciting disciplines UTP should pursue. Since I am still on a steep learning curve about the university, I will not add to the list.

However, there is a common theme under all the suggestion and that is in order to pursue those areas, imagine if you do not have the best people to propel it. For example, we heard a very exciting talk by one of AAC colleagues, Professor Prasad of University of New South Wales (UNSW) about "built environment". He made it transparently clear as to how exciting this discipline is, and how it can palpably impact humanity. But think of the following scenario: Imagine UNSW without Professor Prasad!

So, if "built environment" is an area UTP wants to pursue, you should with all your might recruit Professor Prasad to come to UTP!

Over lunch, I deliberately sat with UTP's faculty. I happened to sit next to Professor Birol Demiral, who holds the Slumberger Chair in Petroleum Engineering and is the head of the Mission Oriented Research (EOR). I quickly detected that his accent is vastly different from all the other Malaysians sitting around the table. Being inquisitive by nature, I probed into his background and found out that he was a Stanford University-trained scientist whom UTP recruited from Turkey's Middle East Technical University. Our conversation soon got into how his family considered entering into a new life in Malaysia. Indeed, recruiting any talent normally comes with a "baggage" known as "family". I found out that not only was he happy with the university's support of his research (which presumably was the reason why he was interested to come in the first place), he also emphasized that his wife and two sons are very happy in Malaysia because they were able to quickly and seamlessly become interwoven into Malaysia's society and cultural fabrics. In fact, both children are having a great experience in learning to speak Malay and Chinese, an opportunity which obviously would not exist in Turkey.

Colleagues, this example is an important case-study of recruitment. There is no doubt that since Malaysia's research communities are still fledgling, by necessity you will need to tap into the Global community in building your intellectual capacity. In doing so, one must not forget to leverage the newly acquired intellectual strengths to nurture local talent, which in the long run is the only way to sustain a robust growth. Recruiting outstanding individuals from other corners of the world is a multi-dimensional effort. It is not merely professional alone. Rather, it is a combination of professional and personal efforts. From the experience of Professor Demiral, when he decided to uproot himself and his family from Turkey to Malaysia, the decision was made on an admixture of professional as well as lifestyle considerations.

Indeed, this move, which included his family so completely, will allow him to plant his intellectual seeds, deepen his professional roots and nurture his students and other researchers around him in Malaysia. Also, what is truly important to Malaysia is that he will be here for a long time and therefore can train several generations of Malaysian scientists.

I strongly felt that if UTP were able to strategically recruit some 20 or 30 Demiral-like faculty members, who would stay and spread their intellectual wings in Malaysia, and become part of Malaysia's society, then it would be doing something that few, if any, universities in Malaysia have accomplished: which is to plant seeds for greatness. Indeed, I can confidently say that if UTP could do that, UTP will be well on its way to become not only one of the best universities in Malaysia, but Asia and beyond as well!

3. Global trends of higher education

Ladies and gentlemen, in the 19th, 20th and 21st centuries, we witnessed interesting movements in mankind's intellectual center of gravity.

Sir Isaac Newton   James Clark Maxwell

I think no one would disagree with me that the 19th century was European-centric. One individual in that century who symbolized "supreme excellence" in science and technology would be, according to my biased view, James Clark Maxwell. Assimilating the many great scientific accomplishments since the Renaissance, which must include Sir Isaac Newton, Maxwell developed four equations with his namesake which were able to completely portray the illusive concept of radiation, and which even to this day, form the basis of modern science and technology!

It must be noted that it was not merely science and technology which Europe dominated in the 19th century; the arts produced in that period also were superb. For this reason, I often put two supreme human intellectual creations side-by-side, and they are Maxwell's equations and Chopin's *Nocturne*!

The composer and pianist Frédéric Chopin

Two terrifying events happened in the grandest human scale in the first half of the 20th century which made North America, especially the U.S., become the center of gravity of human intellectual and economic efforts almost overnight. Those events were World War I and World War II.

Indeed, WWI and WWII were so brutal and so fundamentally perturbed Europe that within 50 years, a large portion of some of its truly world-class people in sciences, technologies, humanities and the arts were lock-stock-and-barrel dropped into North America. The following set of individuals would symbolize some of the "household names" who came from Europe to North America during that period.

This unprecedented human brain movement took place in only half a century, which by any standard is a very short time. The scale had never before been seen in human history, nor do I believe it will be seen again. The movement was so powerful that it literally propelled the U.S. forward. One of the results of this forward leaping is that its universities became the envy of the world in a relatively short time.

As we move into the second half of the 20th century and eventually emerge into the 21st century, we notice the continual shift of the intellectual and economic center-of-gravity.

In fact, even on the North American continent, the best symbols to show this shift are the two monumental constructs: the Statue of Liberty, which was given by the French to the U.S. in late 19th century, and the Golden Gate Bridge built in the 1930s in California. To me, the former structure is a symbol of the linkage of the U.S. to the "old countries" in Europe and the latter is the opening of North America to Asia.

There is a lesson I have learned about U.S. higher education which I would like to share with you. As you know, in 1903, the Wright brothers demonstrated to the world, with absolutely primitive construction, that man can fly with the aid of engines.

It is remarkable that by 1916, some 13 years after the heroic work of the Wright brothers, MIT had already developed a complete educational aeronautical engineering program, from Bachelor to Master degrees. To do so in such a short time with an academic discipline that had not yet proven to be completely commercially viable (Boeing as a company was barely starting then and initially without much success) requires university administration with *academic bravery*!

Finally, Tun Dr Mahathir Mohamad in his summary comment to the Council asked a profound question: Are Asian universities in general and UTP in particular "relevant" to Asia and/or Malaysia? This question is thought-provoking. It made me remember what another AAC member, Prof. Lord Kumar Bhattacharyya, mentioned over dinner the night before. He said that while working for the Prime Minister of the UK at that time, Margarate Thatcher, she asked the following question during her reign when the British economy was at its worse: *"why are our (UK) universities so good and our economy so bad?"*

We are now in the 21st century. Asian economies, especially in Asia Pacific, saw a growth that has not been seen anywhere on earth. It seems to me it is very natural to ask whether the intellectual shift in the 19th century from Europe to the 20th century in North America will continue to move westward, towards Asia in the 21st century and be fulfilled?

So, please allow me to end by posing some questions to myself and to everyone:

- Do Asian universities have the academic bravery to educate a new generation of Asians with inherent self-confidence?
- Do Asian youth feel that they are surrounded by excellence, just as Europeans did in the 19th century and Americans did in the 20th century?

- Do Asian universities have the appropriate and ubiquitous mindset to fulfill their mission?
- Are Asian universities relevant to Asia and the world?

If answers to these questions are all YES, then I am sure the 21st century could be the century for Asia!

Annex: Members of the AAC

UTP Academic Advisory Council 2010

Chairman
YABhg Tun Dr Mahathir Mohamad
UTP Chancellor

Members

Tan Sri Datuk Dr Yusof Basiron
Chief Executive Officer
Malaysian Palm Oil Council (MPOC)

Datuk Ir. (Dr) Hj Ahmad Zaidee Laidin
Vice President, Academy of Sciences Malaysia

Dr. Øystein Berg
Managing Director
International Programme for Petroleum Management and Administration (PETRAD)
Norway

Prof. Dr. Ing. Klaus Riedle
Former President of Fossil Power Generation, Products
Siemens Power Generation (PG)
Germany

Prof. Lord Kumar Bhattacharyya
Founder & Director
Warwick Manufacturing Group
University of Warwick
United Kingdom

Prof. Dr David B. Prior
Executive Vice Chancellor For Academic Affairs
The University of Texas System
U.S.A

Prof. Dr. Ir. Arjen Evert-Jans Wals
Professor and UNESCO Chair
in Social Learning & Sustainable Development
Wageningen University
Netherlands

Prof. Dr. Feng Da Hsuan
Senior Executive Vice President
The National Cheng Kung University
Taiwan

Prof. Dr. Deo Karan Prasad
Professor, Faculty of the Built Environment
University of New South Wales
Australia

Prof Dr. Dieter Jahn
Senior Vice President
BASF AG Group, Ludwigshafen
Germany

Puan Juniwati Rahmat Hussin
Vice President Education, PETRONAS
Datuk Dr. Zainal Abidin Hj. Kasim
Rector & MD/CEO, UTP

(2010)

16

BINUS UNIVERSITY: My First Trip to Indonesia!

This was a speech for the "Global Leadership Forum: Excellence in Leading Higher Education in a Globalized World", held on July 2, 2013, at Binus University, Jakarta, Indonesia. The author was Senior Vice President, Global Strategy, Planning and Evaluation, National Tsing Hua University.

Rector Harjanto Prabowo and Vice Rector Boto Simatupang of Binus University, members of Binus University's Board of Directors, Professor Christine Ennew, Provost and CEO of Nottingham University, Malaysia, leaders from the 22 members of National Universities Network Indonesia (NUNI,) leaders from Australia, India, Indonesia, Malaysia, Thailand, and United Kingdom attending the Nottingham Global Network workshop, my fellow Forum speakers, distinguished faculty members and students, ladies and gentlemen, I am truly honored to have the opportunity to speak to you today about a subject that is not just critical for Indonesia, but for Asia in general. I should say that this is not only my first visit to Indonesia, it is also my first visit south of the equator. All these make my visit truly exciting!

I think it is bad news for me to be the last speaker of the four. This is because I realized that many of the salient points I wanted to say have already been said, maybe more than once. So I hope what I am about to say you may still find interesting and meaningful.

I have said on many occasions that

"To understand a nation's well being, or the lack of it, examine its universities!"

Ladies and gentlemen, if you look around the world, I am sure you will agree with me about the truism of this statement. While I have limited knowledge about Indonesian higher education, my anecdotal interactions with leaders of education from this fast growing nation in the past six years since coming to Asia, and my last two days of intensive interactions with leaders of Binus University and NUNI members, have convinced me that Indonesia's well being is full of promise!

South East Asia's Overall Landscape

As was mentioned by Professor Brodjonegoro earlier at the Forum, South East Asia is on the move, economically, intellectually and politically. There are several palpable evidences showing us that.

First, consider the proactive and imaginative economic cooperation between China and ASEAN, known as 10+1, and the possible cooperation between China, Japan and Korea with ASEAN, known as 10+3. If this cannot convince the non-believers, I don't know what can.

Second, until about two years ago, due to my own limitation, my interactions were primarily with higher education institutions in Singapore and Malaysia, and to a lesser extent with Thailand and Vietnam. Two years ago, I was invited to make a presentation at the China-ASEAN Education Forum in Bangkok. There I saw first-hand how all ten progressive ASEAN nations were working diligently and together to promote their higher educational systems. Indonesia is certainly one such nation. Since then, I became thoroughly convinced that higher education is a high priority for nation building in ASEAN nations!

Third, in his presentation yesterday at the Nottingham Global Network, Vice Rector Simatupang showed the following slide. I think it is not a stretch of the imagination that sometime in the 21st century, *Indonesian will be the engine of ASEAN, and universities in Indonesia will be the engine of Indonesia!*

Fourth, I think it is quite remarkable that 21st century may be the century of "defragmentation" of South East Asia. Unlike Europe, North

Country	Total land area	Total population	Gross domestic product at current prices
	km^2	thousand	US$ million
	2011	2011	2011
Cambodia	181,035	14,521.3	12,766.2
Indonesia	**1,860,360**	**237,670.7**	**846,821.3**
Lao PDR	236,800	6,385.1	8,163.3
Malaysia	330,252	28,964.3	287,922.8
Myanmar	676,577	60,384.0	52,841.5
The Philippines	300,000	95,834.4	224,337.4
Singapore	714	5,183.7	259,858.4
Thailand	513,120	67,597.0	345,810.8
Viet Nam	331,051	87,840.0	123,266.9

America, Africa, and South America, geographically, the nations of South East Asia are mostly a collection of islands and peninsulas. Yet, with progressive economy and political maturation and tranquility, there will soon be massive infrastructure constructions launched whose long term impact would *de facto* be defragmenting South East Asia. For example, the highly-anticipated high-speed rail from China through Laos, Thailand, Malaysia and Singapore, the underwater tunnel between Malacca, Malaysia and Pulau Rupat island of Sumatra, Indonesia, and the bridge between Sumatra and Java (see the following diagrams) will convince you that such defragmentation will have major sociological, cultural, political and economic impact for a region that is already on the world's radar screen of economic development.

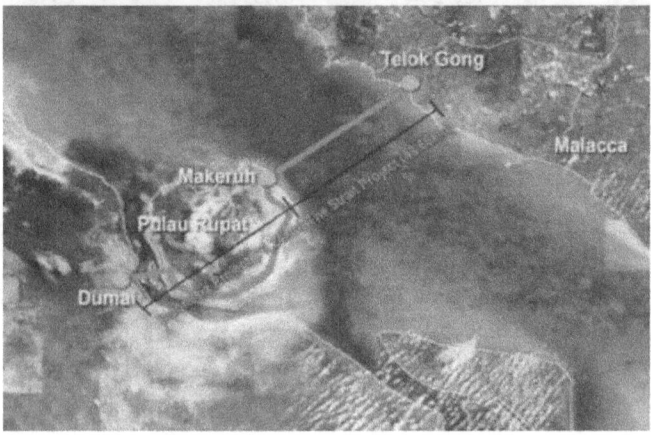

Higher Education Landscape

It is truly remarkable that merely a few decades ago, if there were such a thing as the radar screen of higher education institutions, what would be blinking brightly on it would be primarily western universities.

After WWII and until the 80s, Asian universities were essentially rebuilding or building from scratch. Except for Japan, Asian universities, without significant financial support from the government, were essentially teaching-centric then, with no significant infrastructure for graduate or professional education.

BINUS UNIVERSITY: My First Trip to Indonesia! 135

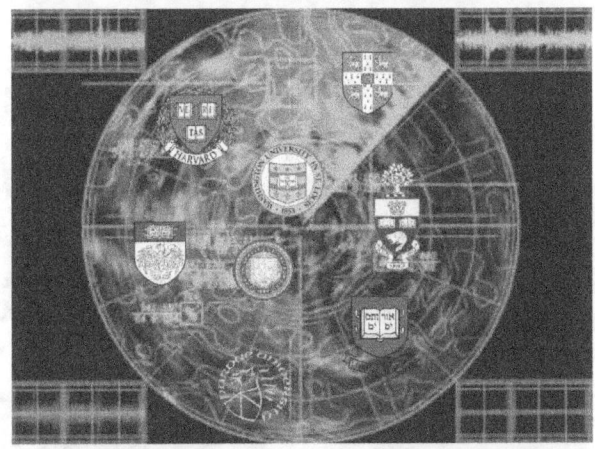

Therefore, just merely a few decades later, higher education in Asia made what I would refer to as a "great leap forward." Today, Asian universities are not only blinking on this radar screen, but they are blinking brightly. Having this new landscape, and with the title of our Forum in mind, I asked myself what would be the most important lesson we in Asia should constantly be striving towards?

Here, I would like to tell you a story and discuss what the moral of the story is. In 1979, I was spending a year as a visiting professor in the Niels Bohr Institute (NBI) of the University of Copenhagen. NBI was

Scanned at the American Institute of Physics

Heisenberg, Werner; Bohr, Niels Henrik David; Rosenfeld, Leon; Delbruck, Max; Bloch, Felix; Waller, Ivar; Fues, Erwin Richard; Stromgren, Bengt Georg Daniel; Kronig, Ralph de Laer; Weizsacker, Carl Friedrich von; Beck, Guido; Nielsen, Jens Rud; Darwin, Charles Galton, Sir; Manneback, Charles Lambert; Brillouin, Leon; Meitner, Lise; Ehrenfest, Paul; Heitler, Walter; Kramers, Hendrik Anthony; Nielsen, Harald Herborg; Hylleraas, Egil Andersen; Dirac, Paul Adrien Maurice founded by Professor Niels Bohr, who did fundamental work in developing quantum mechanics, a branch of science so fundamental that nearly all modern form of high technology critical for our economic well being is based on this. Professor Bohr won the Nobel Prize in Physics in 1922. This following picture taken in April of 1922 was what I downloaded from the American Physical Society archive (isn't Google wonderful). It shows many of the top physicists from all corners of the European continent, who practically "invented" quantum mechanics in the earlier part of the 20th century.

Let's now fast forward to the 1970s. I think we can all agree that 1977 was an epoch-changing year for Asia. It was the year when China terminated its ten painful years of Cultural Revolution. Almost immediately afterwards, in order to reestablish its connection with the outside world, China began sending some of its brightest of the bright globally. One of the first groups, if not the first, was sent to the Niels Bohr Institute. Therefore, in 1979, I met a number of visitors from China who spent a significant amount of time at NBI. One of them was in this photo: Fu-Jia Yang, then professor of physics of one of China's best universities, Fudan University.

Fu-Jia and I became friends since then. He went on to a spectacular career in science and education. He later became an academician of the Chinese Academy of Sciences, the President of his alma mater, Fudan University, and a distinguished member of the Nuclear Threat Initiative (NTI), an organization founded by Ted Turner and the former Senator Sam Nunn. *"The NTI works to strengthen global security by reducing global threats from nuclear, biological and chemical weapons,"* according to its website. His impact on humanity is broad and deep.

To go on with my story, I now have to tell you that Oxford and Cambridge in the UK were founded in 1167 and 1209, respectively. That is approximately a centennial short of a millennium. The founding of those two universities was essentially the beginning of higher education in the UK.

Since Indonesia is not a member of the British Commonwealth, many of you must have wondered why universities in that collection of nations refer to the presidents of their universities as "vice chancellor?" The reason is that according to Wikipedia, "the Chancellor is usually a titular

Professor Fu-Jia Yang

non-resident head of the university." Indeed, the Chancellor is supposed to project the grand image and vision of the university. For example, the Chancellor of Cambridge University from 1976–2011 was none other than His Royal Highness the Duke of Edinburgh. It is also interesting to note that according to Wikipedia, the first Chancellor of Cambridge was instituted in 1246! It is no wonder that this tradition in the United Kingdom is a not just a practice, it is a mindset!

Since their beginning, with nearly a millennium of history, no British universities had ever appointed a non-British individual as their Chancellor. However, on the first day of the 21st century — January 1st, 2001, the unthinkable became thinkable. On that day, Nottingham University (which is so serendipitously represented here in Jakarta in the past two

Fu-Jia Yang, as Chancellor!

days) lit up the higher education universe by fundamentally changing the "rule of the game" and appointing an Asian as its Chancellor.

That Asian is my friend Fu-Jia Yang.

It has been more than three decades since Fu-Jia and I were together at the Niels Bohr Institute. Much science, for him and for me, has passed under the bridge. However, one thing I learned from him then turned out to be my motto for life for whatever I was able to engage in. He taught me that

"Nation building does not begin with science and technology. Nation building begins with properly setting up policies. Any action, and education system is no exception, must be based on vision, mission, strategy and implementation!"

So what are the moral of the story here?

First, it was transparent to Niels Bohr (the person, not the Institute) in the early part of the 20th century that the pursuit of excellence *absolutely* cannot be a "national thing". It must be global. From the very start, Mr. Bohr opened his institute to the world. Indeed, when I was there in the late 1970's, it was one of the few places on the planet earth where I could meet scientists freely from the so-called "Iron Curtain." I remember that during many informal lunches in the Institute's cafeteria, I was able to discuss heatedly and freely on physics, even politics, with scientists from Poland, then Soviet Union, Romania, Bulgaria, then Yugoslavia, along with Americans, Brazilians, Germans, even East Germans, Indians, Chinese, Japanese, Singaporeans and Israelis! It is worth noting that the Niels Bohr Institute was housed in a set of very modest buildings. Except for the 21st century cars parked in front today, it is precisely how I remembered it in the late 70s! Indeed, excellence resides in people, not buildings!

Niels Bohr Institute

Second, the action of Nottingham University — breaking a millennium habit by appointing an outstanding individual who is NOT a British national as its Chancellor — tells me that it is critical that globally aspiring universities in the 21st century must always be on the lookout to break new grounds and dismantle old habits! Indeed, undoubtedly this action by Nottingham University will have a profound impact not only on the globalization of educational institutions between Asia and Europe, it will also exert profound impact between the amalgamation and understanding of Asian and European cultures. In the 21st century, where the earth is "flat" and getting "flatter," this to me is obviously a good direction. If the Chancellor is expected to project grand vision and mission, what better way or ways can the University of Nottingham do so than to install an outstanding Asian?

21st Century Challenges

In the 21st century, because of our unrelenting utilization of natural resources in the 20th century, and with uncontrolled growth of human population, the globe is faced with many hitherto unknown challenges.

For example, I have often wondered how lucky we are that on any day we live on this planet, we are blessed with three grids: electric, water and sewage. Imagine how terrible it would be if we were short of one on any given day?

Yet a very high percentage of our fellow human beings do not have such necessities.

In addition, the globe is faced with the following challenges:

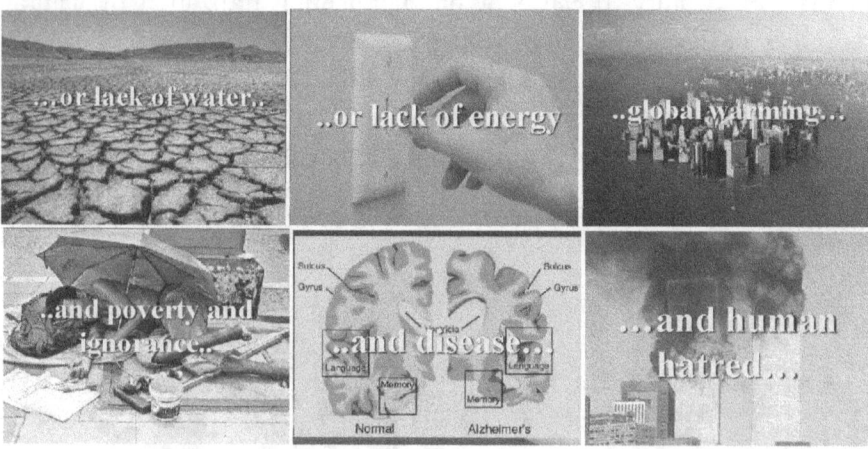

These challenges are the challenges for all of us, whether we are living in the East or the West. As Asia now is growing economically, so is its responsibility in assisting the globe in mitigating such challenges. Students of today, be they in the East or the West, must understand such responsibilities inherently. The necessary tools to solve these current globally challenging problems are dependent not merely on science and technology, but also on profound understanding of human behaviors, public policies and political courage.

If we place all our hope in solving the above depicted challenges on technologies and management skills, then we may be putting the cart before the horse. This truly puts heavy responsibilities on the shoulders of universities in the 21st century.

Excellence in Leading Higher Education in a Globalized World

To summarize, let me get back to the title of the Forum. I was very pleased to hear Professor Brodjonegoro pointed out that the three fundamental challenges to Indonesian higher education are autonomy, accountability and governance. It so happens that about two months ago, I was invited to a forum organized by Harvard Center in Shanghai. The title of the forum was "**The Futures of Chinese Higher Education.**" The title of my talk was "**Autonomy, Accountability and Governance: Challenges of East Asian Public Universities in the 21st Century**." Because of the cumbersomeness, I have referred to it as AAG.

Autonomy Accountability Governance

AAG is a complex and complicated issue for higher education in the 21st century in Asia. One thing is clear, many Asian nations, such as Japan, Korea, Hong Kong and Singapore, have made the decision to move in that direction aggressively. Perhaps their successes could teach us all about why and the difficulties of implementing AAG. I think in Asia, AAG, especially autonomy, needs exceptional courage and profound understanding from both governments and universities, a courage I think is in short supply. As I summarized in my Shanghai talk:

> "Clearly, direct government control of research universities is absolutely not conducive to the intellectual, cultural and economic contributions which the research universities can and are expected to make to societies, to nations, and to humanities."

For Indonesia, I think this is very exciting because you are now in the fledgling era of wanting to build a higher education system that will be good for modern Indonesia. As Indonesia becomes one of the leading nations of the world, its universities must also be in line to assist humanity to mitigate the challenges. In order to build world-class universities, I am convinced that seriously taking AAG into account is not a luxury but a necessity. This is the time where government, universities and society in Indonesia to work hand-in-hand to reach this lofty goal.

Finally, before I end my talk, may I take this opportunity to acknowledge my Binus University hosts. From the moment I was picked up at the airport until this evening when I will depart, I have found nothing but warm friendship and exciting and forthright discussions.

Thank you so much.

(2013)

The New Era

17

"One Belt One Road", Supercontinent and Neo-Renaissance: The Development of Universities in the 21st Century and Beyond

Contents of this speech were delivered at Peking Normal University, Peking University, Shanghai University, Ningbo University Ningbo, China, Sichuan University, National Taiwan Normal University, Huazhong University of Science and Technology, Nanyang Technology University in Singapore, Binus University in Indonesia, and Hing Wah High School in Malaysia.

Preamble

This content of this article occupied a large portion of my thinking hours about higher education in the past couple of years.

It all began in December of 2013 when I had to give a talk at the historical first Joint Meeting of the League of European Research Universities (LERU) and Association of East Asia Research Universities (AEARU). In this meeting, a large percentage of presidents of the 23 top research universities in Europe and 17 top research universities in East Asia came under the same roof in Hsinchu, Taiwan, to discuss what the responsibilities of these universities are and how to carry out the solemn educational processes.

In preparing this talk of great significance, I examined the websites of all the LERU universities from Europe. I noticed that they were more or less created just before, during or right after the Renaissance, somewhere between the 13th to the 17th centuries. A few were even created before that period, such as Oxford University (1096) and Cambridge University (1209). For the Asian universities, they were all created during or after the middle of the 19th century, the oldest one being Tokyo University, which was created in 1877, essentially immediately after the Minji Restoration. The youngest is the Hong Kong University of Science and Technology (1991). In this sense, European universities from LERU are "old or very old" universities and Asian Pacific universities from AEARU are "new and very new" universities. Bringing these two groups of educational leaders together with vastly different time scales surely could, and did, create a great deal of sparks about issues confronting higher education, past, present and future.

Supercontinent and New Silk Road

With that as background, I asked myself a series of questions.

First, I asked a question which had puzzled me ever since I was a young boy. For as long as I can remember, one of my hobbies has been staring at maps (I cannot tell you what joy I have had ever since there is Google Maps!), especially the map of the world. I have always wondered the following. Even to the most casual observer, it is clear that North America is a well-defined landmass. So are South America and Africa. Australia and New Zealand are by themselves in the southern hemisphere. I have often wondered: why are Europe and Asia not regarded as one continent?

One rationale I provided for myself was that it probably had something to do with the distribution of human beings in this large landmass: Most of the people in this landmass either were/are concentrated on its western end, hence Europe, and eastern and southern end, hence Asia! Of course, there is also the so-called western Asia, which the western world refers to as the "Middle East!"

It seems to me that throughout history, people on both sides of this large land mass, either for economic, cultural or military reasons, have wanted to link up the people of the two ends of this landmass. Indeed, the well-known military expositions of Alexander the Great and Genghis

Khan, and the natural creation of the Silk Road, surely are some of the best manifestations of this desire.

Second, I am sure we all noticed that even though in the 60's, Japan had created the first high-speed-rail known as Shinkansen, it wasn't until the end of the 20th century and now the 21st century where this transportation infrastructure proliferated. Remarkably, this proliferation happened both in the western end of this landmass, i.e., Europe, and in the eastern end, i.e., Asia. Perhaps the most spectacular development is the creation of a national high-speed-rail system in China in the 21st century. Barely 15 years into the 21st century, China has made the colossal decision to vastly upgrade its national transportation infrastructure by constructing some 16,000 kilometers of high-speed-rail. Except for the extreme western and southwestern ends, the high-speed-rail system has linked up nearly every corner of this vast nation. I should point out that to date, not a single inch of high-speed-rail has been constructed yet in the North or South America continents.

With this as preamble, propelled by significant economic and political maturation and coupled with the high-speed-rail technology gaining sufficient sophistication, the next step of transportation development in the large land mass of Europe and Asia would be the linking of Europe and Asia with a high-speed-rail system.

I think everyone would have experienced the following. If you fly from Hong Kong to London, your experience is confined to those two cities only. Imagine if you can take the high-speed-rail from Hong Kong to London — you would gain a profound understanding of nearly everything in between. It is for this reason — making people come into contact with one another — that rail transportation can initiate economic and cultural, even political transformation.

In fact, it is certainly true that the very large percentage of air travelers in Asia and Europe tend to go from one end, such as Beijing, to the other, such as London; the vast in-between, which includeds much of Asian Russia, five resource-rich independent republics — Kazakhstan, Kyrgyzstan, Uzbekistan, Turkmenistan and Tajikistan — are literally not on the radar screen of travelers. Once we have a high-speed-rail system linking Europe and East Asia, the Central Asian nations will literally all light up, economically and intellectually!

This is why an Asian-European high-speed-rail system as a "New Silk Road" can and will inevitably instil a new mindset in people of this vast landmass, that they are from a "Supercontinent". As a side note, in that landscape, one would no longer wonder whether Israel is a European or an Asian nation!

Third, having some of the leading academic leaders from LERU and AEARU sitting down together under one roof for two days, it is natural they ask the following question: What could be the fundamental purpose of higher education? After all, Europe has the oldest form of universities, represented at the meeting by LERU members, and Asia has the youngest and probably hungriest universities in the world. Also how can some of the best universities in Europe and Asia shoulder together many of the responsibilities to overcome challenges humanity faces in the 21st century? Surely this is a rare if not unique opportunity for East and West higher education decision makers to examine seriously how these universities could together be beneficial to mankind. Indeed, when Europe and Asia becomes a "supercontinent" later on in this century and beyond, what can one expect from them?

Having the presence of LERU universities in this meeting, it seems to me that the proliferation of universities during the Renaissance era could be an excellent case-study for us to draw lessons from, about the fundamental importance of universities and about the future development of higher education in the "supercontinent" era.

Fourth, by Asia, I meant Asia Pacific and South Asia. Due to my lack of understanding of the history and culture of Western Asia, or what is known commonly as the Middle East, I will not discuss that section of Asia. I should point out, however, that Western Asia did and still does play a large and fundamental role in the vast Asia–Europe landmass.

The Renaissance Era

I am sure most people when asked what they think about the Renaissance will inevitably mention names like Leonardo da Vinci and Michelangelo (their full names, which no one except the true Renaissance scholars would know, are Leonardo di ser Piero da Vinci and Michelangelo di

Lodovico Buonarroti Simoni, respectively). Unquestionably, da Vinci and Michelangelo and their colleagues opened new vistas for arts, engineering, medicine and science.

If one presses further, I think most people would come up with names like Galilei Galileo, René Descartes, Nicolaus Copernicus, and Francis Bacon as Renaissance giants and Isaac Newton and James Clark Maxwell as post Renaissance giants. Of course, there are many others one can think of, but for the moment let's just concentrate on these great minds who are already very representative of that era.

It is interesting to ask what commonalities these great minds have.

René Descartes in 1604 attended the Collège Royal Henry-Le-Grand. In this school, he was able to learn mathematics and physics systematically, including Galileo's work. I think most of us would remember that in our secondary school days, the first thing we learned about geometry was the Descartes Coordinate system! Indeed, it was Descartes who amalgamated two branches of mathematics: algebra and geometry. Without this amalgamation, many disciplines, science, engineering, architecture and so on would not be impossible. Finally, his immortal words ***Cogito ergo sum (I think, therefore I am)*** essentially define humanity!

Nicolaus Copernicus in 1491 attended the University of Kraków (now known as Jagiellonian University) to study astronomy and mathematics, which this university was at the time already well known for. Later, as we all know now, Corpernicus proposed the correct theory where the Sun as the center of our solar system, known as Heliocentrism, rather than the Ptolemaic system where the earth is the center of the universe. Having done so, he was under enormous pressure from the Roman Catholic Church to "alter his erroneous views".

Galilei Galileo in 1581 attended L'Università degli Studi di Pisa (University of Pisa), originally wanting to study medicine. But for one reason or another, he eventually turned to natural science. The outcome of this change allowed Stephen Hawking to crown Galileo as "the creator of natural science!" It was in the L'Università degli Studi di Pisa where Galileo learned about Heliocentrism. His championing of this correct understanding of our solar system had several centuries of difficulties with the Catholic Church.

As a young 12-year-old child, Francis Bacon entered Trinity College of Cambridge University in 1546 to study theology, logic, mathematics, astronomy, Greek and Latin. In the verbatim of the 21st century, this would be termed as a "Liberal Arts Education!" Armed with such a broad intellectual bandwidth, Bacon became a philosopher, a statesman, a scientist, a jurist, an orator, an essayist and a prolific author! I am especially impressed by his phrase with lasting sustainability: "Knowledge is Power!"

Finally, in the 17th and 19th centuries, Trinity College of Cambridge University accepted two students, Isaac Newton and James Clark Maxwell, whose lifetime work defined modern scientific thinking and methodology. Their work is the foundation of many modern day activities for humanity in the 21st century. Because Maxwell gave a complete understanding of all electromagnetic radiation, including visible light, there is nowadays a common joke that goes *"let there be Maxwell Equations!"*

I have often whimsically commented that between 1642 (or 1643, because there is uncertainty as to whether Newton was born on 1642 Christmas day or January 4th of 1643) and 1644, Nature played a gigantic joke on China. In 1642, Nature handed the West Isaac Newton, the pioneer of scientific methodology. Yet in 1644, it ushered in the first year of China's Qing Dynasty's founding emperor Shunzhi. The former was transformational for the West in its march towards modern enlightenment and the latter marked the continuation and deepening of feudalistic rule of the nation. In fact, during the reign of the second Qing Dynasty emperor Kangxi, a "lock door" policy was initiated, which essentially blocked modern scientific thinking and methodology from entering the country.

Because of my personal academic background, I have often concentrated on the discussions of the works of the great scientific or scientific-like minds during and after the Renaissance in Europe. In fact, I would be remiss if I did not mention that during and after the Renaissance, every form of human intellectual efforts in Europe flourished with gusto as well. One of my favorite Power Point slides is to place the Maxwell Equations next to one of my mother's favorite Chopin Nocturnes to signify that both are two of humanity's greatest and equally important intellectual achievements.

From the above brief discussion, I think no one would dispute that the humanity-defining achievements of the great minds during the Renaissance and the post-Renaissance eras are timeless. So what do they share in common? For sure, it is not their achievements. After all, these were giants in different fields of human endeavor.

Their commonality is that they all have attended universities. I should mention that despite Leonardo da Vinci and Michelangelo not receiving formal university education, their works certainly were one of the important ingredients of the curricula of universities during the Renaissance era!

Many may consider that the achievements of these great minds are the essence of the Renaissance. Yet, to me, the true essence of the Renaissance stands way beyond these isolated great achievements. The real essence of the Renaissance is that it is one of the greatest social movements of humankind: the creation, proliferation and popularization of universities. These institutions became the platforms not just for the great minds but also for tens of thousands of other and nameless youngsters to systematically and effectively obtain a deep understanding of nature and to overcome ignorance for the betterment of humankind.

Indeed, when we think of Nicolaus Copernicus or Isaac Newton, we tend to forget that as students, they had to attend lectures with many classmates at the University of Kraków and Trinity College of Cambridge University, respectively. Their fellow classmates would have received the same level and amount of information as Copernicus and Newton did. Many probably discussed and debated with them, and indirectly assisted Copernicus and Newton in becoming intellectually mature. This was what universities did then, as they do now! Furthermore, while most of the fellow students of the great minds, for one reason or another, did not attain outstanding or noteworthy achievements like Copernicus and Newton, in their own diminutive manner they also were intellectual soldiers during the Renaissance and post-Renaissance periods. As these individuals moved around Europe at the time and were immersed in the social fabrics, it was natural that collectively, they defined the intellectual landscape of the time and were as important as Copernicus, Newton and other great minds. To me, all these students who studied in universities for several centuries rendered the Renaissance and the post-Renaissance the greatest human transformational era.

This to me is the fundamental reason for the existence of universities!

Universities in Asia Pacific

In the 19th and 20th centuries, two important events in Asia Pacific could arguably have been fundamental in creating the new era of Asian universities. The first is the Minji Restoration of Japan (1868–1912) and the second is the Xinhai Revolution of China (1911).

It was during the Minji Restoration era that some of the best Japanese universities, such as the AEARU members — Tokyo University (1877), Kyoto University (1897) and Tohoku University (1907) were created. Many of these universities were given the prefix "Imperial" in the beginning. This adjective was dropped in 1945 when WWII ended. Unquestionably, these Japanese universities today are undoubtedly intellectual leaders of Asia today. Indeed, by creating these universities as knowledge centers of the country, one could argue that Japan was the first nation to create a "knowledge economy"!

While it was not the Xinhai Revolution's intention to proliferate universities, many universities in China were nevertheless created at or during that era. The most spectacular example was how Tsinghua University was created. The reasons for the creation of this university were complex. People who are interested should Google the term "Boxer Rebellion Indemnity Scholarship Program". This program was one of the primary incentives for Tsinghua University to be created. Many leading Chinese intellectuals in the beginning of the 20th century were associated with this program and their impact on Chinese higher education, even to this day, cannot be ignored nor underestimated.

Asia, especially Asia Pacific, was turbulent, if not violent, in the first half of the 20th century. This was especially true during the period after WWI and the end of WWII, and spilled over to the Korean Peninsula (even to this day). After WWII, especially near the end of the Vietnam War, the economies of many Asian countries began to show a definite upswing tendency. Terms like "little tigers" designating the rise of Singapore, Hong Kong, Taiwan and South Korea were invented for that phenomenon. It is fair to say that for Asia Pacific, the 20th century began when colonialism was still prevalent and ended when many Asia Pacific nations emerged as independent economic powers.

The change in the economic landscape in the 20th century was accompanied by a profound change of perception by the West about the East. I remember someone once asked me what the best manner to characterize this perception was. After thinking about this long and hard, I found that the best way to demonstrate it is via the Nobel bylines of two Asian Nobel laureates. They are Rabindranath Tagore from India who had the great honor of being the first Asian to be awarded the Nobel Prize in 1913 and Gao Xinjian, the last Asian to win the Nobel Prize in 2000 in the 20th Century. Remarkably, both won it in the literature category!

The Nobel byline for Tagore in 1913 is: *"because of his profoundly sensitive, fresh and beautiful verse, by which, with consummate skill, he has made his poetic thought,* expressed in his own English *words, a part of the literature of the West"*, and for Gao in 2000, it is: *"for an œuvre of universal validity, bitter insights and linguistic ingenuity, which has opened new paths for the Chinese novel and drama".*

In these elegant words one can detect the tremendous change in attitude of the West towards the East. The most telling words in the 1913 Nobel byline for Tagore, which was only thirteen years after the initiation of the Nobel Prize and 36 years before India achieved independence, is *"...a part of the literature of the West"*! Perhaps it was natural for Westerners to put these words together when colonialism was still so real, in practice and in the mindset. However, by the time Gao won the Nobel Prize in 2000, Asia had completely transformed. There is clearly new understanding between East and the West. Indeed, the words *"...opened new paths for the Chinese novel and drama"* was an utter tone reversal of the 1913 Tagore byline!

Inherent Self-Confidence

In the 19th century, Europe, building on several centuries of the Renaissance, rose to become the global intellectual epicenter. A most telling aspect of the European dominance was to compare the pioneers of thermodynamics between Europe and the U.S. While nearly all the names one can think of in this important scientific area are Europeans, such as Sadi Carnot, James Clark Maxwell, Hermann Helmholtz, Ludwig von Boltzmann and so on, the sole and lonely scientist from the U.S. who could hold a candle to his European counterparts was Willard Gibbs of Yale University.

Basking in the global intellectual epicenter landscape, having people like James Clark Maxwell and Frédéric Chopin producing profound humanity's understanding of the universe and heart throbbing beautiful and gregarious music must surely have endowed European young people of that era with a deep sense of "inherent self-confidence," allowing them to realize that "the best is right here!"

It was also interesting that after WWI and WWII, which propelled one of the greatest intellectual migration from Europe to North America mankind had ever seen (for this, I suggest the book *Hitler's Gift* by Medawar and Pyke), this "inherent self-confidence" was also transplanted in North America, especially the U.S. This migration coupled with the fledgling rise in intellectual quality of universities in North America to become the envy of the world. I believe that the words *"There are those who look at things the way they are and ask why? I dream of things that never were and ask why not!"*, uttered by Robert Kennedy were the clearest manifestation of this "inherent self-confidence"! Indeed, the outstanding universities dotting the U.S. landscape after WWII made young people in North America come to the realization that "the best is here!" as well!

As is obvious, higher education in Asia Pacific in the late 20th century, especially now in the 21st century, is lifting off. For example, in the 80s, with the exception of some of the best universities in Japan, none of the Asia Pacific universities would blink on the global higher education radar screen. The situation is now different. Indeed, many of the AEARU universities are now constantly being mentioned globally. Yet, even within this landscape, I think one of the greatest challenges of universities in Asia Pacific today is how to bring the "inherent self-confidence" in our young people to the level of Europe and North America in the 19th and 20th centuries, respectively.

It is my belief that just as North America, the boost of "inherent self-confidence" of young people came about by the enormous infusion of European intellects in the first half of the 20th century. By the same token, to lift the "inherent self-confidence" of Asia Pacific's youth to a new and unprecedented level will also, in my opinion, requires new infusion of ideas, if not people. It is with this as preamble that I believe the formation of "supercontinent" can and will have tremendous impact for this eventuality.

In 2009, I made a summary talk at a conference organized by the Asia Development Bank about "Global Economic Crisis: Industrial Reconstruction." I said the following regarding "inherent self-confidence":

> *"Throughout the 20th century, Asia was psychologically "coupled" to the West, and understandably so. With superior economic and intellectual strengths, it is quite natural that Asia viewed the West as the 'standard of excellence.' However, after such a period as this with the West so palpably exposing its social & economic weaknesses, this may be the first time in the modern global economy that Asia can psychologically "DECOUPLE" from the West. This is not to suggest that Asia should decouple economically and intellectually from the West; rather, I am talking about a "psychological decoupling" to undo a sense of reliance on the West, without which it is unlikely that Asia will develop a deep sense of inherent self-confidence and without which the 21st century is surely not to be the "Asian Century."*

It is very clear that universities in Asia Pacific are all taking the building of "inherent self-confidence" to heart and the efforts to promote it in the 21st century are palpable!

Supercontinent, Neo-Renaissance and "One Belt One Road"

When I presented my talk in December of 2013, I was concerned whether the "supercontinent" concept might be too radical a mindset change by a large percentage of the world's population living on this landmass. After all, the idea of Europe and Asia as separate continents have been deeply ingrained in the minds of people for many centuries, if not millenniums. I was also uncertain whether there would exist an international champion who has the "political courage" and the "know-how and how-to" to push forth the completion of infrastructures in order for the concept to become a reality.

That concern was alleviated when I came to the University of Macau and learned about President Xi Jinping's push forth one of China's new and bold global economic and intellectual transformational projects known as "One Belt One Road". This term is a short form for the land-based "Silk Road Economic Belt" and oceangoing "Maritime Silk Road." In fact, in hindsight, I realized that Xi's pronouncement was two months before the LERU-AEARU conference in Hsinchu. Had I known that fact during the conference, my talk would have sounded less tentative and far more positive.

The stage seems to be set for the creation of a Neo-Renaissance.

As I have emphasized previously, one of the greatest achievements of the Renaissance was the creation, proliferation and popularization of universities throughout Europe. Facing European challenges then (which *de facto* is the equivalent of Global challenges of today,) the universities produced penetrating minds who were able to overcome deep ignorance, the greatest challenge at the time.

The challenges facing humanity today are much larger and deeper in scale. They are, for example, lack of water, lack of energy, warming of the globe, ubiquitous poverty, wide spread ignorance, incomprehensible human hatred, diseases, corruptions, population explosion and so on. The survival of the earth as a planet depends on how these challenges are tackled. Indeed, to overcome such challenges would require not just science and technology, but understanding of different cultures, human psychology, public policies as well as political courage. These are challenges totally unimaginable during the Renaissance. While during the Renaissance universities would not and need not deal with such issues, they surely must in the universities today.

This is where the creation of a Neo-Renaissance in the supercontinent comes into play. In the supercontinent, Eastern culture and Western culture will crisscross, admix and even collide in the universities at every corner of the supercontinent. New and creative thinking by the neo-greats will no longer be strictly having under their belts Western points-of-views. Their thinking will be a combination of East and West. Bringing "inherent(ly) self-confident" Easterners and Westerners together in the supercontinent to face new challenges, the neo-Galileos, neo-Copernicus-es, neo-Descartes-es and neo-Newtons with a supercontinent under their feet, I am confident they and their fellow students can and will find solutions hitherto unknown to overcome the new global challenges.

Epilogue

In the beginning line of *A Tale of Two Cities*, Dickens wrote "*It was the best times, it was the worst of times*." While these words except for one caveat apply equally to the Renaissance and the future Neo-Renaissance eras, the time scale of transformation for these two eras are vastly different, at least by several orders of magnitude.

What is Neo-Renaissance and how can a supercontinent enhance its formation?

First, in every higher education administration corridor today, one can inevitably hear the words "rapid transformation" uttered. Yes indeed, things change fast and universities do not seem to change fast enough. During Renaissance times, a student would meet his/her peers face-to-face within the same university or at most in the same continent, with difficulty. In the neo-Renaissance era, a student within the supercontinent, with high-speed rail transportation, would meet his/her peers electronically as well as face-to-face in the same supercontinent and have the warm feeling that they come from the same continent with ease. In this sense, the intellectual activities would literally light up from one end of the supercontinent to the other much faster, unlike the days of the Renaissance, where intellectual activities would light up across Europe, but took centuries! With modern forms of transportation and communication, maturation could come much faster, even within a century!

Second, in the supercontinent, not only will universities from the two ends of the landmass will be amalgamated in spirit, so will many institutions in between in Central Asia as well. Such an intellectual admixture has never happened in human history before and the outcome can be expected to be spectacular.

There is an old Chinese saying: 百年树人, or, "It takes a century to rear a person!" This means that one must be patient in establishing an educational tradition. One sees that a large number of universities in Europe and Asia today would design strategies in the next 10 to 20 years. With the idea of supercontinent coming on line in the coming century, I think it is absolutely necessary and important for a university's leadership in the supercontinent to develop educational strategies that keep what could happen in this century and beyond in mind!

As I mentioned earlier, had President Xi Jinping not initiated the bold "One Belt One Road" project, I think initiating the mindset of a supercontinent and the creation of a Neo-Renaissance would be a vision, if not a mirage. With the "One Belt One Road" project, I am very confident with our discussion here they could be realized, maybe as soon as the end of the 21st century, if not sooner!

Thank you.

(2015)

18

"Basic" and "Practical": The Dilemma of Modern Research Universities in the 21st Century

This was the opening comment at the "2014 Britton Chance Center for Biomedical Photonics (BCCBP) of Huazhong University of Science and Technology (HUST)". The author was Senior Vice President, Global Strategy, Planning and Evaluation, National Tsing Hua University.

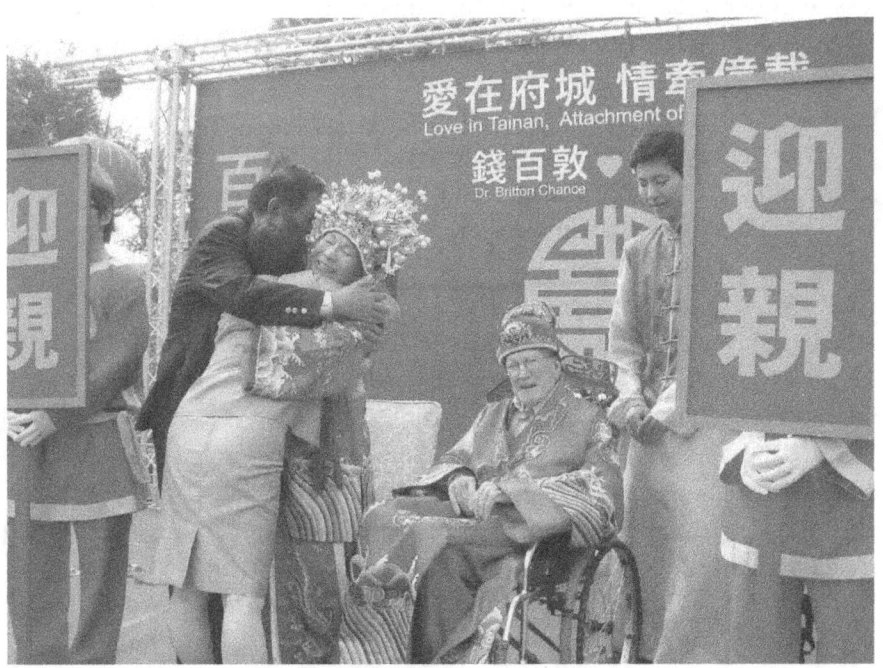

Britton and Shoko getting married in 2010

President Ting (丁烈云), my fellow colleagues, good morning. This is the sixth meeting in eight years of the BCCBP advisory committee. It's the second one since our dearest friend and intellectual leader Britton Chance is no longer with us. But I can assure everyone that we all can feel his intellectual presence.

I am sure I speak for all my fellow members of the committee to say that so far it has been a great intellectual journey for all of us. The Center is named after one of the greatest intellects of the 20th century, our good friend the late Professor Britton Chance.

The intellectual, technological and technological transfer progress made by the Center is, to say the least, breathtaking. There is no doubt in our minds that BCCBP is today not merely a shining example for HUST, but it is one for Wuhan Optics Valley.

President Ting, the visionary and substantive speech you delivered a few minutes ago was indeed exciting for us to hear. Despite the fact that you have just assumed the Presidency of this great and vast university for less than two months, it was obvious that you have already captured the essence of the importance of BCCBP and how it can and will assist HUST to become an outstanding teaching and research institution for China in the 21st century.

Your comment outlined a fundamental challenge for research universities in the 21st century, which is how to balance between the "basic" and "practical". From your speech, I sensed that there indeed is some urgency for HUST to tackle this challenge head-on. Of course, such a challenge is hardly the prerogative of HUST. It is one confronting all aspiring universities in every corner of the world.

In a nutshell, Present Ting, you raised the question as to how a modern research university such as HUST should balance its operation between "basic" and "practical". As you had so acutely stated, what should be the optimum balance between these two extremes?

Serendipitously, just yesterday morning, I received an email from Academician Bai Chunli (白春礼), President of the Chinese Academy of Sciences (CAS). In this email, Academician Bai enclosed a copy of CAS's recently-published white paper entitled "Towards Excellence in Science". The white paper discussed a multitude of issues confronting science and scientists in the modern day. Among them, one which caught my special attention and is relevant to today's discussion was the section entitled

"Assuming the Social Responsibilities of Scientists". President Ting — perception wise, "Social Responsibilities of Scientists" are code words for how the development of science should be the economic engine for society, a subject which in your speech, you had stated in an even more elegant manner.

Your comment and the comment by Academician Bai prompted me to think about two personal experiences which I hope you will allow me to share with you.

First, about a decade ago, I had the privilege of having a lunch with a Vice President in charge of research at a large-scale technological company. Our discussion quickly centered on what could be the role of a research university when industrial research activities were all rapidly diminishing or, worse, being eliminated. This person made a rather startling suggestion to me that *"universities should closely be aligned with industrial directions and conduct research that would have near-term meaning (to industries)."* I recall that my kneejerk reply to him was: *"I believe a hundred years from now, my university will still be here. I am not sure if your company will be!"*

Second, I was in the presence of a powerful U.S. Government Official and two high powered medical doctors to discuss the modern applications of medical instrumentations. This official asked us: "What is PET?" With that question, I noticed that the two doctors immediately wanted to launch into a long discussion of the clinical functionality of PET. After they uttered a few words, the official showed some impatience and gently said: "Oh, I mean, what does PET as an acronym stand for?" To my utter surprise, the two doctors looked bewildered. I then interpreted that they were not absolutely sure what it stood for. So, to save the day, I jumped in and said "Sir, it stands for Positron Emission Tomography." Then the official followed up with another question: "I am not a scientist. Can you tell me what a positron is?"

President Ting, I mentioned these two examples to illustrate how profoundly difficult the challenge HUST and National Tsing Hua University are facing today is, in finding the right balance between "basic" and "practical".

The first example clearly indicates to us that if a university's research landscape is utterly dictated or dominated by industrial needs, it could indeed be a dangerous course of action. I think the dismal outcome of companies such as XEROX and Eastman Kodak could serve as clear warnings for us.

The second example tells us that while we are pursuing "practical" aspects of research, which we must, in view of what modern societies demand of universities, it would be dangerous for us to abandon the "basic" part of education. The products of research universities, namely, students, should not and must not be merely highly skilled technicians. If these products lack the basic knowledge for them to have the necessary intellectual bandwidths, how could they develop compassion for their fellow human beings?

President Ting, one of my most respected scientists in the 20th century turns out not to be merely a great scientist, but a scientific administrator. His name is Vannevar Bush. Immediately after World War II, Bush recognized inherently that in order for the U.S. to be a powerful scientific intellectual country, the nation must allow the faculty in research universities to conduct what is now known as "curiosity driven research". Bush also recognized that this could only be done if it was a national policy. With that in mind, he suggested to the United States Government to set up the National Science Foundation. In hindsight, I cannot imagine today what the U.S. research landscape would be like if the country had not had a man like Bush with such farsighted vision. I think you would agree with me that many national funding agencies, such as the Mainland's National Natural Science Foundation and Taiwan's National Science Council were all modeled after the NSF.

I think if you look at the scientific career of Britton Chance, from developing sailing technologies in his teens, to developing the radar to combat the Nazis, to biochemistry and biophonetics, you will see that all were deep intellectual pursuits and technological innovations. I am confident that there was not a single day that would go by where he would not be absolutely driven by his profound sense of curiosity. Perhaps Britton's life could give us a guide as to where the illusive balance of "basic" and "practical" is.

At the moment, I do not have a definitive answer for the challenge you and I are facing as university administrators. However, in the past three decades since I became acquainted with the Mainland, especially with its higher education infrastructure, I saw a palpable and significant transformation, and much of it was for the good. So, with that in mind, I have every confidence that with great leaders such as yourself and your predecessor, President Peigen Li (李培根), China will eventually find the right balance between "basic" and "practical".

In a sense, I am confident that China will fulfill the "education dream" of my good friend and our fellow BCCBP board member Academician Fu-Jia Yang (杨福家).

China is an ancient country with deep respect and practice of scholarship. Couple this with its 21st century economic growth, it must also now carry the global responsibility of the late President of South Africa, Nelson Mandela, who uttered the following immortal words: "The most powerful weapon to change the world is education!"

(2014)

19

Challenges Faced by Asia Pacific Universities in the 21st Century

This speech was made at the "Forum on Cultivating Globally Competent Human Resources", sponsored by Asia University and Commonwealth Publishing Group, held on October 19, 2010, at the Asia University, Taichung, Taiwan. The author was Senior Executive Vice President, National Cheng Kung University.

Starting from second from left, Professor Ramamoorthy, Provost Benjamin Wah, Professor Raymond Yeh, President Jeffrey Tsai, President C. L. Liu and DHF

President C. L. Liu (刘炯朗校长), Chairman of this panel, President Jeffrey Tsai (蔡进发校长) of Asia University, our most hospitable host, Professor Raymond Yeh (叶祖尧博士), who was the Chairman of the University of Texas at Austin's Computer Science Department when I was a physics post-doc in that university, Provost Benjamin Wah (华云生校长) of the Chinese University of Hong Kong, Professor C. V. Ramamoorthy of the University of California, Berkeley, and last but not least, our keynote speaker, Joel Brinkley, and fellow students from Asia University (in Taiwan, since there are two others in Japan and South Korea), good afternoon. This is such a great honor for me to be on the same stage with such an august group of individuals and with the students of Asia University.

I must congratulate the administrators, faculty and students of this fast growing and fledgling university, Asia University, for organizing this Forum. This event is a clear manifestation of the breadth and depth of this young but aspiring university, which is propelled by great leadership.

I am also excited to be in the presence of such a distinguished individual, Joel Brinkley, a Pulitzer Prize Laureate. When I was growing up as a physicist, it took me quite a while into my career to realize that Nobel Laureates, such as Richard Feynman, look like human beings and not a "diagram". I am equally pleased today to see that a Pulitzer Prize Laureate also looks like a human being! But of course, he inherited great journalistic genes, being the son of the great David Brinkley, whom many of us in the U.S. in the 60s and 70s learned to watch every night on TV! As the son of a journalist, I was naturally fascinated by Joel Brinkley's discussion about the responsibility and role of how a journalist should report a story. From his talk, I learned one thing which he repeated several times, and that was what he referred to as the *"unintended consequences"*. Furthermore, the many case studies mentioned in his speech also had another important concept embedded in it, and that is that *history* is, or should be, our best teacher. Many of you may have heard the famous quotation from an American writer called Pearl S. Buck who said that *"If you want to understand today, you have to search yesterday."*

Also, as a senior administrator of a university in Taiwan, I am very much touched by Professor Raymond Yeh's palpable interest and wisdom about what skill sets a university student in Asia Pacific should have in the 21st century in order for him/her to be a meaningful contributor to society, nation and the world at-large.

I am so inspired by these two talks that I hope you do not mind that I will try to amalgamate as best I can these two themes of Brinkley and Yeh. The best way I know how is to bring out a case study.

The case study I would like to center on belongs to today's hot social topic for higher education in Taiwan in particular, Asia Pacific in general. The topic of today's Forum is to discuss about Cultivating Globally Competent Human Resources. I am sure you would agree with me that the cultivation of such human resources must originate with the best higher education system, which must be, at least in part if not in total, how we structure our higher education. To this end, I would like to focus on a closely connected issue, and that is the issue of the global ranking of a university. I have chosen this topic because I just returned from a meeting for "Asia's Top University Executives" in Tokyo where this topic was discussed extensively. The meeting was organized by the largest scientific publication company in the world, Elsevier.

At the meeting, there was a talk by Professor Alan Johnson. The title of his talk was "Challenges of Research Management: An Australian Perspective." Professor Johnson was the former Deputy Vice Chancellor (which is equivalent to Vice President in most non- British system universities) of the University of Adelaide.

The primary message I took away from Professor Johnson's talk is "how to improve the ranking of your university". The ranking which Professor Johnson focused on is the so-called Shanghai Jiao-Tong University Academic Ranking of World Universities (AWRU[1]), although for today's discussion how such a ranking was carried out is of less relevance. I should mention that there are so many rankings out there now in the public domain. Often, and especially for Asian universities, they provide very different and often conflicting results. I would be surprised if the average citizen on the street is not utterly confused by them. No doubt, such a discussion has a great deal of resonance in Asia Pacific for the following reasons.

Undoubtedly, in the past several decades, Asia Pacific universities had received, and will continue to receive in the foreseeable future, significant funding from their respective governments. This is due *in part* to Asia Pacific governments' recognition of the profound value of higher education as an engine to move citizens up the ladder, economically and/or intellectually. Such movement can and will transform society and nation, for the better, I might add. Also, *in part* because they have the financial might to do so! For example, in Taiwan, there is the additional funding from the so-called 五年五百亿, or "Five Years Fifty Billion" (New Taiwan Dollars, which is approximately US$1.7 billion) beyond the normal funding for the twelve top universities (顶尖大学). Likewise, in Mainland China, there are two massive projects known as 985 (985 工程) and 211 (211 工程) to infuse funding to improve the qualities of Chinese top universities.

Since the highly visible government (extra) funding *de facto* comes from tax payers' contributions, it is a natural consequence that there will

---

[1] http://www.arwu.org

be intense and palpable social anxiety to demonstrate return on investment, or ROI. However, unlike a corporation, where ROI can easily be measured by the intake of profit on an annual quarterly basis, ROI for a university is almost by definition amorphous and not easily quantifiable, for sure not within the time scale of one year.

With this as background, and even with the ubiquitously understood ancient Chinese proverb 十年树木，百年树人, or *"It takes ten years to grow trees, but a hundred to rear people,"* it is no wonder that with explosive economic growth in the region naturally propelling society's impatience about having tangible results in a short time scale, the "global ranking of universities" which gives an annual "number" representing "quality" became a "quantifiable" ROI index for universities for the society to hold on to.

An "unintended consequence", as Joel would say, of such rankings, is receiving intense media interest and having the results reported with profuse frequency all across Asia Pacific. Without a doubt, we the administration of universities must be proactively driving the issues of ranking, or more broadly, the issue of quality of education, and not be led by outside forces. To be proactive, universities must not give the perception (*and we know that perception is reality*) that because of ranking pressure, we are deviating from the fundamental mission of a university, which is to educate generations after generations young minds with knowledge and the responsibility to improve quality of life for humanity. After all, the ultimate reason for research is for humans to have a deeper understanding of their surroundings, whether they be physical or humanistic, from which better understanding of human relations with one another and with the environment can emerge and innovations can be the natural outcome.

There is another issue I like to bring up today, although I am not sure what is the "unintended consequence". However, from history, I am confident that it must be profound! The history I learned is by noting that Charles Eliot, Harvard University's president in the late 19th and early part of the 20th century said that "... *a university, in any worthy sense of the term, must grow from seed. It cannot be transplanted from England or Germany in full leaf and bearing... . When the American university appears, it will not be a copy of foreign institutions, or a hot-bed plant, but the slow and natural outgrowth of American social and political habits.... The American college is an institution without a parallel; the American university will be equally original."*

I rest my case with the fact that in today's world, no one would view Harvard University as a copy of Cambridge University in Great Britain or the University of Gottingen in Germany. (*I am treading on dangerous ground here by heralding Harvard University when it is so obvious that in today's Panel, it is* de facto *or at least nearly a University of Illinois Champagne/Urbana and UC Berkeley "mafia"!*)

Purely by serendipity, all the universities represented at this meeting in Tokyo last week, from Japan, South Korea, Mainland China and Taiwan, have a common underpinning, and that is they all stand on the same foundation of Confucianism. For example, one cannot but help to take note that the oldest university in our group, Sungkyunkwan University (成均馆大学校), was founded in 1398. *"to offer prayers and memorials to Confucius and his disciples, and to promote the study of the Confucian canon."* I think there is no doubt that Confucianism for Asia Pacific would surely be a component, certainly an important component, of Asia's *"social and political habits,"* as I so boldly paraphrase Charles Eliot. With globalization in mind in the 21st century, in which Western culture is virtually and palpably embedded in the Asia Pacific society, it seems to me is imperative that Asia Pacific universities should and must find a way to harmonize these two seemingly different cultures, Eastern and Western. Perhaps by amalgamating these two vastly different cultures, one could create a new intellectual ambience; Asia Pacific universities could develop a new and novel roadmap for all our young minds in the 21st century so that they could serve humanity appropriately.

I would say that if universities in our region could do this, then we have taken an important step towards the goal of this Forum!

Thank you so much for your attention.

(2010)

20

Why Canadian Universities should Collaborate with Asia

This article was co-written with Harvey Weingarten. Harvey Weingarten is president of the Higher Education Quality Council of Ontario and President Emeritus of the University of Calgary. Da Hsuan Feng was Senior Vice-president, Global Affairs, Planning and Evaluation, of National Tsing Hua University in Taiwan. The writers urged the Canadian players to seize the existing opportunity, to delay no more.

After two trade missions to Asia in as many months, Prime Minister Stephen Harper signalled that Canada's economic future should be less reliant on the U.S. and more focused on opportunities with Asia. A number of recent reports have underscored the economic benefit to Canada of increasing trade with Asia, and the new task force report for the federal government entitled "International Education, a Key Driver of Canada's Future Prosperity" speaks to the importance of positioning and branding Canada's higher education internationally.

These arguments and analyses suggest that we should think carefully about how Canada's colleges and universities could engage effectively with their Asian counterparts. Right now, Canada, and much of the rest of the world, measures the worth of its universities by a set of metrics largely shaped by U.S. models. But as Yale University president Richard Levin notes, within a relatively short time Asian universities will be among the best in the world. There is considerable controversy in Asia about whether the American model is the best way to serve the economic and social requirements of their countries. This disquiet provides a significant opportunity for Canada to link its postsecondary system to a part of the world that will likely dominate higher education in the not too distant future. The massive investment in higher education in a host of Asian countries is nothing short of breathtaking. China is investing billions annually to raise the world status of nearly 100 of its universities. Consider, For example:

- the annual budget for Tsinghua University in Beijing has reached an eye-popping US$1.8 billion this year;
- over the next 10 years, China expects to increase university enrolments by 25 to 40 percent;
- Taiwan is investing the equivalent of $3.4 billion in additional funding over 10 years for just 12 of its 64 public universities to increase their competitiveness and drive a number of them into the ranks of the world's top 100;
- Singapore invests 20 percent of its annual budget in education and strategic research and development;
- Macao, a Special Administrative Area of China since 1997, is investing $1 billion in a new campus for its premier university — on a site in mainland China offered to it by the central Chinese government. The campus, to be open in just three years, is accompanied by an aggressive program of faculty recruiting;
- in 2010, India proclaimed its intent to increase the number of world-renowned institutes of technology from seven to 16.

Why is this an opportunity for Canada? Asians like the welcoming and modest attitude and style of Canadians. As the 2012 report by the Council of Canadian Academies on the state of science and technology in Canada revealed, researchers in China and Korea have a "notable and growing" affinity for publishing with Canadian collaborators. Asians also recognize and appreciate the significance that a number of Canadian universities have achieved world-class status. And, perhaps most importantly, Canada's vibrant and extensive Asian communities, especially in Toronto and Vancouver, provide an obvious welcome and effective link to many Asian communities.

What does Canada need to do to further its engagement with higher education in Asia?

First, it must recognize that there is potential even beyond China and India. Malaysia, Korea, Indonesia, Viet Nam, Thailand and the Philippines are also moving aggressively on higher education and provide important opportunities for collaborations and engagement with Canadian counterparts. Also, since Asian countries are planning collaboratively — 10 Southeast Asia nations participate in the Association of South East Asia Nations — Canada must think holistically and strategically about the entire region. As it already recognizes in its trade and economic policies, Canada must diversify beyond an almost singular focus on the U.S. By 2050, Asia's population is expected to reach 5 billion and 35 percent of world GDP. Canada cannot afford to lose the opportunity to affiliate with a part of the world that by many indices will significantly influence, if not dominate, global affairs.

Second, Canada should palpably participate in the vibrant discussion within Asia's higher education sector about how to reshape the nature, purposes and processes of higher education. It is clear that Asians, once exposed to what is going on in Canada, are motivated to learn from the Canadian experience. In turn, Canadians have much to learn from their counterparts in Asia. The action in higher education will inevitably move from the U.S. and Europe to Asia. It's already underway and Canada is well advised to affiliate with their agenda.

Finally, Canada should recognize that the limited number of Canadian universities that have attained world-class standing represent the foundation, and often the initial point of intersection, between the two regions. Canada must preserve its current slate of top 100 universities and is well advised to drive some of its near contenders to that status, a concern underscored by the most recent Times Higher Education World University Rankings. The prominence and economic power of Asia allows it to be very selective. Asians recognize and will work with the best. Through engagement of its top universities, Canada will engage other institutions, thereby uplifting its own higher education sector.

In the global marketplace, Canada cannot be just about oil, gas and minerals. It has fine educational institutions, brains and ideas. These are the currencies — as much as commodities — around which the world will organize itself. Canada has a chance, but it cannot delay.

(2012)

21

A Tale of Three Speeds: Challenges for Southeast, South Asia and Taiwan Universities (SATU) in the 21st Century

This is the opening comment made at the "2010 Southeast, South Asia and Taiwan Universities (SATU) Presidents Conference", held on October 2, 2010, at National Cheng Kung University. The author was Senior Executive Vice President at the university.

"The ultimate challenge for Asian universities is as follows: In the 19th century, Europe reined supreme in nearly all forms of intellectual achievements. Universities in Europe were second to none then. In the 20th century, North America reined supreme and universities in that continent became the envy of the world. And still is, I might add. So with wealth created in dizzying speed in Asia in the 21st century, will that be coupled by robust intellectual achievements, and universities in the region become some of the best in the world? I am convinced they will. But the long and arduous road is still ahead of us!"

Good morning, distinguished leaders from universities throughout Southeast Asia, South Asia and Taiwan. My name is Da Hsuan Feng. As Senior Executive Vice President of the host institution and as Secretary General of SATU, I am truly honored to have the opportunity to say a few words to this august body.

But before I do so, I am reminded by a great 1999 movie entitled *The Matrix*. In this movie, the heroine Trinity said the following memorable line: *"Morpheus believes he is the ONE.."*

Quite by serendipity, *SATU is also the ONE* since SATU means ONE in the Malay language!

Frankly, I am quite in awe today to see some one hundred higher education leaders, many are presidents, under one roof. In my many years as an administrator in the U.S., I do not recall ever seeing such a gathering, for sure not of this magnitude. Since coming to Asia, I noticed that SATU is one of the many such gatherings. This is clearly a manifestation of the higher education dynamism in Asia today, and signals the progressive nature of the region.

As a former Southeast Asian who was born in India, it gives me unabashed reason to greet my friends and colleagues with warm kinship from my former homelands, Singapore, Malaysia and India.

Ladies and gentlemen, since it was inaugurated by former President Kao (高强) and later promoted with vigor by President Lai (赖明昭), the SATU conference has emerged once every two years as an important brainstorming platform for a large fraction of universities leaders from one of the most robust and rapidly developing regions of the world. As such, I am confident that you will agree with me that we must take full advantage in these two days to collectively contemplate the unprecedented and quite unchartered responsibilities of higher education for this part of the world in the 21st century, a century on the one hand holds great promise for humanity and on the other guarantees enormous, rapid and unimaginable social, political and economic changes and upheavals. Even better, I hope we can collectively design a roadmap for universities to be relevant to the societies we are embedded in, the nations we belonged to, and the world we are part of!

Asia a century ago bears no resemblance to Asia today. Then, a large part of Asia, for sure the part represented by SATU delegates, was under the grips of colonialism. Economically and politically, the region was close to "bankruptcy." Human hardship of unimaginable scale was ubiquitous. This complete switch of landscape within a century, if I may be so bold to say, places universities in our region today in a particularly interesting and precarious position. As leaders of universities, it literally forces all of us to think out-of-the-box, to ensure that universities do not become "irrelevant". Indeed, business as usual, as the cliché goes, can no longer be the *modus operandi*!

To allow us to focus on the grand scenario, for this year's SATU conference, we have given the mission as follows: **"The Next 10 Years: A Decade of Innovation, Advancement, and Sustainability"** (高等教育未來十年之目标：创新、精进与永续发展) We did so because it is our humble belief that this mission is one of the most important challenges confronting 21st century universities. Of course, as leaders of the best universities in our region, you are more equipped intellectually and experience wise to give in depth answers to this mission than I can. Hence it is my hope that what I am about to say will perhaps give you some more fruits for thought. This mission is indeed timely. In fact, it is part of a much bigger challenge. There are serious grand challenges confronting humanity today. Allow me to name just a few: the looming of pandemics, energy shortages, ignorance and severe poverty, lack of tolerance and hatred of fellow human beings. I think universities in general, and universities in our region in particular, are lighthouses dotting this turbulent sea. Some of the solutions to these grand challenges, if not all, must come from non-silo thinkers with bold visions and innovative skill sets. Hence, is this not the mission of universities around the globe in general, in our region in particular, to nurture such *"non-silo thinkers with bold visions and innovative skill sets?"*

Flat Earth and Three Speeds

In today's world, universities need to take seriously what Thomas Friedman called the "flat world". I would argue that the flat world is due to three very different "speeds". I made this argument a few years ago in an international conference of bioscience chairpersons. Since then, I have thought more about it and would like to share it with you.

First, it is the speed of light. As everyone knows, almost to the point of being a cliché, this is how the internet, a technology which leverages the speed of light, has fundamentally altered the way mankind thinks and interacts. For those not scientifically minded, the speed of light is about 671 million miles an hour. Pretty darn fast, I would say. For all practical purpose for our small planet, it is instantaneous!

Then there is the second speed. It is the speed to move large objects like you and me. Here I have a more personal anecdote. In as recent as the early 50s, students going from Asia to the U.S. to pursue higher education usually went by boat. That journey took three weeks from origin to destination. Imagine what was in the mind of a student making that trip. He/She may have to accept the fact that he/she may not see his/her homeland for a long time. Even more painful, he/she may have to entertain the thought that he/she may not see his/her family for a long time. This was one of the reasons why many tears were shed in the docks at departure. However, today's transportation speed is roughly the speed of sound (768 miles per hour or technically it is called Mach 1). While it is still a far cry from "Beam me up, Scotty," the 21-day sea voyage has been reduced to between 10 to 12 hours of flight, from take-off to touch-down. This is roughly a factor of 40 increases in speed. Tears are certainly not necessary in this paradigm!

My message to students going abroad nowadays to pursue your dreams is as follows: do not for a moment think you will be free from your parents because they will see you in no time!

Finally, there is the third, subtle speed. It is the speed of turning vast amounts of data and information into useful knowledge. This is unlike just a few decades ago, where data and information came to one in the form of paper publications. However, I think we can all agree that data and information are useless if they cannot be processed into knowledge. That in itself places a boundary condition on how much one person can consume in finite time. The "slowness" of information *de facto* allows a person greater freedom to spend more time to contemplate what was being read and turned it into some form of understanding and better still, knowledge and innovations! Today, that freedom of having more time is absent because data and information is coming to one like a tsunami. Comprehension of information is a complicated human intellectual effort.

I was informed by cognitive scientists that it involves nearly every dimension of human existence, from raw intelligence to cultural background. With this complication, how do universities of today educate our students well enough so that they can in the shortest time digest vast amounts of information and turn it into useful knowledge?

So what *can* we learn from all this? There is an old Chinese saying: 读万卷书不如行万里路, or, *"Studying ten thousand books is not as fruitful as traveling ten thousand miles"*! Armed with the modern day three speeds, this means that human beings are going to all corners of the globe, and intellectual and economic developments, achievements, and for that matter, failures, are no longer regionally confined. The success or failure of a region or a nation, one may argue, to a large extent will depend on how globally enlightened and how often and how high a percentage its population travel to all corners of the globe. Indeed, the global grand challenges I mentioned earlier are now the responsibilities of all, not a few.

From an individual university's perspective, it can no longer serve merely a local region, catering to regional needs. As we move more and more into the 21st century, the three speeds will melt more and more national boundaries. Universities will almost be coerced, if not forced, to cater to a wide region. In fact, it could be global. As such, they will overlap, geographically, internetwise and people-wise, with other universities far away.

Research Questions

Embedded in the three speeds paradigm, I think never before have university administrators needed to be more cognizant of the global issues I outlined above. The question is how or whether one should tackle unsolved problems that have a much broader scope, with the ultimate aim of benefiting humanity. I should stress that this is not to say that one should not carry out intellectual efforts that are based on curiosity. Indeed, I am quite sure that it was entirely due to the curiosity of Watson and Crick that DNA was discovered! On the other hand, it is also true that there is now an explosive knowledge growth, coupled with an ever explosive growth of technologies (as recent trends would tell us, many of such technologies are still waiting to be invented!), so much so that they embolden us to ask broader questions. Imagine for this example of DNA, if people could travel easily, if there were no high speed networks and computers, if the barrier between information technologists and genomists was not lowered, and if there was no deep understanding of the science, the renowned Human Genome Project could not be completed so soon, if at all, and neither could one begin to think about "system biology", bioinformatics, post-genomic disease research and so on.

Therefore, with "ranking" of universities notwithstanding, administrators of universities should be fully alerted about the fast transformation of the intellectual landscape and encourage university communities to pursue what the late D. Allan Bromley, the Science Advisor of President George H. Bush (or Bush Senior) referred to as "grand challenges". A university should and must create a comfortable yet competitive ambience whereby working on such grand challenge problems, from funding to infrastructure to seamless communication, is not only highly encouraged, but given high priority!

When I entered graduate school in physics some four decades ago, I had to select a spectrum of "physics problems" to make contributions to. While most of these problems were exciting and unsolved, the upper bound of the scopes could be considered as rather restrictive and hence most would not fall into the definition of "grand challenges". I am sure that my biology friends, my chemistry friends, my mathematics friends, my engineering friends, or whatever field one happened to select then, had similar restrictions. While this paradigm is still quite prevalent today because of the silo structures in universities, more often then not one now hears researchers asking questions of a much general and broader nature.

Let me give you one example: *"How can we ensure that transportation of grains in a particular region is secure and seamless?"* Obviously a plethora of knowledge is needed to deal with this problem, from agriculture to economics to network security to human behavioral science to transportation scheduling on a massive scale, to local and inherent culture of the people, and the politics of the region, and the list simply goes on and on and on. However, what is also clear is that problems of this nature can be tackled only because of the interplay of the three speeds I have outlined. Providing solutions to such challenges will require individuals possessing different skill sets, probably distributed and working together in different institutions in different parts of the globe.

Epilogue

The issue at hand is profound and deep. It is interesting how speed seems to alter human behaviors. Indeed, it was the speed of the "zeros" in WWII that was the determining factor for the Japanese to attack Pearl Harbor and not San Francisco. Now, the three speeds, the speed of light for the internet, the speed of sound for travel of physical objects, and proper education to enhance the speed of acquiring knowledge are fundamentally altering human landscape. To wrap up, I would like to quote Charles Eliot, Harvard University's president in the late 19th and early part of the 20th century. He said:

> "...a university, in any worthy sense of the term, must grow from seed. It cannot be transplanted from England or Germany in full leaf and bearing. ... When the American university appears, it will not be a copy of foreign institutions, or a hot-bed plant, but the slow and natural outgrowth of American social and political habits. ... The American college is an institution without a parallel; the American university will be equally original."

Ladies and gentlemen, as leaders of aspiring Asian universities in the 21st century, I think it is worth remembering these profound words of Eliot in the 19th century. In fact, if in the above quotation you were to replace "England or Germany" with "Western" and "American" with "Asian", this quotation could easily be the motto of any university whose leaders are present today.

There is a phrase in Confucius' *Analects* which states: 工欲善其事，必先利其器 or "*The state of art depends on the state of your tool.*" I discussed a great deal about creating the right ambience and conditions for a university to pursue excellence to benefit humanity. The challenge for all of us is whether the "tools" of the university, the administrative structure, is at the state-of-the-art level so that excellence is simply a natural outcome.

The ultimate challenge for Asian universities is as follows: In the 19th century, Europe reined supreme in nearly all forms of intellectual achievements. Universities in Europe were second to none then. In the 20th century, North America reined supreme and universities in that continent became the envy of the world. And still is, I might add. So with wealth created in dizzying speed in Asia in the 21st century, will that be coupled by robust intellectual achievements, and universities in the region becoming some of the best in the world? I am convinced they will. But the long and arduous road is still ahead of us!

I am merely touching the tip of the iceberg here. However, it is nevertheless a very serious challenge and I urge all of you to give all you have, your energy, your wisdom, your knowledge and your regional and global connections, to provide the best answer to the mission of this Conference. The future of our region may depend on you coming up with the most appropriate solution. If we could start this process now, then SATU would be a huge success, and it will indeed be the ONE!

Thank you so much for your attention.

(2010)

22

"Google my late father?": What could or may Happen to India, China and United States in the 21st Century?

This was a speech for a conference titled "The Dragon and the Elephant: Understanding the Development of Innovation Capacity in China and India", organized by the National Research Council's Board on Science, Technology, and Economic Policy, co-organized by The Levin Graduate Institute of SUNY Woodrow Wilson International Center for Scholars Urban Institute Athena Allianca, held on September 24–25, 2007, at the National Academy of Sciences, United States National Academies' headquarters. The author was Senior Executive Vice President, National Cheng Kung University, Tainan, Taiwan.

I am truly honored and a little embarrassed to participate in this meeting on issues that have profound implications for me personally, for the U.S. and for the world.

I have to admit that today I am here under two "false pretenses".

The first is that the organizers invited me some months ago to come as the Vice President for Research and Economic Development of the University of Texas at Dallas. On September 1, three weeks ago, I became the Senior Executive Vice President of National Cheng Kung University in Tainan, Taiwan.

The second is that I stick out like a sore thumb in this august group of individuals. After all, I am not an economist, nor a political or social scientist, not even a philosopher. I am merely a theoretical physicist who happens to have been born in India, received all my advanced education, from undergrad to grad to post-doc, in the U.S., and have visited the Asia Pacific region in the past quarter of a century well over a hundred and twenty times. So my view of this issue is maybe what the Chinese would refer to as 井底之蛙, or the view of the sky of a frog at the bottom of a well!

In October of 2005, at the Annual Convention of the Indian Institute of Technology North Texas Alumni Association, I was invited to give a keynote speech, which I titled ***India, U.S. and China: Tripartite or Trinity in the 21st Century***? How pivotal these three nations will be for the world in the 21st century will depend very much on the intertwined relations between them.

Allow me to share something with you that is deeply personal but which I believe has profound implications in what we are discussing at this conference. I mentioned earlier that I was born in New Delhi, India. Besides the obvious reason that my mother (an American-educated pianist) was there at the time, the whole family was there because my father (an NYU JD in 1937 but who never practiced law, only journalism) was the chief English editor of the Kuomintang's Central News Agency. A few weeks after my speech in Dallas, my son amazingly was also admitted to NYU's law school. When he went for his interview, he dug-up information about my father. After my father died in 1950, he seldom entered my mind. My son's action actually surged my interest in my father. A few days after my son's action, one Saturday morning, while I was net surfing, I suddenly had the urge to Google my father! I was not sure of the precise English spelling of his name, so I just typed in "Paul Feng" and "India".

What came out from the search startled me! Hooray for Google!

The result of Google's search produced a website[7] containing a mesmerizing article by an author named Manoj Das (I am hoping that maybe one of our distinguished Indian participants in this conference would know this gentleman) with the title "Forging an Asian identity." It was published in *The Hindu* on January 7, 2001.

---

[7] http://www.burmalibrary.org/reg.burma/archives/200101/msg00016.html

The entire article is worth reading by all but the passage that startled me and which I would like to share it with you here is as follows:

> "...We in India have debated as much as other Asian countries have, about issues like the desirability of Western influence on our culture, its inevitability or otherwise, and the relation between tradition and modernity. Like the May Fourth Movement in China which championed western values and ideals in the 1920s, we too had voices against our traditions and they were given a reasonable hearing. An exchange in experiences of this kind would no doubt be highly educative."
>
> For quite some time, Indian literature for the common Englishman meant what Rudyard Kipling and the like wrote. For long, India's window as well as that of the West on Chinese life has been Pearl S. Buck's Good Earth. But when I read Lu Hsun, a number of his short stories and The True Story of Ah Q, I realised that despite the realism in the works of Pearl Buck and other gifted writers, Lu Hsun's work had an authenticity that could be expected only of a native of China. I do not propose to display my meagre knowledge of Chinese literature here, but what I propose is a strong and well-planned academy of Asian literatures to take care of the great need to know one another.
>
> "And who could take any effective step in that direction? For me, the answer came from the first Prime Minister of India, Jawaharlal Nehru. (Ladies and Gentleman, the following passage almost knocked me out of my chair!) **Speaking to Mr. Paul Feng of the Central News Agency, he said on January 20, 1946, "If China and India hold together, the future of Asia is assured." This holding together need not be confined to diplomacy; it can, by all means, be a psychological force that can work wonders in the realms of creativity... ."**

I said in an IIT speech in October 2005 that "*....In preparing (this speech) I realized that it must have been my background that the organizers were zeroing in on. The more I thought about it, the more I am convinced. Indeed, I am a product of these three great nations and so I may have some unique personal perspectives about them....*"

Having read the article about my father, I am even more convinced that that is why I was at that conference in Dallas, and why I am here today!

I should mention that all of you have heard much about these three nations on a daily basis. Someone once told me that *"if not for the constant claim in U.S. that China and India are taking all the jobs away from Americans, all the international news in this country would be on global terrorism."* Is it not ironic, maybe even a little amusing that the "bad" news about China and India is bringing some mental relief to the general population in the U.S.?

Still, there is no doubt that in the 21st century, U.S. interactions with India and China will continue to increase, in depth and in complexity. Also, in the 20th century or the centuries before that, whenever you have two or three powerful nations, wars inevitably would break out. I cannot, however, foresee the day when the U.S., China and India will have wars. If nothing else, the way businesses and intellectual exchanges that will be discussed extensively in this Conference would bind the nearly 3 billion people, or nearly half of the earth's population on earth, would make wars unthinkable.

If there are no wars, then there must be peace. If there is peace, the people of these three nations must think of ways to not just co-exist (the English language has a great word to describe such a co-existence: it is "**tripartite**") but exist together for the benefit not only for themselves, but humanity in general (another beautiful word: "**trinity**").

Let me tell you a very short form of my life story to try to convince you that India, the U.S. and China should and can be more a trinity than a tripartite!

I grew up in Singapore and my parents sent me to Chinese schools. That will explain why I absorbed so much traditional Chinese culture. In fact, the elementary school I went to was organized by the Kuomintang, and every morning before classes began, the entire faculty and students gathered in the athletic field to sing the national anthem of the Republic of China (which by then only had sovereignty in Taiwan) and the traditional three bows to Sun Yat-Sen, the father of modern China, as well as the Republic.

Singapore was a British colony (making me a British subject!). For this reason, education in Singapore, even Chinese schools, would have English as a subject. It was in learning English that I had my first real exposure to India. My first teacher in English was a jovial gentleman of

Tamil decent. I remembered that besides being a great teacher (he taught me the rudiments of this difficult language), he was also enormously proud of his heritage and culture.

In my 1st year of senior high, something horrible happened: war broke out between India and China. While the conflict was quite remote from Singapore, I remember there was a great deal of anxiety about its outcome. Unfortunately and understandably, there was also demonstration of nationalism, from both the Chinese and Indian communities in Singapore. I am sure while Nehru was able to foresee the grand Asian picture, this war between these two Asian giants "broke him" and soon after he died.

I came to the U.S. after high school and became thoroughly "Americanized". Several things happened in the past several decades — while on the one hand I became more and more an American, I also became more and more aware of China and India.

First, no sooner than I arrived in the U.S., China detonated an atomic bomb. As you may have noticed, I said nothing about China after I arrived in Singapore. The reason was simple: There was virtually no news about China in Singapore at that time. China was *de facto* a blackhole! Therefore, the fact that China was able to explode a sophisticated atomic device, which required a great deal of technical knowledge, was certainly an eye opening experience for me.

Second, throughout my graduate school days, many of my fellow students came from India. Outstanding institutions such as the University of Delhi, Banaras Hindu University (don't you just love that name), University of Calcutta, Tata Institute for Fundamental Research and Saha Institute of Nuclear Physics (in Saltlake, outside of Calcutta) started to enter my psyche. I was both pleased and excited to learn about the fact that India, the country of my birth, has a large number of outstanding universities.

As I became more educated in physics, I began to learn about how great science flourished in India well before many other Asian countries. Perhaps the most remarkable Indian scientist, who was the first Asian in science to win the Nobel Prize (in 1930) was Sir Chandrasekhara Venkata Raman. I should mention that the next Asian who received this accolade was Hideki Yukawa of Japan 19 years later in 1949. The first two Chinese (and only after they received all their advanced training in the U.S.) were T. D. Lee and C. N. Yang in 1957, some 27 years after Raman. It is interesting to note that the byline of Raman's prize is:

"for his work on the scattering of light and for the discovery of the effect named after him."

Nearly every scientist today would know the Raman Effect. Perhaps in my mind the most remarkable achievement of Raman was that he received his entire education, and did his ground breaking work in India. If you have not done so, I would urge you to read the Nobel acceptance speech of Raman which you can get from the Nobel website.[8] It is the most heartwarming scientific writing, and Raman did it without a single equation! By the way, I was asked to review a proposal recently by one of the funding agencies in the U.S. I rejected it instantly because in the proposal, Raman Effect was spelled "Ramen Effect"! I said that anyone who could not tell the difference between great science and noodles should not be funded!

One should remember that while the accolade belongs to Raman and Raman only, it must be underscored that great scientific achievements are seldom solo performances. Raman's achievement must imply that India's scientific conditions — while it may not have been as robust as Europe when Raman was doing his work — the culture of world-class scientific research must have been quite prevalent for him to achieve greatness. Therefore, if one fast-forwards to today, it should not come as a surprise that India's technological prowess did not grow from vacuum. It stood on solid foundations.

Third, perhaps one of the most memorable moments in my life in the U.S. (before the morning of 9/11) was on a cold day in January of 1972 in Beijing, I watched on TV with awe when Nixon descended from his Air Force One, with his hands protruding in order to shake the hand of Zhou Enlai. Compare this with what happened in 1954 when the U.S. Secretary of State Dulles refused to shake Zhou's hand, and deeply insulted not just

---

[8] http://www.nobel.se

Zhou but all Chinese. This single gesture of Nixon was certainly one that initiated the thawing of the icy relationship between these two nations.

As we all know, the Chinese "open policy" began after the fall of the "Gang of Four" in 1977. In these 30 years, the world was totally transformed. Technology, especially information technology, profoundly and fundamentally transformed the world. In hindsight, having enormous populations in China (1.4 billion) and India (1.3 billion), how can one NOT expect that these two nations will not be transformed and impact the world. 1976 was a defining year for modern China. Mao died on September 9, followed immediately by the spectacular collapse of the so-called "Gang of Four", thus bringing closure to ten painful and devastating years of "Cultural Revolution", and ushered China into a new era. I am sure historians will undoubtedly consider the new era as the "miracle of the world in the 20th century". In 1976, China was at the verge of a complete meltdown, economically, technologically and intellectually. Having quarter of humanity, and a land size spanning nearly half of Asia, such a meltdown would have horrifying global implications! Yet, no meltdown occurred.

One of the fundamental reasons, in my mind, as to why no meltdown occurred was due to the Herculean contributions of tens of millions of Chinese intellectuals. In their darkest hours, enduring the hardest of hardships and suffering the deepest personal humiliations, they maintained palpable hope for themselves, their family, their professions and China. Indeed, even without personal liberty, both physical and mental, they remained important pillars of the nation, holding up its dignity and searching for dim light at the end of a long and dark tunnel. The current state of China, and its impact on the Asia Pacific basin, is in no small part due to these brave individuals.

China of the 21st century is fundamentally a different country from the days when the Communists first took power in 1949. India in the past two decades also has transformed, or some would call it, reinvented. China of the 50s gave the perception of fear. Indeed, when I was growing up in Singapore, what we were constantly reminded was China's "Red Menace". India in the 50s gave the perception of a desperately poor third world country.

Today, the perception of China and India are nations profoundly interested in becoming, and probably already are, economically strong and intellectually robust. As I see it, China and India in the 21st century have at least the following challenges which did not exist in the 50s.

First, there are unquestionably vast increases in international commercial activities. While there were none in the 50's and considerably less before the 90's, the amount ballooned significantly in the 90's and beyond. With a large internal market and large and reasonably well-trained workforce in the hundreds of millions, one would expect that there will be no slow-down of this trend.

Second, while the percentage is still small, but because Chinese and Indian populations are so large, *in absolute number* there are now sizable middleclasses, and they are growing rapidly. For example, for China, even if the middle class makes up as little as 10 percent of the population (which I am sure would be an underestimation), in absolute number it is around 130 million, which is a third to a half of the US population. It is well known that the middle class will demand a better environment, better health care, better education for their children, and a higher standard of living. All of these demands will place significant pressure on China's and India's soft and hard infrastructure. There is no doubt in my mind that this sector of the population will significantly impact both countries.

Third, for both nations, there is a growing private sector and it is undeniable that the wealth in the nation is slowly flowing into the hands of that sector. In India's case, it is obvious. In China's case, my interactions with China in the past decade, I find that the percentage of friends who work for and/or started private businesses are increasing quite rapidly. For example, I was told that as high as 80 percent to 85 percent of the wealth generated in Zhejiang Province now arises from private sectors. These are welcome sign not just for China and India, but for the world as a whole.

Fourth, fast and at times uncontrolled and unstructured economic growth can bring undesirable elements to the society, such as degradation of the environment, shortage of the necessary resources to propel the growth and worse, the tendency to cut corners. These issues can significantly lower the quality of life and could lead to conflicts, national or international.

Fifth, as in all modern nations in the 21st century, one should not rely on the inherent human instincts to be ethical. Mencius (孟子) said that "*ren zhi chu, xing ben shan*" (人之初, 性本善) or "Human at Birth is Ethical." Whether this is true or not, I argue that we should not take this chance and see how each of us may turn out in real life. To this end, modern nations must be nations of law. Some recent spectacular examples in the corporate and academic worlds, which in the U.S. is the genesis of SOX, or Sarbane-Oxley Compliance, clearly indicate to us "ethical indoctrination" should never be left to individuals.

Finally, I cannot help but think a little "blue-sky" at this point of my speech. If we look around the globe in the 20 century, perhaps the most interesting political and economic development is Europe. Before WWII, countries in Europe with profoundly different cultures, languages and political systems had major conflicts. Wars between these nations were bloody and protracted.

Yet, after WWII, with Marshall Plan from the U.S. and with the recognition that "united we stand," European Union, or EU (欧盟) was created.

So, can one think that in the 21 century, there could actually be an AU, or Asian Union (亚盟)? After the French and Germans, who were bitter enemies before WWII, decided to be proactive parts of EU, and with US closely aligned with the concept, EU was created! So, can one not have nations in Asia, encouraged by the two giants India and China, working closely with US, to form AU?

Imagine that perhaps one day in the future a person can actually hop on a bullet-train in Seoul, Korea for Mumbai without having to show once his/her passport to anyone! Imagine the economic explosions and expansions, for the region and the globe that can come from such a scenario. Imagine the improvement of the "quality-of-life" for all people in the world if Asia Pacific and South Asia, with more than half of the world's population, propelled by India and China, and assisted by U.S., become AU in the 21st century!

Imagine!

I hope I have given you my very personal, very limited and probably very bias view about these three great nations. I am upbeat about their futures because I think all three have deep intellectual strengths. From my personal experiences and perspectives, I believe that US, India and China have far more in common then not. All are powerful nations in their own right. However, if they can work together, with mutual respect as the underpinning, the world will show a sigh of relieve.

It is clear to me that the condition, which took entire 20 century to mature, is ripped for these three nations to regard themselves as a "trinity" and not a "tripartite." Due to their individual successes, I believe that these three nations should and need to shoulder a major part of global responsibilities to ensure that the world can be a better place for all humanity in the 21 and beyond centuries.

Thank you.

(2007)

New Ideas

23

A Game-Changing Model for Higher Education?: On University of Nottingham Ningbo China (UNNC)

The author was Special Assistant to the President for Global Strategies and International Relations and Professor of Physics, The University of Texas at Dallas, when he wrote this article.

Preamble

Ever since on November 14, 2006 I was bestowed the great honor of UNNC's honorary professorship, many people both in the U.S. and China wanted to know whether UNNC is a "foreign branch campus of Nottingham." While this is a natural assumption, the answer is negative. In fact, I believe that if UNNC succeeds in its mission, it could be a game changing model for higher education. Thus, I like to take this opportunity to clarify the status of this university. I should say that any erroneous information I provided here is entirely due to me.

What is UNNC?

The name Nottingham notwithstanding, UNNC is by legal definition a Chinese university on Chinese soil. In accordance to Chinese law, it is forbidden for foreign university to establish a campus or campuses on Chinese soil. Therefore, to depict UNNC is indeed a Chinese university, the subtle difference between a foreign university campus, or "University of Nottingham **in** Ningbo, China" and an independent Chinese university, or "University of Nottingham Ningbo China" should be noticed.

While legally UNNC is autonomous (独立法人), it also has a deep connection with a foreign university, namely University of Nottingham. The top administrator of a university, namely the "President" of the University, according to Chinese law, must be an individual who holds Chinese citizenship. Indeed, the first and current President of UNNC is Academician Fu-Jia Yang (杨福家). Obviously, the rules and regulations of higher education institutions established by Chinese Ministry of Education need to be adhere to.

University of Nottingham in the United Kingdom

In UK, University of Nottingham, a comprehensive university with about 30,000 students, is one of its top global universities. In the past decade, it has consistently been ranked in the top 10 in the country, and in the world top 100. In 2003, a current faculty member, **Sir Peter Mansfield**, and a former faculty member, **Dr. Clive W.J. Granger**, received the highest global scientific accolades, the Nobel prize, in medicine and economics, respectively.

Two Pivotal Individuals for the establishment of UNNC

As in any game changing effort, it usually is the vision of a few individuals. UNNC is no exception. In establishing of UNNC, there are two individuals who played major, if not pivotal role. Without their complimentary visions and actions, it would be difficult to envision that UNNC can be created. They are **Sir Colin Campbell**, Vice Chancellor, or VC, of University of Nottingham in UK and **Academician Fu-Jia Yang** in China.Both cannot have more different backgrounds and life experiences. Yet together, they seem to be able to dovetail their demeanors at the right time at the right place to be the change agents for higher education at the global level.

Sir Colin Campbell, Vice Chancellor of University of Nottingham

In UK universities, the Vice Chancellor, or VC, is the chief executive officer (equivalent to the President in a US university). A lawyer, or barrister, by training, Sir Colin Campbell is indeed a remarkable global visionary. From what I could read about him, in the decade of the 90's, Sir Colin already instinctively recognized that in the new century, China's influence, whether it be intellectual or economic, will be globally felt. To this end, he intuitively understood the necessity of University of Nottingham "going global." Yet, for Sir Colin, "going global" apparently does not simply mean making contacts with foreign universities, which at the grass roots level happen frequently anyway, or to enhance a greater number of foreign students, or to establish some presence in some foreign countries. For him, it is to alter innovatively its fundamental and internal culture of University of Nottingham. To this end, he made the truly bold, unprecedented and historical recommendation in 2000 to the University Court (equivalent to the Board of Trustees of an American university) that a Chinese citizen, Academician Fu-Jia Yang, be its Chancellor.

It should be noted that by deep and profound tradition, the ceremonial Chancellor position of any British university is usually an enormously and socially known dignitary. For example, at the extreme, the Cambridge University's Chancellor is none other than the Duke of Edinburgh, husband of Elizabeth II, the Queen of England. Indeed, for as long as British universities have existed (Oxford University began in 11th century) there have never been a Chinese citizen who holds the Chancellor position in any one of them. By appointing Academician Fu-Jia Yang as University of Nottingham's Chancellor, Sir Colin literally "broke the mode" and was able to leverage this position to begin his process of fundamentally creating an internal cultural transformation. Indeed, by extrapolation, Sir Colin has significantly expanded the role of a Chancellor!

Academician Fu-Jia Yang

Apparently, appointing Academician Fu-Jia Yang is precisely "what the doctor's ordered!" By "game changing," such an appointment has instant "shock value" for the media in China, UK and beyond. The world suddenly took notice that University of Nottingham is doing something that is tradition altering and is making a serious attempt to trail blaze in the 21st century in creating a new paradigm for higher education.

Fu-Jia Yang is without exaggeration one of the most visible and highly respected academicians in China. He is also one of the most well connected and well networked individuals globally. His impressive resume includes the following: He was one of the first in 1962 to be sent to a western university for advance research (Niels Bohr Institute of the University of Copenhagen) after the Communists took power in 1949. He was the former President of one of China's best universities, Fudan University. During his tenure, he initiated many exciting and innovative programs, including merging one of the best medical schools in China to be a part of the university. In 1990, Yang was elected to be an academician of the Chinese Academy of Sciences, the highest academic accolade in China, for his exceptional contributions in utilizing small accelerators to study material properties. Yang takes being an Academician very seriously because he considers being one is not merely a supreme honor, but a responsibility to be executed and the opportunity to be a "change agent" for China. He is also a member of the world renowned Nuclear Threat Initiative, an organization for the mitigation of weapons of mass destruction, co-chaired by two distinguished individuals: U.S. Former Senator Sam Nunn and the well known media mogul, Ted Turner. Finally, in the last three decades, ever since China resumed "open door policy," Academician Yang has been a visible and vocal in advocating that Chinese higher education must be proactive in globalization.

I am not sure whether there is a direct correlation or not, but since Academician Yang became University of Nottingham's Chancellor, the number of Chinese students for this British University shot up significantly, from under 100 in the late 90's to now well over 1000 of today. In addition, many notable Chinese or Chinese Americans have appeared on campus. Very well known individuals such as the **Honorable Chen Zhili** (陈至立), Councilor of the State Council of the People's Republic of China and former Minister of Education, **Academician Lu Yongxiang** (路甬祥), President of the Chinese Academy of Sciences and **Professor T. D. Lee** (李政道), one of the two Chinese Americans to first win the Nobel prize appeared on campus to receive Doctor of Science or Doctor of Humanities, *honoris causa*, from University of Nottingham. While the events may be considered as ceremonial, the fact that so many being honored in this manner also signaled to the world, both in perception and in reality, that a profound change in the internal culture of University of Nottingham is taking place.

The Stage is Set for UNNC

Creation of UNNC require the serendipitous aligning the stars! The first is to have the above mentioned two individuals, Sir Colin, the VC and Academician Yang, the Chancellor of University of Nottingham. It seems to me that both individuals complement each other exceedingly well, in ability and in vision. Their strong and sustained collaboration of is one alignment. Indeed, UNNC must satisfy Chinese legal boundary conditions on the one hand and, on the other hand, down the road must enhance the tremendous global reputation enjoyed by University of Nottingham currently.

Obviously without the push and clear mission articulation on the UK side by Sir Colin, and by the same token, without the push, articulation, and finding the right venue and team on the Chinese side by Academician Yang on the Chinese side, especially the painstaking process of explaining that UNNC to the education authorities in China is indeed a Chinese university, it is difficult for me to see how UNNC would be here today.

Sir Colin and Academician Yang are two individuals who are almost unique to carry out such tasks in their respective countries. For example, having Academician Yang assuming the Chancellorship of University of Nottingham in UK makes him the absolute perfect candidate to be the first President of UNNC. To overcome the so-called *"vision without funding is a hallucination,"* it was critical that both Sir Colin and Academician Yang worked hand-in-hand to locate the right team in China to carry out the arduous task for finding the venue and the enormous funds that was required to jump start the process. Indeed they did, and still do. Being one of the most famous native-sons of Ningbo, and that this city is also the hometown of a significant number of intellectual and economic giants, both in and out of China (Ningbo has one of the highest, if not the highest, number of native-sons who are Academicians), and a city government absolutely hungry in creating a new city which is both economically and intellectually strong, viable and sustainable, selection of the City to create UNNC is obvious.

Of course, the fact that 2003, the year that the concept of UNNC being articulated coincided with the year University of Nottingham faculty members received two Nobel prizes, certainly did not hurt the effort!

All these culminated the old cliché that *"if one had to choose between being smart or lucky, always choose lucky!"*

UNNC now

Four years into its operation, UNNC is still in its infant stage. So whether this "experiment" will ultimately be successful, satisfying its metric of success, or not remains to be seen. However, the initial vectors are all pointing in the right direction.

For example, the following are now already in place.

- The ceremonial effort of bestowing the Honorary Chen Zheli the honorary degree in University of Nottingham has already, according to its website[9], reaped the benefit of her having *"agreed to launch the Chinese Policy Institute, a quality-oriented think tank which will produce top quality research and policy papers on selected topics to help build a more informed dialogue between China and the UK and to guide business and government strategies"*! This is certainly an area where I believe US could take note. There is of course a Johns Hopkins University–Nanjing University Center which serves more or less the same function for nearly two decades already. It would be interesting to see whether these two Centers can get together and compare notes.
- All courses in UNNC are delivered in the English language. This makes UNNC absolutely unique in China. In my discussions with the many students there, I certainly found them to be far more fluent in the English language then students from standard Chinese universities. Also, the fact that UNNC is in an entirely Chinese environment, there is probably no danger that there is diminishing abilities of Chinese literacy of the students. Thus, down the road, I can see that there will be a new cadre of young intellectuals emerging from UNNC who are

---

[9] http://www.nottingham.edu.uk/China

fluent not only languages of both countries, but also culture, mannerism, and inherent ways of doing business.
- As an example of the "flat world," students at UNNC and University of Nottingham share the same internet resources. In the so-called post-internet era, this is a critical component for modern universities. The fact that UNNC and University of Nottingham is literally "joined at the hips," makes this a particularly exciting paradigm.
- A large number of faculty members at UNNC are seconded from University of Nottingham. While I was there, I met two of them and both at extraordinarily excited about contributing to this experiment.
- A teaching quality assurance system is now in place to ensure that UNNC and University of Nottingham have the same standard. The necessity of such a system, as I mentioned earlier, is obvious.

Impact on Chinese higher education landscape

It is probably still too early to tell whether the UNNC experiment will be successful or not. It is certainly too early to tell whether it will impact the Chinese higher education landscape down the road. However, I am confident that if it can satisfy the merit criterions, the impact on Chinese higher education landscape can be enormous. UNNC has very different ways of doing things, compare to the vast ocean of universities in China.

As in any great effort, this was initiated by visionaries and technocrats, exemplified by Sir Colin and Academician Yang. At this moment, to see this effort grows and matures, these visionaries and technocrats must continue to guide UNNC, since it still has some distance to go before it can reach a stage of self propelling. The issue of interest here is whether there will be equally visionary leaders waiting in the wings to continue this great march. From what I have been observing in the past several years, especially in the recent visit, I am confident that those individuals do exsit and can pick up when the batons are ready to be passed.

As a good chemist friend once told me, "*if you just let a small drop of red ink into a beaker of clear water, it will alter its entire complexion!*" In a sense, UNNC could be such a small drop of red ink!

(2008?)

24

Private Universities: A Future Force in Global Leadership in Asia Pacific

This was a speech made in Malaysia when the author was Director of Global Affairs and Special Advisor to the Rector, The University of Macau.

Abstract

Unquestionably, Asia Pacific saw a spectacular surge of economy in the latter half of the 20th century. With economic boom, and accompanied by the population who were high on education to begin with, it naturally induced an unprecedented explosive growth in higher education, both in scale and intellectual depth. However, as Asian societies regard education as a government business, the growth and *modus operandi* of higher education were essentially "relegated" to the government. In this speech, I will discuss the fundamental importance of a nearly "forgotten" component of higher education, namely **private institutions**. I will discuss some examples where private institutions not only are critically important in their own right, but they could very well be the missing incentive for a far more robust higher education model in a nation. I will also discuss what and how one may render private universities outstanding.

Preamble

Distinguished colleagues, please allow me to thank you for inviting me to speak at this very timely topical conference on higher education excellence in Malaysian. As a youngster who grew up in Singapore and at one point in my life held a Malaysian passport, the well-being of this region is always dear to my heart.

Higher education is the pulse of a nation. When it is strong, so is the nation. If there is one national issue which should be absolutely above politics, it should and must be education! In addition, as someone who had devoted nearly 20 years of my professional careers to promote higher education globally, I felt that the main theme of this conference cannot be timelier. So, please allow me to congratulate the organizers of this conference for being so visionary.

The issues confronting Malaysian higher education as I see it is complex, multidimensional and convoluted. It is not a subject one could cover in finite time. In view of this constraint, I will only confine my discussion on what I see as the role of private universities in Malaysia. I hope there will be other conferences in the future where some other important and fundamental issues of Malaysian higher education infrastructure, hard and soft, could be discussed.

Case Study: Korean vs. Taiwan Universities

As someone who was an administrator in the past decade and a half in public universities (The University of Texas at Dallas, National Cheng Kung University, National Tsing Hua University and now the University of Macau,) how and why did I pick this topic? I think this may appear to be especially unusual because in Taiwan, private universities are hardly on the higher education radar screen nationally.

Please allow me to tell you how I came to this revelation! I could almost pinpoint the moment when I suddenly was alerted to the importance of private universities in a higher education landscape. On January 27–28, 2010, several colleagues and I at National Cheng Kung University were graciously hosted by the then President of Seoul National University (SNU,) President Jang-Moo Lee. Our mission to SNU was surgical. We were there to learn about the mission, process, and internal and external challenges for SNU to enter into its profound transformation, the transformation of **corporatization**. As some of you probably know, SNU since 2011 made the bold move to do just that.

On the evening of our departure from Seoul, we were warmly hosted to a sumptuous dinner by a longtime friend of mine, Dr. Jung Uck Seo. Dr. Seo is a renowned builder of science and technology in Korea in the past forty years since his return from the U.S. after completing his education at Texas A and M University. He was a former Minister of Science and Technology, a CEO of several high-tech corporations, and a member of the Board of Regents of his alma mater Texas A and M University. During my tenure at the University of Texas at Dallas, I was extremely fortunate to have invited him to be a distinguished member of the scientific advisory board.

After the dinner and just before we bid farewell to one another, Dr. Seo said one of the most profound and absolutely out-of-the-blue statements about Korean higher education in our two days of meeting. He said that

> *"some twenty years ago, if you were to ask me which universities in Korea would be top twenty in the country, I would probably find 15 national universities and 5 private ones. Today, the situation is completely reversed. This tells me that Korean higher education has come of age!"*

Knowing Dr. Seo was a loyal Seoul National University alumnus, such a statement stunned me. This comment was made while I was still working in a Taiwanese university where I had noticed that Korean universities were surging ahead in intellectual strength. However, I had for as long as I could remember considered Taiwanese and Korean universities were similar if not identical in characteristics, cultural and functionality. Therefore this comment made by my good friend Dr. Seo hit me like a ton of bricks!

In order to understand more deeply what Dr. Seo meant, I started to do some homework regarding Korean higher education. What I discovered completely altered my thinking about Asian higher education. To get some precise information about this rather remarkable comment, I began examining two popular systems of ranking of universities: the Shanghai Jiaotong University and Times Higher Education (THE) rankings. As I have said emphasized about such rankings, however you like them emotionally and/or intellectually, by themselves they could only convey information within their restrictive boundary conditions. Together, they may convey something more global.

Shanghai Jiaotong University 2014 Ranking of Korean Universities in the Top 500 Globally

1. Seoul National University (101–150) (Nat)
2. KAIST (201–300) (Nat)
3. Korea University (201–300) (Pvt)
4. Sungkungkwan University (201–300) (Pvt)
5. Yongsei University (201–300) (Pvt)
6. Hanyang University (301–400) (Pvt)
7. Kyun Hee University (301–400) (Pvt)
8. Pohang University of Science and Technology (301–400) (Pvt)
9. Catholic University of Korea (401–500) (Pvt)
10. Ewha Women's University (401–500) (Pvt)

Times Higher Education 2014 Ranking of Korean Universities in the Top 400 Globally

50. Seoul National University (Nat)
52. KAIST (Nat)
62. Pohang University of Science and Tech (Pvt)
148. Sungkyunkwan University (Pvt)
201–225 Korea University (Pvt)

201–225 Yonsei University (Pvt)
351–400 Ewha University (Pvt)
351–400 Hanyang University (Pvt)
(**Pvt means Private and Nat means National**)

The data of these two ranking systems completely corroborated with the statement of Dr. Seo. In the SJTU ranking, except for the top two heavily funded public universities, SNU, a comprehensive university and KAIST, a technological university, the rest are all private universities. The situation is even more striking for the THE ranking. In the eight Korean universities in the THE top 400, only SNU and KAIST are listed. It is also worth noting that "student to student" and "professor to professor," Postech, a private university, competes well with KAIST, a public university! Indeed, in the campus of Postech is the only state-of-the-art synchrotron radiation facility in Korea!

Shanghai Jiaotong University 2014 Ranking of Taiwan Universities in the Top 500 Globally

1. National Taiwan University (101–150) (Nat)
2. National Cheng Kung University (201–300) (Nat)
3. National Tsing Hua University (201–300) (Nat)
4. National Chiao Tung University (301–400) (Nat)
5. Chang Gung University (401–500) (Pvt)
6. National Sun Yat Sen University (401–500) (Nat)
7. National Yang Ming University (401–500) (Nat)

(*There are 7 from Taiwan in the top SJTU 500 of which only 1 is private. There are 10 from South Korea in the top SJTU 500, of which 2 are national universities.*)

Times Higher Education 2014 Ranking of Taiwan Universities in the Top 400 Globally

155. National Taiwan University (Nat)
251–275. National Tsing Hua University (Nat)
276–300. National Chiao-Tung University (Nat)
351–400. National Cheng Kung University (Nat)

351–400. National Sun Yat San University (Nat)
351–400. National Taiwan University of Science and Tech (Nat)
(***In the top 400 THE ranking, Taiwan has 6 universities, of which none are private. For Korea, there are 8, and only 2 are national!***)

Clearly, the complete opposite of the Korean and Taiwan situations deserves greater examination.

First, without the slightest exaggeration, the palpable rise of the quality of private universities is challenging the national universities intellectual leadership in Korea. In Taiwan, the dominance of national universities is nearly absolute, if not total, in public perception and in reality. The fact that the private universities are literally at the heels of the public universities in Korea must imply that the public ones, in fact there are only two, SNU and KAIST, absolutely cannot sit on their laurels! It is worth noting that the seven years I spent in Taiwan's two top public universities, I never felt palpable "intellectual presence" of Taiwan's private universities! A very good friend of mine once mentioned to me that for Korean families, having sons and daughters accepted to private universities are "**no shame**!" In fact, it is quite an honor. In Taiwan it is quite the contrary. In my seven years, I had often heard from parents something to the effect that "my son/daughter is not very smart, and therefore he/she could only get into a private university!"

(This statement was made notwithstanding that there are terrible public universities in Taiwan!)

As the old saying, "competition is never a bad thing!" A cursory survey of the data, it is clear that in global competition, Korean universities have surged ahead of Taiwan universities. While there are many factors for Taiwan universities down-sliding in ranking, I am convinced that one of them is that the public universities felt no competition from the private counterparts and felt no necessity to "reform" or "reinvent." They are too happy in their comfort zone!

It is worth mentioning that effective January 1, 2011, Seoul National University made a giant move in "corporatizing" the university, in that the university will hitherto be operated by a Board of Trustees, similar to that of a State University in the U.S. Of course, what it means is that the Korean government will not dip its hands into SNU's business. I am absolutely convinced that one of the reasons why SNU would take such a bold move was because they felt the palpable competition coming from the private universities!

Second, I was astounded by the fact that one of the top private universities of Korea, Yonsei University, with 40,000 students, has an annual budget at ~$2.8 billion U.S. dollars. To be able to operate with such a large annual budget must imply that the university has a very healthy endowment and a robust fund raising engine. There is an old American saying, which is *"vision without funding is hallucination!"* The same is true with operating a university, especially a private one. To be able to meet its financial obligations year in and year out, it is critical that the private universities must have sound and healthy financial war chests. We often talked about the great private universities in the U.S.

Let me give you some numbers of their endowments.

Harvard University: $36 Billion (2014) $26 Billion (2009)
Stanford University: $22 Billion (2014) $12 Billion (2009)
Princeton University: $21 Billion (2014) $12 Billion (2009)
MIT: $12 Billion (2014) $8 Billion (2009)
Caltech: $2 Billion (2014) $1.4 Billion (2009)
University of Pennsylvania: $10 Billion (2014) $5 Billion (2009)

It is worth underscoring that as a small and young Korean private university (28 years of history, 400 faculty members and 3500 student), Pohang University of Science and Technology (Postech) has an endowment of US$1.3 Billion. In many ways, this is comparable to Caltech! There is NO comparable private institution in Taiwan.

These numbers tell us that one of the real strengths of these private universities is that operationally they are financially independent from the Government. While great universities such as Harvard compete fiercely for the research funding from the U.S. Federal Government, the running of the university is absolutely not dependent on it! I know of two anecdotes which can give us a clear indication as to their independence.

The first is mentioned to me by Chancellor Fu-Jia Yang, former President of China's Fudan University and former Chancellor of the University of Nottingham of UK. In one of his visits to Harvard, he learned that when the U.S. Secretary of Education made one of his visits to Harvard, the President of Harvard actually had no time to meet with him because he had *"more important guests he needed to entertain."* Presumably the importance of the guests is measured by how much donation they were going to make to Harvard.

The second is during the 350th anniversary celebration of Harvard University, President Ronald Reagen was invited to attend as a guest of honor. For this ceremony, *"Harvard University has decided to grant no honorary degrees at its 350th anniversary celebration next year, cutting short a heated debate among its faculty and alumni over the prospect that President Reagan would be among the degree recipients."* Imagine having such a backbone when the university's financial viability depends on the government! For Korean private universities operating with such a strong financial situation must imply that it is quite, if not very, independent from government interference. This is clearly not the case for Taiwan's private universities. No private universities in Taiwan would have such backbones in dealing with the Ministry of Education.

I think there is something profound here that is worth underscoring. In my seven years Taiwan, I did notice more and more funds raised by the university from the private sector. Indeed, many building constructions in National Cheng Kung University and National Tsing Hua University were generously funded by the private sectors. However, I had seldom noticed any significant infusion of funds from the private sectors for intellectual enrichments, say in the form of endowed chairs or a vast multi-year research institute on a timely topic of global importance. It is not obvious that the private sectors of Taiwan understand how critical it is for educational purposes to support the intellectual effort of higher education. One gets the feeling that the private sectors felt that such is, or should be, entirely the responsibility of the government! Whether the government, *a la* the Ministry of Education, understands the operations of universities, private or public, is debatable. I do not know whether Korea private sector has overcome this hurdle, but the fact that their private universities are financially strong must imply to me that this hurdle must have been partially, if not fully, overcome.

Third, the relationship between the Government of South Korea and higher education institutions must have reached a substantially more mature and sophisticated level then between the Government of

Taiwan and the higher education institutions. The fact that there are significant similarities of South Korea and Taiwan in culture, economy and social structure, the rise of private universities in Korea must imply that the Government (*a la* Ministry of Education) maintains a relatively "hands-off" attitude towards the private educational institutions. In the South Korea higher education landscape, the strong private universities will get stronger intellectually and financially and the weak ones either diminish in statue, or find alternative ways to survive, or simply shut down. In Taiwan, the opposite is true. Government is deeply involved in the operations of private universities! Despite the fact that there is looming danger of population drop, the Ministry of Education still cannot propose a reasonable policy to deal with its imminent eventuality.

Fourth, just as private universities in the U.S. are "legally owned" by the respective Board of Trustees (BOT,) so are the private universities in South Korea. This ownership must imply that there is or must be very clear legal and ethical codes and conducts the BOT must adhere to. There is a very subtle point about such ownership. Both private universities BOTs and the Board of Regents (BORs) of public universities are financially and intellectually responsible for the well-being of the university. However, there is a subtle difference here. Public universities ethical conducts of funds are governed by government auditing, while the private universities funds must have strong internal auditing system. For this reason, ensuring the financial robustness of private universities, with careful management and highest ethical conduct, present and in the future, must be transparent or it could easily be abused!.

Indeed, the cliché of "slippery slope" here is very operational! In addition, it also may imply that philanthropic contributions of higher education, especially for private universities are socially and governmentally acceptable and encouraged. Academic structure of private universities must allow the presidents to engage in vigorous fund raising activities, just like those in the U.S.

It is worth noting that there are only few countries in the world where private universities could challenge the dominance of public universities. U.S. is of course an off-scale example, while Japan and now South Korea are two whose private universities are highly visible at the societal level!

Lessons Learned and Implications for Malaysia

As I have mentioned from the outset, I am an outsider looking into the Malaysian higher education landscape. With that in mind, let me based on the aforementioned Korean and Taiwan case study to cast some light on the situation in Malaysia.

Malaysia, Taiwan and Korea have some similar characteristics as can be seen from the following table.

Country	Population	Number of Universities	Ethnicity
Korea	51 million	~230	Primarily Single
Malaysia	30 million	~100	Multi
Taiwan	23 million	~160	Primarily Single

By the 21st century, all three regions "exploded" with the number of higher education institutions! Having such a large number of "universities" could itself be a challenge, and could degrade the quality and quantity of higher education. That unfortunately is even more complex and is beyond the scope of this discussion.

Still, I think with the size of the population in the tens of millions and "large" number of universities, it makes a compelling case to compare Korea, Malaysia and Taiwan.

First, there is no doubt that the top rated universities in Malaysia are public ones. According to the 2014 QS ranking, they are as follows:

1. Universiti Malaya (UM) (151)
2. Universiti Kebangsaan Malaysia (UKM) (259)
3. Universiti Sains Malaysia (USM) (309)
4. Universiti Teknologi Malaysia (UTM) (294)
5. Universiti Putra Malaysia (UPM) (376)
6. International Islamic University Malaysia (IIUM)
7. Universiti Malays ia Sarawak (UNIMAS)

I picked QS and not THE or SJTU rankings is because no Malaysian universities appeared in the former and only Universiti Malaya appears in the latter. These seven Malaysian universities are all public ones. In Malaysia, there are a number of private universities, such as Multimedia University (MMU), Universiti Teknologi Petronas (UTP) and Universiti Tunku Abdul Rahman (UTAR) and of course Sunway University and others. At the moment it is fair to say that the private ones are not challenging the public ones and are not "*at the heels of the public ones.*" I think at the moment in Malaysia, the situation is more like Taiwan and less like Korea. The pros and cons of the Taiwan and Korea I mentioned before are also very likely applicable to Malaysia as well. For example, the apparent Taiwan's higher education stagnation could be what is facing Malaysia's higher education as well when the dominance of public universities is so complete.

Second, it is well known globally that the success of Malaysia as a nation is that it is one where multi-ethnic groups have lived and prospered harmoniously together. Yet, one of the most surprising and somewhat depressing aspects of Malaysia is that many of Malaysia's talented young people do seem to either *voluntarily* or *involuntarily* wanting to pursue higher education outside of the country. For example, it is no secret that Malaysia's immediate neighbor Singapore does tap quite a bit into the talented pool of youngsters here. The same is true, although for a much lesser extent for Taiwan, and now also Hong Kong, Mainland China and even Macau, and to a much lesser extent UK, U.S., Australia and New Zealand. In my many visits to Singapore, I met many outstanding people in leadership in various arenas there and I found out that many actually came from Malaysia. I suspect once a youngster leaves Malaysia for tertiary education, it is very likely that he/she will develop a subsequent career also outside of Malaysia. This *de facto* constituted a "brain drain" from which Malaysia suffers quite a bit. For a progressive nation like Malaysia, I am sure that this issue is or should be very high on the agendas of the Government.

So what makes this brain-drain occur in Malaysia? The national universities such as those listed above, for one reason or another, are essentially out-of-reach and/or out-of-bound by some of these talented Malaysian students. At the same time, to date the private ones in Malaysia have not yet measured up in quality to the top national universities in order "fill in the gaps" to absorb and retain these talents for Malaysia. So, in order to find their intellectual challenges, these outstanding students, whom I am sure are encouraged by their parents as well, have to seek opportunities abroad.

As I have clearly depicted in the comparison of Malaysia, Taiwan and Korea, Malaysia as a multi-ethnic country is rather unique and it is one which outsiders like me cannot and may not fully comprehend the political complexities. But education as I said from the beginning is the life line of a nation. If there is one issue which must stand above politics in a nation, it surely must be education. Nevertheless, it is this reason, and even if there were no other reasons, that some of the private universities such as Sunway University should and must "fill in the gap" for Malaysia's national well-being to prevent further erosion of brain-drain which I am confident is hurting Malaysia as a forward and robust nation in Asia Pacific in the 21st century.

However, the rise of private universities should not merely aim at "filling the gap." That alone, while it is important at this point in time for Malaysia, is not sufficient for the creation of a world class private university in the country. The creation of such a private university may help the country in the short run, but just like Korea, it should profoundly carry the intellectual burden and well-being for Malaysia in the long run. The creators of private universities in Malaysia must aim not just high, but higher!

So my friends, how and what sort of world class private university should one envision in Malaysia?

First, the private university should and must be financially independent. The examples of Korean private universities (e.g. Postech) tell volume about how financially strong is important. Pohang Steel Company provided and is still providing enormous and generous financial backing of the university. Can Malaysian's private sector support at least one world-class private institution? I have no doubt it can!

Second, just as all world-class private universities worldwide, there must be an outstanding "Board of Trustees" who can provide profound intellectual and/or deep financial support for the leadership of the university, *a la* the President. The BOT constitution must be clear and transparent. What powers they have and NOT have must be clearly spelled out. A member's term limit must be clearly specified. It should not be too short so he/she is rendered powerless or too long so he/she becomes entrenched. Any university must be a "not-for-profit" organization. Therefore, members of the BOT must be individuals who could do this arduous job in a *pro-bono* manner but have the deep interest in education issues as well as time and energy to serve. Each member must understand that the highest ethical standard is demanded of him/her. He/she also must understand his or her role on the BOT as well as the true mission and meaning of that particular university he or she is serving. For a Malaysian private university initially, the selection of the members of the BOT is a sacred effort. I cannot underscore enough the profound importance of the structure and operations of a private university's BOT. I would even go as far to say that the "rise and fall" of a private university depends on the quality of its BOT!

Third, search for a leader as the President who is intellectually powerful and visionary, sets high threshold as well as non-compromising attitude for intellectual quality, must be eloquent and profound in substances in speeches delivery, and politically courageous and savvy with smooth management skill. For a successful private university, the President is not just the spokesman for the university he/she serves, but is an advocate for higher education for the nation.

Fourth, tt must be remembered that building a university must be a "slow or fast" evolution and not a "revolution"! The best example I can think of who fits this bill is Harvard's president of 40 years, from 1869 to 1909. His name is Charles Eliot. He had one famous line which is:

> *"... a university, in any worthy sense of the term, must grow from seed. It cannot be transplanted from England or Germany in full leaf and bearing. ... When the American university appears, it will not be a copy of foreign institutions, or a hot-bed plant, but the slow and natural outgrowth of American social and political habits... The American college is an institution without a parallel; the American university will be equally original."*

With that, Eliot transformed "Harvard into Harvard" after 40 years of presidency.

Epilogue

If my analysis of Malaysia is at least not completely off the mark, it seems to me that in higher education at least, it is unquestionably at a cross road. One could continue on the current path and face a somewhat uncertain if not an undesirable future, or the private sector could jump in and create an entirely new era. It is my sincere hope that the example of Korea and Taiwan show us some useful indication as to which path Malaysia may prefer to take.

Good luck Malaysia!

(2015)

25

Residential College and Asia Today

This was a speech made at the inaugural high-table dinner event of Chao Kuang Piu College (曹光彪书院, 澳门大学), held on November 12, 2014. The author was Director of Global Affairs and Special Advisor to the Rector, The University of Macau.

Good evening, distinguished guests. This is truly an honor you bestowed on me to have this great opportunity to speak to you at the inaugural high-table dinner event of Chao Kuang Piu College.

The title of my talk is **Residential College and Asia Today**.

Before I begin, let me say to all the superbly attired students this evening that there is a "book" which I know you would read every day. I have to confess to you that it is also a "book" I read every day.

As an incurable teacher, I cannot help but want to ask you what is the name of this book?

(I am so pleased that one student immediately said: FACEBOOK! Bingo!)

Let me also welcome all of you to go to my FB, whose account is my Chinese name in traditional characters: 冯达旋! I welcome all of you to become my FB "friend!"

For everyone here today in the University of Macau, you are experiencing something unprecedented for Asian universities: you are experiencing one of the most comprehensive Residential College systems in Asia Pacific!

An optimist would call you a PIONEER, while a pessimist would call you a GUINEA PIG! Whether you are a pioneer or a guinea pig, this is an experience of a lifetime that money cannot buy! Hopefully, after four years of education in the University of Macau, with Residential College as the "living component" under your belt, not only will you be on your way to become an expert in your field, you will also gained a deeper and comprehensive understanding of yourself, of Asia, and of the world.

Have you ever wondered what is the geopolitical mindset platform all of us are standing on today? My friends, something remarkable happened in the 20th century, which I shall call East-West MINDSET TRANSFORMATION.

Allow me to tell you two episodes to illustrate this mindset transformation.

In 1913, the great Indian behemoth Rabindranath Tagore was awarded the Nobel Prize in literature. The Nobel committee gave the following byline to illustrate Tagore's contribution:

> "... he has made his poetic thought, expressed in his own English words, a part of the literature of the West..."

Yes, "part of the literature of the West" was what was stated. These words were naked manifestation of colonialism! It reflected vividly the Western mindset in the beginning of the 20th century which transparently demonstrated a true sense of "superiority!"

In last year of the 20th century, i.e. year 2000, another Asian won the Nobel Prize in the 20th century. It also happens to be in literature. His name is Gao Xingjiang 高行建. For his contribution, the Nobel committee stated the following:

> "... has opened new paths for the Chinese novel and drama..."

From these two Nobel bylines, we could sense the enormous and fundamental East-West mindset transformation of the 20th century.

Even though the 21st century is still in its fledgling era, we also are observing something that was unimaginable in the 20th century.

Besides the fact that many Asia Pacific countries have constructed the a vast and far reaching national high speed rail system, there is now a real possibility that **just when you youngsters are ready to launch your professional careers**, you will be able to take a high speed rail from Beijing to Jakarta, from Beijing to Europe!

Such infrastructure construction will surely induce a new era of Political, Cultural and Intellectual TRANSFORMATION! This transformation will give rise to a magnificent intellectual boulevard for young people in Asia to develop their views of themselves and their lives in the 21st century.

Therefore, my dear young friends, are you psychologically ready to face this new reality?

With this in mind, the University of Macau must prepare you for this eventuality, which is just around the corner. Unfortunately, such preparations generally cannot be accomplished in a classroom. That is why we have Residential Colleges!

So, please allow me to tell you what Residential College must do to get you prepared for this eventuality. Indeed, what "bag of tricks" as I call it you must at least have to prepare you for the future?

Trick 1

A residential college must become your global platform

The Residential Colleges, like of Chao Kuang Piu College, must and will have students from all parts of the Globe, living and bonding together. By living together, by learning about each other's culture on a day-to-day basis, especially each others' "unusual" behavior because of the inherent cultural differences, you will gradually learn to understanding, and more important, appreciate, challenges facing your friends by wearing HIS/HER shoes! With this under your belt, you can be competitive and productive in all corners of the world.

And my good friends, you will be a GLOBAL CITIZEN!

Trick 2

Residential College must assist you to develop a profound sense of intellectual courage.

Master Liu mentioned earlier about some of the great minds such as Newton, Bacon, Maxwell and Nehru who all, as you know, were once in residence at Trinity College of Cambridge University. We tend to think of them as individuals of greatness, which of course they were, and amazingly, after many centuries, still are. Yet normally we do not think of them as students who once lived in Trinity College, which they were, being nurtured and challenged by peers and their College Master or Fellows. Such experiences were surely some if not all of the reasons as to how they developed skill sets to think the unthinkable, and ultimately the courage to perform an academic "Hail Mary!"

Just like Newton, Bacon, Maxwell and Nehru, I believe that by interacting on a day to day basis with faculty and students in many disciplines in a Chao Kuang Piu College on equal basis, it can undoubtedly stimulate in you a deep sense of intellectual courage. Once again, I am sure that the classroom setting is incommensurate to such a form of interactions. It is for this reason that the University of Macau has bestowed its Residential Colleges to shoulder such a solemn responsibility!

Trick 3

Inherent Self Confidence

Whatever concentrations our students intend to pursue in the University of Macau, it must be well-equipped to assist them to carry out their newly endowed responsibilities of building a better world for their fellow human beings in the 21st century. To do so, the University of Macau must equip you with inherent self-confidence to mitigate and conquer the global challenges in the 21st century.

What are some of the global challenges would require your wisdom to mitigate?

First, on a daily basis, there are three networks which we all enjoy. They are the water network, electric network and last but not least, sewage network. Just imagine what life would be like if you do not have access to one of these three networks. My good friends, large proportions of your fellow human beings do not have access to at least one, if not all three!

Let me also just list some other immediate challenges: lack of water, lack of energy, global warming, poverty and ignorance, disease, human hatred and uncontrolled population explosive growth and so on.

In today's world, as responsible global citizens, to mitigate such global challenges, you cannot merely be equipped with technical knowledge. You must also be aware and understand human behaviors, you must learn how to execute public policies and of course, you must know the true meaning of political courage!

To shoulder such responsibilities, Asian students must have a mindset of inherent self-confidence and that it should not be confused as arrogance.

Just like Trick 1 and Trick 2, Trick 3 is not something you can learn directly or by osmosis from your classrooms. These are something you can acquire from your peers and from your experiences you inherited in the Residential College you live in!

Summary

In summary, let me repeat the salient points of the three tricks.

Trick 1: A residential college must become your global platform.
Trick 2: The residential college must assist you to develop a profound sense of intellectual courage.
Trick 3: Inherent Self Confidence

In 2009, I was invited to summarize an Asia Development Bank Conference on "Global Economic Crisis: Industrial Reconstruction." I like to share with you what I said then:

> *"Throughout the 20th century, Asia was psychologically "coupled" to the West, and understandably so. With superior economic and intellectual strengths, it is quite natural that Asia viewed the West as the 'standard of excellence'. However, after such a period as this with the West so palpably exposing its social & economic weaknesses, this may be the first time in the modern global economy that Asia can psychologically "DECOUPLE" from the West. This is not to suggest that Asia should decouple economically and intellectually from the West; rather, I am talking about a "psychological decoupling" to undo a sense of reliance on the West, without which it is unlikely that Asia will develop a deep sense of inherent*

self-confidence and without which the 21st century is surely not to be the "Asian Century."

Yes, my good young friends, let me repeat this in Chinese:

从心理上与西方脱钩!

Psychological decoupling!

Thanks.

(2014)

26

New Angle on Obama's Recent Speech on "Affordable Higher Education"

This was written when the author was Senior Vice President, Global Strategy, Planning and Evaluation, National Tsing Hua University. He felt that the university offering high quality opportunities to U.S. students can be considered as the first salvo of Asian Universities.

On August 22, 2013, President Barak Obama made a ground breaking comment at the University of Buffalo on higher education affordability.[10]

In my mind, the timing of the Obama's speech cannot be better since it was delivered at the heel of a recent bold announcement by outstanding Asian university, National Tsing Hua University in the Republic of China, to set up an information session in Santa Clara for high school students in the U.S. to consider pursuing higher education in NTHU in particular, Asia Pacific in general.

Although in preparing for this important information session, we in NTHU have given serious and extensive consideration about our "ways and means" of recruiting, e.g. via Facebook[11] as well as a video clip[12], this comment by President Obama made me think of a new angle as to why what NTHU is doing at this point in time is so profoundly important for U.S. and Asia Pacific.

---

[10] http://www.whitehouse.gov/the-pressoffice/2013/08/22/remarks-president-college-affordabilitybuffalo-ny
[11] http://www.facebook.com/NTHUinfo
[12] http://youtu.be/AmFHgX92n18

The bottom line is that while U.S. higher education becomes more and more important to achieve a quality life and less and less affordable to its young citizens, many Asian institutions, such as National Tsing Hua University are "crescendoing" in quality and ambiance in the past three decades, becoming more and more "friendly" to outsiders, and are truly affordable (1/3 to 1/5 the price, or higher, of an education in a great U.S. university.) Furthermore, the rise of these Asian institutions, and NTHU is no exception, was an indirect, if not direct, result of U.S. assistance since the 50's.Thus, in the 21st century, I think the time has arrived for these outstanding universities in Asia such as NTHU to, in some sense, to "return the investment" of the U.S.

Why?

Since the 50s, tens to hundreds of thousands of students from the Republic of China (Taiwan) pursued their advance education in the U.S.. Most, if not all, received some form of financial assistance from the universities they attended. Today, in all the outstanding universities in Taiwan, such as NTHU, a very high percentage (as high as 80 percent to 90 percent) of the faculty members have doctorates from some 100 outstanding research universities in the U.S.

There is no question, across Asia, because of political maturity and economic surge, societies in the region have made breath taking transformation. It is no surprise that one of the fundamental causes of this transformation was, and still is, the enormous quality growth of higher education institutions in the region.

It is natural to ask why higher education institutions had become significantly "better" in Asia. The reason is undoubtedly because of the enormous pool of talents available which the universities can tap into. That pool of talents, for NTHU in particular, other outstanding universities in the Republic of China in general, is formed by students who went to the United States in the 70s, 80s and 90s. While some returned immediately after completing their doctorates, many stayed on to work in universities, research institutes, national laboratories and industries (or all the above) in the U.S. before coming to the Republic of China. Quietly, in the past two to three decades, National Tsing Hua University, like many outstanding ROC universities today, can stand shoulder-toshoulder with some of the best in the U.S., in quality and ambiance.

There is something special about National Tsing Hua University as a prototype of outstanding universities in the Republic of China. Like I said, it is "housed" by faculty members with deep U.S. experiences. For example, for the President, the four Senior Vice Presidents as well as the four Vice Presidents of NTHU, all have doctorates from outstanding U.S. universities. In fact, two of the four Senior Vice Presidents do not have Mandarin as their mother-tongue! With that, one could imagine that despite the well known government interference which fortunately is slowly being mitigated, while maintaining its Asian perspective, NTHU has admixed into its campus an ambiance of a Western, especially U.S. characteristic. In addition, with globalization now a "mindset" and not a "lip-service", NTHU has made enormous progress (although more is still needed) so that it can be "non-Taiwan friendly" in many dimensions.

It is with this and more in mind that I believe that NTHU's ground breaking effort of an information session for U.S. high school students to pursue a global education is merely the tip of the iceberg.

It is not inconceivable that in a decade or two, for an outstanding high school graduate in all corners of the United States, the selection of a college to attend will not just be the pool of state universities or outstanding private colleges in the country, but many of the outstanding Asian universities, such as National Tsing Hua University, across the Pacific! That day, I have no doubt, will surely come!

(2013)

27

Mindset of the Soul: The Meaning of Liberal Arts Education

This was a dedication to the memory of the author's teacher, John F. Ollom (1923–2013), delivered at "The First Conference on Liberal Arts Education" conference, held on April 19, 2014, at Nottingham University Ningbo China. The author was Special Advisor to the Rector and Director of Global Affairs, University of Macau.

Preamble

President Fu-Jia Yang, university leaders from Asia and the U.S., colleagues and students, good morning.

Ever since President Yang and I met in the Niels Bohr Institute more than thirty years ago, I have followed his illustrious career diligently and I must say that I have been deeply impressed by his more than three decades of dedication towards improving and transforming the education of China.

A few months ago, President Yang invited me to come to talk about the theme of the conference, **Liberal Arts Education**. Although I accepted the invitation, I must confess I accepted with apprehension. The source of my uneasiness arose from the fact that ever since I began my academic career nearly forty years ago, I essentially spent all my time in what is called "research universities!" As a "cocoon" professor of physics, my life, day in and day out, revolved around teaching physics, writing technical papers as well as proposals to funding agencies, mentoring students in research projects and last but not least collaborating with colleagues, nationally and internationally, on research projects. I therefore must confess that I had not spend a great deal of my thinking hours on this topic.

As the famous American oil-well firefighter Red Adair said so eloquently: *"If you think it's expensive to hire a professional to do the job, wait until you hire an amateur."* So today I am here only as a deeply interested amateur.

The 21st century is transformational for Asia, in economy, politics and culture. The meaning of higher education in the region is no longer merely an academic issue, but a palpable one. What kind of students should we produce that would be relevant to today's world? I think it is partially this challenge, if not entirely, that prompted Asian educators such as Professor Fu-Jia Yang to begin to seek answers in the meaning of liberal arts education.

With that as background, in preparing this speech, I made the assumption that one of the reasons I was invited to speak at this meeting must have been because of my experience of studying in a small liberal arts college in New Jersey in the mid-sixties. So in preparing my speech, I subconsciously thought about what that experience had impacted me later on in life.

My Liberal Arts Education at Drew University

Half a century ago, as an unsophisticated youngster from Singapore, I entered Drew University in Madison, New Jersey as a freshman. Madison is your typical small town in New Jersey, which is approximately 40 miles west of New York City. I have to confess I went to Drew University not because of its enormous global reputation, which it did not and still does not have, but because it was kind enough to offer me a scholarship as well as opportunities to be a dishwasher in the university cafeteria to cover my living expenses.

One can literally locate small liberal arts colleges just like Drew University scattered in all corners of the U.S. For example in New Jersey alone, there are more than 20! Just like Drew University, the liberal arts colleges in the U.S. are institutions primarily engaging in teaching undergraduates.

The fact that Drew is called a "university" is because it has three "schools": undergraduate studies, graduate studies and a theological seminary. When I entered in 1964, there were less than 1,000 undergraduate students and the graduate, which primarily engaged in studies of theology and philosophy, as well as the theological seminary which trained Protestant Ministers, had less than a combined population of about 200. I checked recently from Google that its undergraduate population has "soared" to 1,600 and graduate students and seminarians around 800.

The real difference between Drew University then and Drew University now is that the tuition in 1964 was around $800, and today, $45,214!

Let me describe for everyone here the Chinese students' landscape in the U.S. in the 60s. First, it was a post Korea-conflict era, where China had a great deal of internal conflicts and the U.S. and China were certainly not in the best of terms, to say it mildly. Although it would be unthinkable today, in that era, there were no students from Mainland China in the U.S. Of the Chinese students that you found on U.S. college campuses, the majority were from Taiwan, less from Hong Kong, and a tiny number from Southeast Asia. I was one of the tiny number.

The students from Taiwan, all had to complete their undergraduate studies first, and the males needed to complete a two year military service, before they were allowed to come to the U.S. to pursue their Master and/or Doctor of Philosophy degrees. In fact, I would say that nearly all the Taiwan students pursuing graduate degrees were scattered in some 150 or so research universities in the U.S. For this reason, in small liberal arts colleges throughout the U.S., you would find next to none students from Taiwan. It is interesting that in today's higher education landscape in Taiwan, there were a great deal of murmur of "liberal arts" education on campus. Yet, there were essentially no one in the educational leadership level who would have had any exposure to the **Liberal Arts Colleges** that were, and still are, so pervasive in the U.S. The situation is quite the reverse for students from Hong Kong. Just like me, many actually went to such colleges, before entering professional or graduate schools.

Back to Drew University in 1964 when I was a freshman. Coming from Asia, where "big" means "good" and "strong," especially when I had the intellectual appetite to literally swallow as much physics knowledge as I possibly could in the shortest time, I could not be more disappointed when I first arrived at Drew University. To be perfectly honest, when I entered the campus on a cool August (80F would be cool for someone coming directly from Singapore,) my heart literally sank.

I was an impatient young man then. I was impatient because I wanted to become a physicist as soon as I can. I remember I carefully studied the university course catalogue. I thought I learned enough about what first year physics is all about that I wanted to immediately take the "more advanced" courses listed in the catalogue, such as thermodynamics and mechanics. As for the non-physics courses, I thought that I would take an English language course so as to fill in my inadequacy of my language skillset.

Words of Professor John Ollom: My Motto

Professor John F. Ollom
delivering a lecture in elementary physics at Drew University

In the first week of orientation, I remember I went to the university gymnasium where the course registration process took place. I filled in a form stating what courses from the catalogue I wanted to take. The nice lady looked at my form and asked me very politely: *"Victor, have you discussed this with your advisor?"* When she saw my bewildered expression, she immediately said: *"Let me see who your advisor is. Oh yes, he is Professor John Ollom, chairman of the physics department. Please go see him. He is a very kind gentleman, and you will find him very helpful!"*

Please don't think that the physics department of Drew University is anything like that of a physics department in one of China's top universities today. According to the web, Fudan University, where President Fu-Jia Yang was once president, now has some 70 physics professors. If you added up all the research staff members, plus graduate and undergraduate students and postdoctoral fellows, the department could have as many as a thousand people! Well, in this sense, the so-called physics department of Drew University then is the antithesis of Fudan University's physics department. The department then consisted of two full time persons and three part time instructors. The two full time persons were Professor John Ollom, the Chair, and an older white-haired gentleman whose name I could not recall who served as the laboratory assistant.

Following the suggestion of the lady at the registration table, I went to the oldest building of Drew University where Professor Ollom had a tiny office. He greeted me with a warm and firm handshake. I then presented to him the form which stated the courses I had intended to take. He looked over and said something that to date, became my motto, and my life long definition of "**liberal arts education**"!

He said: *"Victor, in Singapore, your teachers and classmates must have trained you to become an engine of physics exercise-solving. That is indeed an excellent first step. I hope that in Drew University, when you are confronted by the subtleties of physics, you and I could together look into why Newton and Maxwell were so intrigued by the mysteries of the universe and how they went about understanding them!".*

"Also, Victor," Professor Ollom went on to say, *"you are still young, time is on your side. You have plenty of opportunities to learn the physics you wanted to learn in the next four years. You know, in our Seminary, the*

great theologian Reinhold Niebuhr comes often to lecture. Why don't you go listen to some of his speeches? **I am sure he will take your mind to where it has never been before***! It doesn't matter whether you understand what he said. Just by being in his presence I am confident you will learn by osmosis!"*

Professor Ollom continued to say *"When you have time, do try to read the editorials of the New York Times in the library as often as you can. By doing so, you will not only get the pulse of the nation, but you will also learn how educated Americans write!"* I did read the *New York Times* editorials religiously in my four years at Drew University!

If there is such a thing called SOUL, then these words uttered by a great educator must touched it!

About a decade ago, there was a movie entitled "Crouching Tiger, Hidden Dragon" (卧虎藏龙). Well, because of Professor Ollom's unpretentious personality, it took me a few years before I realized what I had as a teacher was indeed such a tiger and dragon.

Professor Ollom grew up poor in one of the poorest States of the U.S., West Virginia. During WWII, he completed his military service by being a research assistant at the famous "Manhattan Project" in Los Alamos. After the war, he became a graduate student and completed his doctorate thesis in 1952 under the mentorship of John van Vleck at Harvard University. Interestingly, I learned much later on in life that one of his roommates at Harvard University was someone I got to know when I was spending a year at the Niels Bohr Institute (NBI) of the University of Copenhagen. That person was the co-director of NBI, Professor Ben Mottelson, who together with the son of Niels Bohr, Aage Bohr, won the Nobel Prize in physics in 1975!

As the world knows, together with Phil Anderson and Nevill Mott, van Vleck was the 1977 Nobel Laureate in physics for their work on *"fundamental theoretical investigations of the electronic structure of magnetic and disordered systems."* It is often that people refer to John van Vleck as the "father of magnetism"!

Professor Ollom came to Drew University right after Harvard, and made teaching his call to life. However, something that was equally important to me was that he also worked in the world famous Bell Laboratories in Murray Hill, which is essentially a short ten minute drive from Madison. There he continued to carry on a robust program of research in magnetic materials.

I once saw a very thick book on his table which listed him as an author. It was a book on the classification of magnetic materials. I asked him with awe in my eyes: "Wow, you did this?"Professor Ollom answered in his typical diminutive manner, "Ah yes." Yes, no fanfare!

Once I discovered that Professor Ollom was the student of the great van Vleck, I often fancied myself as the "grand-student" of van Vleck!

As I mentioned earlier, Professor Ollom had a very unpretentious personality. He was highly respected by many of his world class colleagues in Bell Laboratories. The three half time instructors of Drew University turned out all to be outstanding and full time scientists there. They were recruited by Ollom. For this reason, all the courses that were not taught by Professor Ollom, were taught by these three gentlemen. One unusual aspect about their teaching was that, because they all had real day jobs, all the classes were understandably conducted either in the evenings or on weekends!

The three instructors' names were Arnold Boxer, Julian Bowen and Hans Goldstein. Thinking back, despite the fact that there were only a hand full of physics majors at Drew University, these instructors were very conscientious and serious about their duties as teachers. I especially remember vividly that Dr. Boxer, a chubby and joyful fellow, taught excellent courses. He usually came to class around 7pm and lectured for about an hour. Then he would discuss with us about the subtitles of the problems, not just solving them, but how they could be relevant to real life.

But my recollection about these three teachers were not just confined to the fact that they gave me a great physics education, but that they were absolutely unselfish about sharing their life experiences with me. They considered their mission as teachers first, and being physicists second. For example, after the night classes, which officially ended around 9pm, Dr. Boxer would hang around with us for as long as we students wanted to talk to him, about life and science, in the most general terms. For example, it was through Dr. Boxer that I became aware of his ancestry, which was Jewish immigrants from Eastern Europe. I also learned how much Jews respected scholarship. I remember vividly he mentioned that the Jewish culture was fearless in "debating issues." He often jokingly told me that "Jews can argue just about anything. For example, we could vehemently argue about how many Angles can dance on the tip of a pin!" The point was, Dr. Boxer said, not what the outcome of the argument would be that would be important, but that one could learn to think critically in carryout the argument. *"As a professional, you guys will need to learn how to do this well to be successful!"*

Such an informal form of education, and thinking back it was very intense and that went on for my entire four years at Drew University. Without being conscience of their impact, they often as Dr. Ollom would say, *"Took my mind to where it has never been before!"*

I left Drew University not just having more knowledge in science, but more knowledge about myself, and more confident what I could do in my life. As President Fu-Jia Yang always emphasized, a college life must change a student. Drew University certainly did that. These were true "liberal arts education" I had to endure, or enjoy, during my four years at Drew University. I have to admit that they would, and have, lasted me a lifetime!

Liberal Arts Teachers

I should mention that my teachers were not unique to Drew University. In fact, according to the 1998 physics Nobel laureate, Professor Dan Tsui, during his days at the liberal arts college which he attended, Augustana College in Illinois, he was greatly inspired by his physics teacher Donald McLaughlin. In his honorary Doctorate degree ceremony speech, he specifically mentioned that his scientific achievements *"had its genesis at Augustana College."*

It should also be mentioned that one of the most outstanding higher education leaders in Asia who is the founder of the now famed Hong Kong University of Science and Technology, Chia-Wei Woo, was also the alumnus of a small liberal arts college called Georgetown College in Kentucky. I have no doubt his legendary multi-dimensional careers had their genesis in his early liberal arts education.

In my many years of professional careers in the U.S., I met many such outstanding teachers in various liberal arts colleges, such as Peter Collins, Morris L. Clothier Professor of Physics of Swarthmore College, Jerry

Golub, John and Barbara Bush Professor of Physics at Haverford College and Alfonso Albano, Marion Reilly Professor of Physics of Bryn Mawr College.

Without any doubt, teachers like Ollom, Boxer, Bowen, Goldstein, McLaughlin, Collins, Golub and Albano, were what I would call the archetypical "liberal arts educators!" Undoubtedly they love their professional research, but they love to inspire students more. Also, they love but not spoil their students.

Liberal Arts Education is "Mindset of the Soul"

My friends, just like the thousands upon thousands of youngsters, without the slightest hesitation, my four years at a liberal arts college like Drew University impacted me profoundly. I completed my liberal arts education based on the Motto of Professor John Ollom. In those four years, in every class I attended, whether it be philosophy, religion or quantum mechanics, in every seminar I attended throughout my professional life, in every concert I attended, every time I read an editorial, every time I read a book, every time I wrote a paper or an article, in science or otherwise, and every time I prepared a talk, including this one, I did so under the liberal arts edification. My liberal arts education was not just my shadow, it was me! When I completed my Drew University education, I finally understood what "liberal arts education" was!

In Asia today, there is a sweeping interest in "Residential College" system. For example, the ultimate example of this idea is of course Trinity College of Cambridge University. Often we have equated "Residential College" with "Liberal Arts Education." According to my personal and meager experience, I would say that "Residential College" is the structure of "Liberal Arts Education," but not necessarily its inherent meaning. That is to say, to have a successful "Residential College," "Liberal Arts Education" must be its soul. Vice versa is not necessarily so. In fact, the entire Drew University set up, if you like, is a "bigger size" Residential College.

If I may, I would like to emphasize that "liberal arts" is not and must not be just an action, not just a set of courses and not just learning processes. What is perhaps most important is that it is "**the mindset of**

the soul." This mindset will accompany the person for life who had the pleasure and privilege of receiving such an education. In fact, I am confident that nearly all, if not all the liberal arts colleges in the U.S. had the mission of instilling "mindset of the soul" in all their students.

In his latest book "**In Defense of a Liberal Education**," Fareed Zakaria said in his concluding remarks the following: "*Because of the times we live in, all of us, young and old, do not spend enough time and effort thinking about the meaning of life. We do not look inside of ourselves enough to understand our strengths and weaknesses, and we do not look around enough – at the world, in history – to ask the deepest and broadest questions. The solution surely is that, even now, we could all use a little bit more of a liberal education.*" Yes my friends, these are elegant words which in my mind corroborated with **the mindset of the soul**.

I think the search of "**the mindset of the soul**" for students in universities is either lacking, or only in its fledgling stage in Asia today. But I think that in the flat world, the moment has arrived for all educators in Asia to work seriously and collectively to find the best form of liberal arts education that will fit the rephrase of what Harvard's president Charles Eliot said in the latter half of the 19th century, namely a "*slow and natural outgrowth of Asia social and political habits*."

Thank you very much for your attention.

(2014)

28

California Institute and Technology (Caltech) and National Southwest Union University (NSWUU 国立西南联合大学): An Unexpected and Extraordinary Similarity in Different Space-Time

This was written when the author was Senior Vice President, Global Strategy, Planning and Evaluation, National Tsing Hua University.

The entire world **knows** California Institute of Technology (better known as "Caltech") as a world class university. Very few people in the world **know** about National Southwest Union University (NSWUU 国立西南联合大学, or "西南联大" in short) since it lasted only eight years (1938 – 1946) in a remote southwest province of China, Yunan.

But in my mind, if there ever were a university in Asia which resembled Caltech, it would be NSWUU.

On surface, Caltech and NSWUU could not be more starkly different. Caltech, founded in 1891, is now basking in sunny California, armed by a US$1.7 billion endowment, is one of the world's great, maybe greatest, institutions of higher learning. Today, Caltech shows no sign that it is slowing down. In contrast, NSWUU founded under inhuman stressed situation in 1938 when the war of resistance with Japan was initiated and operated with "below shoestring budget" and essentially existed only eight years when WWII ended. Leaving only its College of Education in Yunnan, which today has evolved into a massive Yunnan Normal University (云南师范大学), all three universities returned to their homes in Beijing and Tianjin respectively in 1946.

So how could one compare these two universities?

I had an opportunity to visit Caltech about two months ago and the original site which NSWUU were situated in Kunming, Yunan Province in China a few weeks ago. While both institutions were on my radar screen for many decades, visiting them physically for the first time gave me a close-up perspective which I did not have before: that both institutions are eerily similar in characteristics. A few words about NSWUU, which I am sure few people in the world are familiar with. Details about the history and operations of NSWUU could be found in a book published by Stanford University Press entitled "**Lianda:** *A Chinese University in War and Revolution*." The author John Israel is an old China-hand.

When the Japanese initiated an all out attack on China defined by the so-called 7-7 incident (七七芦沟桥事变), which occurred on July 7, 1937, Chinese government at the time made a conscience effort to ensure that the intellectual strengths of the nation would be preserved and not be decimated. To this end, three top universities at the time, Tsinghua University and Peking University in what is today Beijing and Nankai University in Tianjin were banded together and through unimaginable hardship moved nearly 3,000 kilometers away in 1938 (often many of the students and faculty went by foot) to Kunming, Yunan Province. Throughout its eight years of existence, Kunming, and thus NSWUU, were constantly suffering under aerial bombardment by the Japanese air force.

Something which could only be described as **miraculous** happened in NSWUU in those eight years (1938–1946) which I do not believe even the most strategically minded educators and political leaders at the time could have anticipated. NSWUU not only survived, but became the intellectual heart and soul of China! The intellectual propensity and intensity are what drove me to compare Caltech with NSWUU.

First, just as the successful launching of a rocket which needs a strong launching pad, I am a firm believer that the founding or fledgling president or presidents of a great university should be its launching pad.

In its fledging days when the vocational school Thrope College was renamed as Caltech in 1920, the trio of three great visionaries, **George Ellery Hale**, a renowned astronomer and a Caltech trustee and director of the Mount Wilson Observatory, former MIT President **Arthur A. Noyes** and physicist **Robert A. Millikan** came to Caltech. According to the *Athenaeum* of Caltech[13], "...*this trio positioned the California Institute of Technology as a world-class center for teaching and research*

---

[13] http://www.athenaeumcaltech.com/Default.aspx?p=DynamicModule&pageid=342358&ssid=243574&vnf=1

in engineering and science." It is worth underscoring that the leadership of Millikan is probably defined by his immortal quotation "*Fullness of knowledge always means some understanding of the depths of our ignorance; and that is always conducive to humility and reverence.*" The leadership of these three great intellect and administrators became the launching pad of sending Caltech into its world class intellectual orbit of today.

Quite remarkably by sheer historical accident, there were also three great intellects and administrators who guided NSWUU. They were **Mei Yi-qi** (梅贻琦), **Jiang Meng-ling** (蒋梦麟) and **Zhang Bo-ling** (张伯苓), the presidents of Tsinghua University, Peking University and Nankai University at the time, respectively. In fact, these three gentlemen formed the Executive Committee (常务委员会) which run NSWUU. Since Jiang and Zhang also had other duties with the government, Mei became the Chairman of the Executive Committee and became the *de facto* president of NSWUU during those eight years. Mei's immortal quotation "大学者，非谓有大楼之谓也,有大师之谓也" or "*A great university is made not by great buildings, but by great scholars*" and Jiang's immortal quotation "教授治学,学生求学, 职员治事, 校长治校", or "*Professors profess, students learn, staff handle matters and the president operates the university*" thus became the spirit of NSWUU! Hence just like Caltech, these three men became the launching pad of NSWUU.

I should also mention that in 1956, Mei came to Taiwan and initiated the Hsinchu Tsing Hua University. It is in this sense that the Tsing Hua University also had the great fortune of inheriting NSWUU legacy!

Second, both Caltech and NSWUU are "tiny" schools. Almost from the start, Caltech maintains a small faculty of about 300, and a student body of 900 undergraduates and 1100 graduate students. Likewise, for NSWUU, according to John Israel, even at its prime, it has only about 170 faculty members and 2,000 students.

When I visited Caltech two months ago, President Jean-Lou Chameau of Caltech made a specific point that throughout its history, Caltech made a conscientious effort of not expanding the university. In fact, according to Chameau, to not "expand" is not a natural human behavior but throughout its history Caltech has strictly adhered to the mission of being "small and beautiful."

I do not know if NSWUU could survive beyond the eight years, or whether or not it would expand. But because of the war condition of the time, the university did not and probably could not expand beyond what it was. So by design (Caltech) or by externally imposed war condition (NSWUU), both universities are embedded in a small university culture with an extraordinarily high level of intellectual intensity!

Third, since 1920, Caltech collected the best of the best intellects to be associated with the university as students or faculty. In fact, thirty-one (31) Caltech alumni and faculty are Nobel laureates. Household names, besides Robert Millikan, such as Carl Anderson, Richard Feynman, Linus Pauling, Murry Gell-Mann, Ken Wilson, Theodore von Kármán, Douglas Osheroff, Gordon Moore (of the world famous Moore's law in IT) and many more will forever be in the scientific and technological who's-who! In this regard, I would be remiss if I did not mention the father of China's rocket program Qian Xue-Sen (钱学森) who also taught at Caltech in the late 40's and early 50's and eventually left Caltech not by his choice.

Again, by sheer historical accident, NSWUU collected the best of the best in China under one roof. Great minds and house hold names in science, such as Ta-You Wu (吴大猷), Chen-Ning Yang (杨振宁), Tsung-Dao Lee (李政道), Kun Huang (黄昆), Hao Wang (王浩), Luo-Gen Hua (华罗庚) and Shiing-Shen Chern (陈省身), and in humanities and social sciences, such as Xiao-tung Fei (费孝通), You-Lan Feng (冯友兰), Cong-Wen Shen (沈从文), Yi-Duo Wen (闻一多) and Ziqing Zhu (朱自清) will forever be in the world's intellectual who's who.

Indeed, it is worth underscoring that even to this date, NSWUU, under extraordinarily difficult war time conditions, is (was) the ONLY Chinese university anywhere in the world where two of its students, Chen-Ning Yang (杨振宁) and Tsung-Dao Lee (李政道) won the Nobel Prize!

Epilogue

Pitching the brightest of the bright together in "tight quarters," in the form of a tiny university, naturally there would be intellectual explosions in Caltech and NSWUU. Some 66 years after the formal closure of NSWUU, five universities in the Mainland and Taiwan inherited its legacy: Beijing Tsinghua University and Peking University, Nankai University, Hsinchu

Tsing Hua University and Yunnan Normal University. In a sense, NSWUU was the launching pad of these five universities.

Today, because of different political, cultural and intellectual conditions, each has made its mark in the world of academics, and each has taken on a different flavor. But it is undeniable that despite their differences, there is a thin thread that links them together spiritually, and that thread is the precious eight years of National Southwest Union University.

To me, that is an Asia Pacific miracle!

(2012)

29

Is Nobel Laureate Shuji Nakamura a Scientific Genius?

This is an important reflection on the social norm and judgement of academia, academic qualification, and the education system. Shuji Nakamura is Nobel Laureate in Physics, widely recognized as pioneer in light emitters based on wide-bandgap semiconductors.

On February 17th, 2015, I was invited by the Chancellor of the University of California Santa Barbara (UCSB) Dr. Henry Yang to visit his institution. As we were chatting casually over lunch at a university cafeteria, Dr. Yang suddenly said: "Let us drop by the office of Dr. Shuji Nakamura. If he is in or available, you can say hi to him!" We did, and indeed saw him. Dr. Nakamura was obviously in the middle of doing something, but because it was the Chancellor of the University, he was willing to stop what he was doing and meet with us!

I was of course overjoyed by this gesture of Dr. Yang because I know how successful UCSB is in developing "heterostructure" electronics!

I asked Dr. Yang what the secret(s) of UCSB's success is/are. He answered by giving me the story about two of their Nobel Laureates:

Shuji Nakamura
Professor of Materials and of Electrical and Computer Engineering
2014 Nobel Prize in Physics

"For the invention of efficient blue light-emitting diodes, which has enabled bright and energy-saving white light sources"

and

Herbert Kroemer
Professor of Electrical and Computer Engineering and of Materials
2000 Nobel Prize in Physics

"For developing semiconductor heterostructures used in high-speed and opto-electronics"

Both gentlemen worked on "heterostructural" opto-electronics.

"We realized," Henry said, "that in the Northern part of California, there is a place known as Silicon Valley where there are literally tens of thousands of outstanding engineers working on single element (silicon) technology. There is no way we could possibly compete with that down here in Santa Barbara! So we picked an area not being pursued there!"

This is a profound statement which took me several hours to digest. Professor Kroemer's Nobel award was 14 years ahead of Professor Nakamura. In a span of time of this length, and with the contributions from two giants, there is no question that UCSB is one of the best places, if not the best, in the world in this business.

What Henry was telling me was that for a fledgling university to be successful, one must realize what it could do, and do well, so that it could be one of the best in the world. Just following what the crowd is doing will most likely only end up with second-rate work, or disappointment.

While the short meeting with Dr. Nakamura was a great honor and pleasure for me, I could not help, during my meeting with him, but to think about how deeply perturbed I was when right after the announcement of him receiving the Nobel Prize was made on October 7th, one person in Taiwan who was supposed to be an LED expert made some disparaging comments about him in the media. The comments were essentially about his "lack of proper academic credentials" and "how he seemed to understand very little about physics." If I am not mistaken, he even said Nakamura is not a "scientific genius", presumably because he lacks proper training!

I remember I wrote a reply to such comments essentially stating that such comments were one of the profound reasons why Taiwan's academic institutions are languishing. There are too many people who revere form and not substance. The quality of the work of Nakamura and his contributions to humankind speak for themselves and will last forever. To add disparaging comments or adjectives to his name is neither necessary nor called for!

The author with Dr Shuji Nakamura (middle) and Dr Henry Yang (right).

(2015)

30

Intellectual Bandwidth: Holy Grail of Education in the 21st Century

This piece was written when the author was Senior Vice President for Global Strategy, Evaluation and Planning, National Tsing Hua University.

So often, one hears in the corridors of any 21st century global higher education institution that "interdisciplinary" is the name of the game for properly educating the workforce. Today, terms are mushrooming to describe this new trend. A term which is murmured often nowadays, i.e. "**interdisciplinary disciplines (ID),**" such as "bio-technology" and "financial engineering," is best manifestation of such a trend. As Virginia Heffernan succinctly wrote in a New York Times editorial on August 7, 2011: "...*Simply put, we can't keep preparing students for a world that doesn't exist*...." So the assumption for this "new" education trend is that in order to prepare students for these unknown future, educational institutions better arm students with an "**ID**" in order to prepare them for the future.

Unfortunately, this is neither true nor feasible in the 21st century, especially with the internet rendering the world flatter and flatter. To show how rapid the global landscape is transitioning to flatness, I recall Thomas Friedman once lamented that when he wrote in 2005 the famous book "The World is Flat," a mere 9 years ago, Facebook or other social-media platforms have not even been invented yet. Just this week, Facebook has announced that the number of people having Facebook accounts in India has reached a eye-popping number of one hundred million. Since India has a population of over 1.2 billion, there seems to be no end to this incredible flat transition. Undoubtedly with this new and rapidly transforming era of the world, it appears that merely by promoting "**ID**" within a university education is hardly sufficient to properly prepare our workforce.

Curiously this dilemma is hardly recent. It is worth examining the issues facing fledgling universities during the Renaissance era, i.e. Europe between the 14th and 17th centuries. During that period of time, perhaps the biggest challenge to humanity was ignorance, especially ignorance about nature. For example, it was firmly believed before the Renaissance that the earth is center of the universe, known as geocentric theory. It was shown during Renaissance period by great penetrating minds such as Nicolaus Copernicus that such an understanding was utterly erroneous. The correct theory of course is what we know today, namely it is the earth and other planets which rotate around the sun, a theory we call today as heliocentric. However, to alter the erroneous understanding to the correct one, Corpernicus and the like had to acquire and amass not merely astronomical knowledge, but all forms of human intellectual effort, including understanding the fundamental rational of geocentric theory and how the Church became so deeply entrenched in such a dogma. It is rather interesting that in a sense, obviously without knowing it, these great minds believed intrinsically the famous dictum of Sun Tzu in the *Art of War* (《孙子兵法》), namely, "**Know thy self and thy adversary; Hundred encounters hundred successes!**" By the time Corpernicus was ready to propose to the world his heliocentric theory, he was already standing on a tall intellectual mountain. Using today's terminology, he had an "intellectual bandwidth" that was second to none.

One may think that the 21st century bears no resemblance to the Renaissance. Therefore, it is indeed curious that we are today facing sort of the same dilemma, but in another format. Education institutions have moved from traditional "disciplines" to "**ID**," hoping that such an effort would be sufficient to meet the needs of preparing students in this new era. In Asian universities, we have seen a surge of transforming universities from "teaching-centric" to "research-centric," from traditional disciplines to ID. Quite often, it is because our universities were driven by the pressure of raising their "global ranking." For example, faculty members that were in traditional disciplines such as chemistry, now become ID such as bio-chemistry, materials chemistry or even the trendy nanomaterials chemistry. Yet, even with such alteration of expertise, the fundamental *modus operandi* of a faculty member remains constant. He/she is as deeply into his/her ID as he/she was when it was merely a discipline. Indeed, faculty members in this new paradigm could be as narrow in their intellectual bandwidth as ever.

Yet, the students' need have profoundly altered. Imagine what a modern 21st century student is faced with. Due to the plethora of information in all dimensions emerging from the flat world bombarding the students, from science to social science, from humanities to engineering, from international relations to global politics, and from the simplest to the most complex, and seeing businesses with certain technologies disappearing before their eyes, students within universities not only could have information digestive challenge, they could easily become hopelessly bewildered, if not confused. Facing such information onslaughts, they could become profoundly fearful about their future.

Within a university, there is now a new "digital river" dividing students and faculty. That river is known as "social media" such as Facebook. Students, especially the undergraduates essentially live by their social media platform. Such is of course not the case with the faculty who communicate with one another and with students with more traditional platforms (of course I am referring to emails as being traditional!) With such a divide, there is now less and less communication between students and faculty. Hence, when students become fearful, the faculty members are no help because due to lack of proper communication they could not comprehend what made the students fearful.

In fact, I would say that in the 21st century, the greatest challenge of students is not ignorance. It is fear for the future.

In today's higher education, the need to increase the overall intellectual bandwidth of a university is as intense as ever. Faculty members can no longer afford merely being experts in their respective **ID**. They need to be cognizant of the world in multi-dimensions. They need to be willing and ready to engage in conversations with students in areas in which they regard themselves as being ignorant. With access to vast information at their fingertips, they no longer could claim to be ignorant on any subject for long. They need to leverage their intellectual power to absorb and comprehend new and alien knowledge. The conversation could be face-to-face, social media-to-social media, or face-to-social media. They need to learn to communicate properly in these new platforms. This is the new intellectual bandwidth that a modern university needs in order to be successful, if not merely to survive, in the 21st century.

While the world is turning upside-down rapidly, universities unfortunately are turning upside-down slowly. This is our challenge. To become robust in this turning, there is little doubt that widening the intellectual bandwidth of all the communities within the universities must be carried out rapidly, or face the danger of becoming irrelevant.

(2014)

On India

31

A Practical Example of the Five Dictums of President Ma Ying-Jeou: National Tsing Hua University in India

These were the opening comments made for a speech for the "International Conference on Sino-Indian Relations in the First Half of the 20th Century", held on January 4, 2013, at National Tsing Hua University, Hsinchu, Taiwan. The author was Senior Vice President, Global Strategy, Planning and Evaluation, at the university.

Ladies and Gentlemen, distinguished guest, good morning.

Happy New Year.

I know you are expecting my boss, Academician Lih J. Chen to be here this morning to welcome you. Well, he was called to attend a meeting which could not refuse. I know that he would probably much prefer to be here than there.

Actually, when President Chen asked me to represent him, I hesitated quite a bit. As you know, I was asked by the organizers to give a talk in this conference. I thought to myself, what could I possibly say this morning that would not simply be a watered-down version of my afternoon talk? That thought gave me moments of discomfort.

Well, as the old saying goes: "*If you have to choose between brilliant or lucky, always choose lucky!*" I was lucky on the morning of December 30, 2012, after a night of tossing and turning, thinking about what I should say this morning. When I woke up and opened my emails, I saw a message from a friend in U.S. who sent me a speech President Ma Ying-Jeou delivered recently. The report was very short, which summarized what

President Ma said. He urged the citizens of the Republic of China, *a la* Taiwan, to be proactive in five efforts, which I dubbed as Ma Ying-Jeou's Five Dictums. They are:

1. 「和平的缔造者」 **Peace makers;**
2. 「人道援助的提供者」 **Humanitarian providers;**
3. 「文化交流的推动者」 **Cultural exchange movers and shakers;**
4. 「新科技与商机的创造者」 **New Science, Technology and Business opportunities creators; and**
5. 「中华文化的领航者」 **Chinese culture helmsmen.**

The only "natural resource" RoC has is its people and the five dictums are precisely built on the strength of people's *skill sets*. Therefore as soon as I read this email, my "kneejerk reaction" was that these dictums are precisely what National Tsing Hua University has been pursuing with vigor in India in the 21st century. Ladies and gentlemen, 21st century is a transformational era for Asia. What was regional in the 20th century is now global in the 21st century. What were deemed improbable and impossible in the 20th century are now probable and possible in the 21st century. What was slow moving in time in the 20th century is now rapid moving in time in the 21st century. Indeed, what was unimaginable in the 20th century is now imaginable in the 21st century. With this as underpinning, Asian research universities in this new century should and must also be transformational, and assume new and solemn responsibilities, for their nations, their regions and for the globe.

What Ma has outlined in the five dictums is to urge the citizens of RoC to leverage their soft-power in establishing global connections. I have a feeling that in the media, Ma's five dictums may be interpreted as whimsical. To me, they outlined a fundamental survival blueprint for RoC in the turbulent and prosperous Asia today. Ladies and gentlemen, think about it. Every dictum mentioned by President Ma is worth pursuing only if it could have a global perspective. I do not know whether President Ma has this grand vision in mind, but to me these five dictums are RoC's *master plan* for "foreign policy" in the 21st century.

There is a renowned Chinese saying by a great political statesman Fan Zhongyan (范仲淹) in the Northern Sung Dynasty who said "*assume global responsibilities as personal*" (以天下為己任). Indeed, in this day and age, if an outstanding research university does not take this as its mission, who can? Hence, by extension, National Tsing Hua University's effort in mobilizing all universities in RoC in developing a sustainable relationship with India is, in my opinion, what an elite research university should be pursuing in assisting the nation and the region for global well being.

We all know that in this new century, RoC is at a cross-road. It is searching for a new and unchartered paradigm so that it will not become irrelevant. Hence, research universities which proclaim to be the halls of learning to understand RoC and its relationship with the world must participate and lead in this search. To this end, it would be detrimental to RoC's research universities not to take these words of President Ma seriously. It seems to me that in the coming decades, whatever RoC universities have been doing well, even excellently since the 80s, **redesigning**, **reengineering** and seriously **incorporating** the five dictums into their goals and mission are unavoidable and desperately needed.

It is with this in mind that I as the Senior Vice President for Global Affairs for National Tsing Hua University thought about the university's very proactive activities with one of RoC's most massive neighbors which happens to be one of the two dominant components of the so-called BRIIC: India.

It is obvious for RoC, that in order for it to have a meaningful existence in Asia in the 21st century, the economic, political and cultural rise of three major countries, namely Mainland China, Indonesia and India, all part of BRIIC, and all are practically surrounding RoC, cannot and must not be ignored. In the 21st century, these three nations, because of their rapid rise in political, cultural and economic arenas, have emerged to be of fundamental importance to and for the world. With Mainland China, RoC's former representative Phillip Ong to India summarized it best: "*Our understanding of Mainland China is not through books, but through our DNAs.*" To this end, the five dictums of President Ma can and have been more or less accomplished in the past decade and a half, especially since Ma was elected as President in 2008. From an academic point of view, I think it is obvious that the interactions between the "two shores", a euphemism for PRC and RoC, have been going on in a gang buster manner. This I think this is not only good for universities, but for the tranquility of the region in general.

With Indonesia, the interaction is more challenging. Indonesia, because of sheer landmass and population, and now political maturation, is unquestionably the key nation in Southeast Asia. With RoC, there are major languages, cultural and religious differences. But, fortunately by tapping into the ubiquitous Indonesian Chinese community, RoC could also reasonably build the 5 dictums relationship with this important neighbor. Indeed, with the assistance of Indonesian Chinese, RoC needs to make special effort to understand the cultural and religious diversity of Indonesia.

The most challenging of the three countries for RoC is unquestionably India. From 1949 until 1995, India and RoC had essentially ceased to have any cultural, economic and technological interactions. Even between 1995 and 2005, the interactions were at a minimum. Despite the fact that India and RoC may have similar political systems, there is no commonality between Indian and Chinese languages. The cultural heritages of India, which are vast and complex, bear no resemblance on the surface with Chinese. In fact, as Ambassador Ong said in one of his speeches recently, one could easily think of a thousand reasons why businesses and universities in RoC do not wish to enter into a relationship with their Indian counterparts. The vice versa is also true.

A wise man once mentioned to me when I was starting my career as a theoretical physicist that I should work on the hardest problem I could find. The reason is because if I could solve that problem, what comes next would be easy. While this may not be the best advice to a young scientist, National Tsing Hua University proactive incursion into India does have such a flavor. Our lack of understanding of the ways and means of Indians made it exceptionally hard in bringing closure to many of the opportunities which came our way. I would say that if it were not the herculean persistence of our Team in the Office of Global Affairs, working handin-hand with all relevant divisions within the university, and inherently understanding that the ultimate goal is of fundamental important to the university, and by extension to RoC and Asia in general, we would not have reached the current plateau of "success." Of course, we still have a long way to go, but all of us are beginning to see a faint light at the end of this long tunnel.

Ladies and gentlemen, with everything I have said so far about India, I hope you will agree with me that it makes this conference of trying to understand India and China in the first half of the 20th century that much more important. Indeed, the best way to understand the culture and ways and means of India, a nation that is so "foreign" to RoC and so vast is *via* history, especially history which people here can identify readily. To this end, the theme of this conference is one such important and profound identification. Once we understand that phase of history in the first half of the 20th century between India and China, it will surely whet our appetite to know more about "**Incredible India**." I hope with this conference, it will be the spark to burn brightly the intellectual prairie of this area. To me this is so important and so far has not received its deserved global attention.

Thank you so much for your attention.

(2013)

32

India and I

This was the keynote speech for the "Conference on Globalization of India-Taiwan Relations and Strategy", held on April 28, 2013, at National Tsing Hua University, Hsinchu, Taiwan. The author was Senior Vice President, Global Strategy, Planning and Evaluation, at the university.

Ladies and Gentlemen: A few months ago, the organizers invited me to give a talk in this important conference about Indian–Taiwan Relations and Strategy. Since I was given a very short time leash, I decided to give the title "India and I." I learned this trick a long time ago, when push comes to shove in giving a title of a talk, it is best to give one that sounds good and allows one the greatest leeway to develop the talk.

To set the stage of this talk, please allow me to give you a synopsis of my background. I was born in New Delhi, India. Hence the genesis of the title of this talk. I left India, holding a British Subject passport as a young baby and returned to China. It is worth mentioning that a British Subject passport is in every way and shape like a British passport, except for the conspicuous sentence in the cover: Bearer Has No Right to Abode in the British Isles!

In 1950, my family moved to Singapore which at that time was a British colony. I grew up in Singapore until 1964 when I left for College in the U.S., holding a Malaysian passport. As some of you may know or remember, to gain Singapore's independence from Britain, it had to first join Malaysia. Of course, a year later in 1965, Singapore and Malaysia separated and thus I became a full fledge Singapore Citizen. This citizenship jumping process finally came to a halt when I became a US citizen in 1982.

My globetrotting were as robust as the changing of my passport. I had been to United Kingdom and Texas as a postdoctoral fellow, a professor of physics in Philadelphia, a visiting professor in Denmark and countless number of visits to Asia until I finally came to Taiwan in 2007 and now in Hsinchu at the National Tsing Hua University (NTHU).

Until about 2009, I have always believed that the fact that my short stay in India during my birth period was at best uneventful, at worse of no serious consequence to me. Little do I know that I had misjudged its significance. A few years ago, entirely through serendipity, I discovered that there was in fact an event in 1946 which happened to my family while we were in India that was truly profound. In fact, this event not only has a profound impact on me, on what we are doing today in this conference, but maybe even on how the Republic of China (ROC) could navigate in this turbulent and prosperous Asia!

How I found out about this event was so remarkable that I gave it a title: **"Google my late father!"**

It was quite an amazing coincidence that both my father and my son graduated from the same Law School of New York University, in 1937 and 2009, respectively. Since my father passed away in the early 1950s, I knew relatively little about him. So after my son entered the same law school, on one weekend in 2007, I suddenly had the urge to find out more about him. Almost subconsciously, I googled him! Not expecting anything I could get from the search, I typed in "Paul Feng India China" in my Google search!

What came out from the search startled me! Hooray for Google! The result of Google's search produced a website[14] containing a mesmerizing article by an author named Manoj Das with the title "Forging an Asian identity." It was published in *The Hindu* on January 7, 2001. The entire article is worth reading by all but the passage that startled me was as follows, which I like to share it with you here.

> "...*We in India have debated as much as other Asian countries have, about issues like the desirability of Western influence on our culture, its inevitability or otherwise, and the relation between tradition and modernity.*
>
> *Like the May Fourth Movement in China which championed western values and ideals in the 1920s, we too had voices against our traditions and*

---

[14] http://www.burmalibrary.org/reg.burma/archives/200101/msg00016.html

they were given a reasonable hearing. An exchange in experiences of this kind would no doubt be highly educative.

For quite some time, Indian literature for the common Englishman meant what Rudyard Kipling and the like wrote. For long, India's window as well as that of the West on Chinese life has been Pearl S. Buck's Good Earth. But when I read Lu Hsun, a number of his short stories and The True Story of Ah Q, I realised that despite the realism in the works of Pearl Buck and other gifted writers, Lu Hsun's work had an authenticity that could be expected only of a native of China. I do not propose to display my meagre knowledge of Chinese literature here, but what I propose is a strong and well-planned academy of Asian literatures to take care of the great need to know one another.

And who could take any effective step in that direction? For me, the answer came from the first Prime Minister of India, Jawaharlal Nehru. (Ladies and Gentleman, the following passage almost knocked me out of my chair!) **Speaking to Mr. Paul Feng of the Central News Agency, he said on January 20, 1946, "If China and India hold together, the future of Asia is assured.** *"This holding together need not be confined to diplomacy; it can, by all means, be a psychological force that can work wonders in the realms of creativity...."*

Yes, my friends, the Great Jawaharlal Nehru, this great Indian statesman made the world renowned comment to my father Mr. Paul Feng that "If China and India hold together, the future of Asia is assured" with elegance and clarity nearly seven decades ago.

I have to admit that when I read this passage, for a moment I was bewildered because in view of the little history I knew about China and India, such a concept never occurred as even possible!

The key word in these immortal twelve words uttered by Nehru is "hold!" I asked myself two questions immediately: "how to hold?" and "what should be the agent of hold?" Clearly Nehru did not specify what he had in mind, nor maybe at that point in history, when China was just emerging from eight years of its bloody war of survival with the Japanese and India was at the verge of gaining independence after nearly three centuries of British colonial rule, were these questions of the highest priority to him. Yet, Nehru clearly was not a man worrying about the past, but a visionary leader. He saw what was necessary to achieve a brilliant future of Asia!

My family left India in 1946. In 1949, when my father was appointed as the English editor of the newspaper Tiger Standard in Singapore, we moved there! Soon after we arrived in Singapore, my father died in an air crash. My mother, a Julliard trained pianist, began her illustrious career as a piano teacher. At that time, Singapore was still a British colony.

One of the first Indian I came into contact in Singapore was my mother's fellow piano teacher, Mr. Paul Abisheganadan. By name, you could tell he was, like many Indians in Singapore at the time, of Tamil descent. He was very dark skin which gave me the absolutely wrong impression that Indians have dark skin.

In my first year of senior high school, something horrible happened. The now well-known 1962 border conflict between India and China broke out. Since the population of Singapore has a large percentage of Chinese and Indians, it was natural that this conflict caused a great deal of anxiety among these respective communities. I learned later that the twelve words Nehru uttered in 1946 became one of the sources of severe criticisms by his countrymen. While Nehru was able to foresee the grand Asian picture, this war between these two Asian giants simply "broke him". Soon after, Nehru died.

Unfortunately, what happened in 1946 has consequences even to this day!

Soon after, I left Singapore and went to the U.S. to begin a new chapter of my life, I began to study physics. As I move deeper and deeper into my career as a physicist, more and more Indians fellow students, teachers and Indian Institutions came into my cognizant. I recall a number of my classmates in graduate schools came from undergraduate institutions such as the University of Delhi, Tata Institute of Fundamental Research, Banaras Hindu University (now became one of the Indian Institute of Technology's,) Bhabha Atomic Research Center and so on.

As I received more physics education, I began to learn about how great science flourished in India well before many other Asian countries.

In this respect, two Indian physicists in the early part of the 20th century deserves to be mentioned prominently. One is Satyendra Nath Bose and the other Vankata Raman. I learned about Bose's work when the idea of a "boson" is fundamental in nuclear structure physics and Raman work on "Raman scattering" is fundamental in all forms of material science.

Even though Bose lived from 1894–1974 and Raman from 1888–1970, their names are still household names in physics today! Raman also has the great honor of being the first Asian to win the Nobel Prize in physics in 1930, nineteen years before the second Asian Hideki Yukawa in 1949 and twenty seven years before the third and fourth Asians Chen Ning Yang and Tsung-Dao Lee in 1957. In fact, the year when Raman won the Nobel Prize, Lee and Yang were merely four and eight years old, respectively!

An intriguing question is as follows: Where does today's Indian intellectual prowess originate from?

I think one can get an inkling about the answer to this complex question by examining the scientific giants of India in the early part of the 20th century. Many Chinese greats during that period, especially those who were given the highest scientific accolades, the Nobel Prize, won it after receiving their advanced training and did the work in Western countries. A significant number of Indian counterparts, such as Bose and Raman, were entirely home-grown! It is important to remember that although the accolades should and must belong to Bose and Raman, it must also be underscored that great scientific achievements are seldom, if ever (Einstein being the only exception I could think of) solo performances. The achievements of Bose and Raman and the likes must imply that India's scientific conditions and landscape at the time, while it may not be as robust as Europe and the U.S., the culture of carrying out world class scientific research must be prevalent. I think this is one of the reasons why India's scientific and technological prowess of today. It did not grow from a vacuum.

In 2003, India's higher education suddenly became known to the world. This was because in that year, one of the most popular national television show produced by CBS known as 60 Minutes had a full documentary about the then seven campuses of Indian Institute of Technology. The reporter for the program made the following stunning comment to the world:

"What is America's most valuable import from India? It may very well be brainpower. Hundreds of thousands of well-educated Indians have come to the U.S. in recent decades - many to work in the computer and software

industries. The best and brainiest among them seem to share a common credential: They're graduates of the Indian Institute of Technology, better known as IIT."

With these words, I and the rest of the world became aware of the IITs of India. So in 2004, I led a delegation from the University of Texas at Dallas to visit three Indian Institute of Technology campuses. They are Bombay, Delhi and Roorkee. From our visit, I understood the meaning of Ms. Stahl's words and saw first-hand how the IITs operated. I became thoroughly convinced of the fundamental importance of these institutions for India as a nation. It also gave me a better sense that India is a nation of enormous potentialities and complexities.

I came to Taiwan in the September of 2007. In the first three and a half years I spent in the National Cheng Kung University, while I climbed a very steep learning curve to understand the "Republic of China ROC" and the "People's Republic of China PRC", India was never a part of the equation of this learning process. Perhaps the most gratifying part of understanding ROC and PRC in that period was that I saw a significant and positive change in the so-called "cross-straits" relationship. In fact, the hostility between the two straits had, and still has, de facto vanished in reality, and more important in the minds of the people on both shores.

When I came to National Tsing Hua University in 2011, India suddenly entered into my consciousness! If nothing else, on campus in this university, one can often see Indian students. In fact, I was informed that nearly a quarter of all the students from India pursuing degree programs in Taiwan were at this university. This was an added bonus of the joy of coming to NTHU.

NTHU is literally joined at the hips with Beijing's Tsinghua University, which is one of the intellectually and politically most powerful universities in the Mainland. This linkage provided me a natural platform as NTHU's Senior Vice President in charge of global strategy to gain a deeper appreciation of the intricate relationship between ROC and PRC. It drew for me a roadmap, however blurry at the moment, of the long term relationship of the two shores.

Also it is very interesting that before coming to NTHU in 2011, my background, my knowledge, the fact that I was born in India, had no platform to leverage what they could do, not in Singapore, in the U.S., in UK, in Denmark, and in Tainan! There is an old Chinese saying, namely "A hero without opportunity to exercise his might" (英雄無用武之地) which fits my predicament precisely. Little did I know that prior to my arrival in 2011, President Lih J. Chen (陳力俊) and Vice President for Global Affairs Wei-Chung Wang (王偉中) had already developed a fledgling effort with India. After I arrived, I saw and participated in a number of exciting and robust activities with India.

The projects underway when I arrived were the active, exciting and ongoing development of five Taiwan Educational Centers in New Delhi and Madras in O. P. Jindal International University, Amity University, IIT Madras, Jamia Milia Islamia University and Jawaharlal Nehru University. More are now in planning.

I have always believed that any major undertaking within a university should have a theoretical underpinning. Therefore the fact that I am now in Taiwan at one of its top universities which on the one hand is deeply connected to one of the top universities in the Mainland, and on the other have the deepest connection to India, made the immortal words of Nehru, "If China and India hold together, the future of Asia is assured" ringing in my ears again.

I started to ask myself the following question: *"India and PRC have nearly 40 percent of the world's population, are extraordinarily education centric, have rich and complex history, have robust cultures, have prowess in science and technology, and literally are sitting next to each other with many thousands of kilometers of borders, how can they play a role for the betterment of humanity in the 21st century?"*

It is indeed unfortunate that history has not been kind to their mutual relationship in the 20th century, thus rendering them with an awkward disposition in the 21st century. Still, in many ways, India and PRC are certainly as starkly different as they are strikingly similar. I dare to say that for the tranquility of Asia and for the world in the 21st century, India and PRC should and need to have the best of relations.

It is thinking in this context that makes me particularly excited to think about how ROC could play in this arena, a role which I believe is unique in the world.

It is well known that in physics, in order for two nucleons (protons or neutrons) to have power, they need to bind together, Indeed, what binds them is an "exchange particle" known as a "meson."

Leveraging this analogy, we can think of ROC which is deeply rooted in Chinese culture, "squeezed" in between two massive and powerful 21st century nations, could play a "meson" role.

As is well known, in the past decade, partially due to the rapid economic rise of PRC, there is in India a noticeable surge of interest in Chinese ways and means. In my recent visits to India, I noticed that such interest is by no means confined to only Chinese language, although that may have been the initial incentive, but to cultures, the thinking processes and deep rooted social habits.

The most obvious rise of this interest is that Indian government is requesting all of its secondary schools, if possible, to offer Chinese as a third language. For a nation of 1.2 billion people, such a request would constitute a herculean human engineering effort! It is therefore truly remarkable that ROC, whose tiny population is 23 million, who has inherited thousands of years of rich Chinese culture, could be a hoard at the disposal of the vast Indian population.

In another era, Nehru inherently felt that India and China (in 1946, there was no PRC or ROC, as we understand them today, only China) need to "hold" together. As I mentioned earlier, at that time, neither China nor India had the time or energy to give much thought to this issue. In fact, at that moment, both nations' futures were unchartered, if not uncertain.

I am certain that Nehru felt intrinsically that by themselves, China and India could exert great global influence. However, together, they could render the world truly exciting for humanity. It is not inconceivable that if India and China were to "hold" together, they could create an intellectual excitement, if not superiority, that is not known in history!

It was indeed unfortunate for Nehru that he lived long enough to see the "breaking up" of India and PRC's relation. The war in 1962 was, I am sure, deeply painful for him as a great visionary, and seeing the vision vaporizing before his eyes.

However, if only Nehru could know what happens in the 21st century, that PRC and India became world powers, and that the war of 1962 prevented the two great powers from "holding together," he would unquestionably be furiously seeking the "hold" agent.

Quite recently, President Ma Ying-Jeou recently urged ROC citizens to pursue the following five dictums with vigor: (1) peace maker,

(2) humanitarian provider, (3) cultural exchange mover and shaker, (4) new science, technology and business opportunities provider and (5) Chinese culture helmsmen. To me, these are, or should be, the mission statement of ROC's "foreign policy" as well as future development. They can also be the mission of ROC in India.

Therefore, Mr. Nehru, seek no more. ROC is that agent. Its 23 million people are the only "hold" agent that can play the "meson" role between the two Asian giants. The robust activities with India from NTHU is now as clear as sunrise. In NTHU, with its deep connection to Tsinghua University and PRC, and now with its robust activities in India, the words of Nehru finally have meaning!

Thus, Nehru's words uttered nearly seven decades ago can and should now be NTHU's India mission statement.

I am deeply grateful that NTHU has decided to take this bold step. I am also deeply gratified that with more than six decades of interaction with India, I could play a part in this monumental mission, for NTHU, for Asia, and for the world.

Thank you, Mr. Nehru.

(2013)

On China

33

Challenges for Higher Education: A Reflection of My 100 Trips to China

This was a speech made at the "International Symposium in Honor of the 70th Birthday of Chancellor Fu-Jia Yang", on June 12, 2006, and an invited talk delivered to China Three Gorges University, Yichang, Hubei, China, on June 18, 2006. The reflection was done after the 100 trips the author made to China, within a span of a quarter of a century. The author was Vice President for Research and Economic Development, Professor of Physics, The University of Texas at Dallas.

Preface

Thank you so much for giving me the honor to speak here today. There is a famous story about a blind person trying to figure out what an elephant looks like. When he touches the tail, he said the elephant looks like the tail. When he touches the ears, he said that the elephant looks like the ears. The reason is because the elephant is huge and unless you can examine both closely and afar, with open eyes, you may not see the whole picture.

Indeed, trying to describe Chinese higher education is akin to the blind man describing the elephant. It is easy to give a biased and maybe even wrong description. Therefore I want to state from the outset that this is my impression of the "elephant," right or wrong.

In the past quarter of a century, I have made 100 visits to China. During this critical period for China, it has emerged from one of negligible global influence to one of major international importance. A quarter of a century ago, having only a small number of institutions and burdened with extremely limited resources, the mission of Chinese higher education was to serve a tiny portion of its population. Thus their impact was limited and questionable. Today, with increased wealth and vast expansion of institutions, in qualities and number, the mission of Chinese universities has also vastly expanded.

Universities of today are no longer merely intellectual engines of the nation, but the economic engines as well. This is true not just for China but all nations. Indeed, in China, the shift from "teaching universities" to "research universities" is obvious. It is also not surprising that with this expansion, new models of higher education began to mushroom, thus creating the understandable excitement and confusion. Indeed, I would venture to say that Chinese high education landscape is still very much in a state-of-flux, and how it will look like when the dust settles is still very much a speculation. My talk will discuss this transformation and some of my personal views and biases of how this transformation may affect the nation and the world in the 21st century.

In September of 1981, with an invitation from the Institute of High Energy Physics of the Chinese Academy of Sciences, I made my "first" visit to China since the People's Republic was established. I call this my "first" visit because the last time I was in China, it was in 1950!

Little did I know that for the next quarter of a century, I would be going to China one hundred times. In each visit, I learned a bit more about this fascinating country, deepened relations, developed new relations and friendships. Each visit, I saw China inched forward, impacting the world a little bit more than my previous visit. Each time I saw China changing, some for the good and some not so good. All in all, I saw a nation literally reinventing itself before my eyes, and the eyes of the entire world.

Since my talk is devoted to a description of my impression of how Chinese higher education has evolved, as a scientist I must give you a sense where the origin of my coordinates are from which I measure progress or the lack of it. To this end, I have to tell you about my immediate impression of China when I landed in Shanghai that October in 1981. I think this defines my coordinate system.

Shanghai's Hongqiao Airport (now a domestic airport, sort of like Love Field in Dallas, Texas) made a deep impression on me. My trip began from JFK Airport, which was one of the largest modern airports, if not the largest, at that time in the world. Some 20 hours later, I landed in Shanghai. I recall when I looked out the window as the plane was descending on Shanghai, I saw nothing but darkness, a very unusual sight for what was a city of at least 10 million. That darkness defined China at the time.

The darkness outside the plane window was my first encounter of the remnants of the "cultural revolution," which ended merely four years before. What I saw was an airport badly, in fact desperately, in need of maintenance. Since China's open-door policy was still at the beginning stage, the airport had very low usage. The only airport I could compare Hong Qian to which I now have some familiarity with was Bulgaria's Plovdiv airport which I visited some nine years later just before the tremendous turnover of Eastern Europe.

As I entered Hongqiao, I had difficulty convincing myself that this airport was supposed to be the entry point of one of the world's most populous nations! Imagine this in your mind, 20 hours before, I was at one of the most modern and plush airports in the world, the JFK airport, serving the largest metropolitan area of the U.S.: New York City. 20 hours later, I was in Hongqiao airport, serving the largest city of China, the most populous country in the world. The contrast could not be more acute!

Unquestionably, the most vivid memory I had during those two hours of lay-over before I flew to Beijing was the sole low-wattage light bulb hanging from the ceiling in the toilet. Darkness in the toilet made "aiming" a real challenge.

China was a different country then. So was its higher education.

Some Comments on Chinese Universities Prior to 1950

My young age in 1950 obviously prevented me from having much memory and precluded me from developing an in-depth understanding about China. Suffice to say that during that period, the Asia-Pacific region was hardly one that projected confidence about its future. Poverty and wars ruled the day. Indeed, country after country, from the Korean Peninsula to Malaya Peninsula, to the islands of Philippines and Indonesia, there were pervasive violent confrontations. Some were due to volatility arising from mixing nationalism with colonialism, some were struggles between peoples of different beliefs, while others were racial tensions and conflicts.

China of course was no exception. After eight years of war-of-resistance (*ba nian kang zhan*, or 八年抗战) and four years of civil war (*nei zhan*, or 内战), Chairman Mao proclaimed on Tiananmen on October 1, 1949, that "Chinese people have stood up". This was as much a statement of national triumph as it was the conditions China was in during that period of time. Frankly, I cannot fathom the devastation in China in 1950.

I have very limited knowledge of Chinese universities before 1949, except to note that during my parents' generation, there were a relatively small number of outstanding universities. Some of these universities had religious affiliation, the most well-known being Yanjing University and St. Johns University (SJU). In fact, one of my wife's cousins, Alpha Chiang, a renowned mathematical economist and the author of a standard textbook on the subject, was an alumnus of SJU. Other elite national universities included Tsinghua University, Peking University, Peking Union Medical Colleage, Zhongshan University, Jiaotong University and the National Central University. These universities had consistently produced high quality and highly motivated students before WWII. Many became not only pillars of China, but the world.

Of course, during the war-of-resistance, one must underscore the contribution of the famous *Xi Nan Lian Da*, or South West Union University (SWUU). Due to wartime necessity, SWUU amalgamated several outstanding universities, including Tsinghua University, and moved to the remote province of Yunnan. Despite operating under enormously difficult conditions, SWUU managed to gather "under-one-roof" the best teachers and students China could muster. It became the breeding ground of some of the truly most exceptional students the world had known. Many distinguished Chinese intellectuals who had an impact on the world scene in the 20th century received their early education or taught at SWUU. A few instantly come to mind: T. D. Lee and C. N. Yang, two Chinese who won the physics Nobel Prize in 1957, their teacher the late Ta You Wu, commonly known as "father of physics" of China. the late S. S. Chern who became known to the world as the "father of modern geometry" and the late Fei Xiaotong, who was one of China's finest anthropologists.

Despite sporadic, limited yet enormous successes, I think it is fair to surmise that in the first half of the 20th century, higher education as it is defined today was still in its infancy in China. What we refer to today as graduate education, for example, was at best rudimentary in nature, at worse non-existent. A small number of universities did offer masters degree programs (for example C. N. Yang did his masters degree in statistical mechanics from SWUU,) but doctoral education/training, as far as I am aware of, was virtually absent. With Europe and North America being the center of gravity of modern science and technology at the time, it is no surprise that China, and indeed Asia in general (with the exception of Japan) lags far, far behind in these areas.

In addition, since the number of universities was vastly inadequate to provide "universal higher education" for the large population (in 1950 the number was approximately 400 million, which is a factor of 3 lower than what it is today,) and the nation was suffering from extreme poverty, I suspect that as a whole the intellectual and economic impact of these universities on China, especially in science and technology, was minimal.

There was another interesting by-product that came out of China's inadequate higher education system. It created a new generation of "abroad-studying-students." In Chinese, these students are referred to as *liu xue sheng, or* 留学生. Interestingly, even though advanced training was at a minimum in China, Chinese educators in particular and Chinese society in general recognized the importance of obtaining such training. Therefore, many Chinese families, especially the educated and/or well-to-do families did encourage their children to go abroad to pursue advanced degrees. Indeed, thousands upon thousands went abroad, to Europe and North America. Both my parents belong to this category. I can say that this generation of *liu-xue-sheng,* upon completion of their education in the West or (after 1949) in the Soviet Union, became the backbone of Chinese science and technology in particular and all forms of intellectual pursues in general of the latter part of the 20th century! I would say that the best example of students studying in England is Kun Huang who did legendary work with Max Born at University of Bristol.

I do not want to give the (wrong) impression that universities in China ONLY emphasize science and technology. In fact, I think it is important to point out that one of China's great universities, *Bei-Jing-Da-Xue,* 北京大学 or Peking University, is as much known for its humanities as it is for its sciences. One of the first presidents of PKU was a man whom I believe is not well known in the West (although he should be). His name is Cai Yuan-Pei (蔡元培). PKU would not be what it is today if it did not have Cai at the helm in its beginning. Indeed, with Cai's leadership, PKU became not just the soul of the Chinese university community, but in fact Chinese history and culture of the 20th century. In this context, I should mention the dilemma of university rankings, which Chinese universities across China are very much in tune with. Indeed, how do we measure the "intangible impact" of PKU on China, with the effort of *Bai-Hua* 白话 (modern Chinese) movement, the May 4th movement, and so on and so forth? Is it even logical to consider that PKU is not a "World-Class University" when it has had a profound impact on China, with nearly a quarter of humanity, for a century?

Back to 1981

Chinese higher education made a "disruptive transformation" in 1954 by carrying out what was called "colleges and departments realignments" or *Yuan Xi Diao Zhen* (院系调整). I suspect that some realignments were due in part to the Soviet Union's influence on Chinese Government in the early 50's. Many outstanding comprehensive universities, such as *National Central University* (NCU) in Nanjing, were dismembered. For example, NCU's arts and sciences departments became the basic building blocks of what is today Nanjing University (for which I am a very proud honorary member of its board of trustees) and its engineering school became first Nanjing Engineering College (NEC) and later Southeast University (*Dong Nan Da Xue or* 东南大学). Interestingly, not all the engineering departments in NCU became NEC. If I am not wrong, its aeronautical engineering department became what is today's Nanjing Aeronautical University, a so-called single-discipline institute, which of course is fairly common in the Soviet Union.

One may trace the dismemberment carried out across the land in the early 1950s to be one of the root causes of the many "mergers" of universities across China today. The two most spectacular mergers, which turned two medium size national universities into mega-size national universities is Jilin University and Zhejiang University. Due to my many years of association with it, and the fact that one of UTD's Nobel Laureate in chemistry Alan MacDiarmid has an institute named after him there, I am quite familiar with Jilin University. After merging five universities in Changchun city under a massive central administration of Jilin University, the campuses of the university are literally dotting the entire city. In fact, there is now a saying in Changchun:

Mei Li De Chang Chun Zai Ji Lin Da Xue Xiao Yuan Li
（美丽的长春在吉林大学校园里）
or
The beautiful Changchun is in the campus of Jilin University.

This merger reminded me of the mega-merger of the Department of Homeland Security in the U.S. after 9/11. By literally "forcing" many human organizations with different cultures, and in this case, many levels of standards, together, there would be inevitable human and logistical complications and difficulties. Since most of these mergers were carried out only quite recently, it is probably still too early to ascertain whether they can produce the intended outcome.

For me, even though there was only scant information about China in Singapore before I left for the U.S. in 1964 and little or no information reported in the U.S. about China prior to China opening its door to the outside world in 1978, I was fortunate enough to learn enough about China to initiate my personal interactions with this vast nation for the next quarter of a century, which began in October of 1981.

There were several reasons for this.

First, I did know that since 1972, when Nixon made the historical visit to China, Asia was on the move to economic transformation. Indeed, when I visited my hometown of Singapore in 1979, one could already palpably feel that the island country was well on its way to become one of the economic tigers of Asia. And indeed that did happen!

Second, while I was a postdoctoral fellow in the University of Manchester in England in the early 70s, I noticed that there were far more journals in the library from China than in the U.S. Careful reading some of them gave me a sense of what was happening in China, something which I found absent in the U.S.

Third and more important as far as I am concerned, was that in the fall of 1979, I had the opportunity to spend a year as a visiting professor at the then global center for nuclear physics, the Niels Bohr Institute (NBI) of University of Copenhagen. As a nuclear physicist, this was a dream come true, an opportunity to learn from maestros of the field. I went to Denmark, full of anticipation.

The scientific depth of NBI did not disappoint me. However, little did I know that something even greater than science was awaiting me in Copenhagen.

1976 was a defining year for modern China. Chairman Mao died on September 9, followed immediately by the spectacular collapse of the so-called "Gang of Four", thus bringing closure to ten painful and devastating years of "Cultural Revolution", and ushered the nation into a new era. Someday, historians will undoubtedly consider the new era as the "miracle of the world in the 20th century". In 1976, China was at the verge of a complete "meltdown", economically, technologically and intellectually. Having a quarter of humanity, and a land size spanning nearly half of Asia, such a meltdown would have had horrifying global implications!

Because of the strong and sustained connections even during the cultural revolution period between China and the father and son of the Bohrs, Niels and Aage, both Nobel Laureates, and the fact that after the cultural revolution China was wailing about utilizing "science" to save the nation (*ke xue jiu guo,* or 科学救国), one of the first batches of the best and the brightest Chinese intellectuals sent aboard, landed in the Niels Bohr Institute. They were

- **Cheng-Li Wu** (昊成禮) of Jilin University,
- **Yong-Siu Chen** (陳永壽) of the Institute of Atomic Energy (IAE or known commonly in China as the 401 Institute),
- **Zhan Xu** (徐湛) of Tsinghua University,
- **Cheng-Lie Jiang** (姜成烈) of IAE,
- **Ding-Chang Xian** (冼鼎昌) of the Institute of High Energy Physics in Beijing,

- **Gen-Min Jin** (靳根明) of the Institute of Modern Physics in Lanzhou, Gansu and last but not least,
- **Fu-Jia Yang** (楊福家) and his wife.

At that time, Yang was the head of the Nuclear Physics Department of Fudan University, already one of China's best universities.

Together with Choy-Hin Lay (赖載興), a fellow Singaporean and now Vice Provost of the National University of Singapore who had just completed his Ph.D. from the University of Chicago and was spending his postdoctoral training at the NBI, this group of Chinese scientists and I became good and life-long friends. In fact, Cheng-Li Wu and I became close scientific collaborators for the next decade and a half!

It should be underscored that most of these scientists went on to great careers. For example, Yang became President of Fudan University, an academician of Chinese Academy of Science (CAS) and now Chancellor of United Kingdom's Nottingham University. Xian became a leading expert in synchrotron radiation and was elected also to be an academician of CAS. The work of Zhan Xu became known in the field of particle physics as the "Tsinghua-trick". The list goes on and on.

I learned from this group the hardship they went through (I still remember the long night discussions with Xu about extreme difficulties he endured and how even without physical freedom, he continued to think about science). All of them had horror stories to tell about their experiences in those ten years. In the next two decades, of the hundreds of scientists I became friends with in China, I would say that none were spared during this period.

Through my friendship with this group of unusual individuals, all of whom have achieved far greater successes than I could ever envision for myself, I had a glimpse of why China after cultural-revolution, with its economy in nearly total disarray, did not simply collapse into the abyss. I hope someday, historians will say that it was because the tens of millions of intellectuals in China, while suffering personal and physical humiliation, never lost sight of the future. Even at its worst, they continued to remain hopeful for themselves, for their families, for their professions and for their nation. Their inner strength was the source of China's profound strength.

Of course, four years before 1981, the ten years of "Cultural Revolution" in China came to a grinding halt and suddenly, China seemed to be on the road of recovery. In August of 1981, the very first batch of four Chinese graduate students, all from Jilin University in northeast China, and two faculty members, one from Nanjing University and one from Jilin University, came to pursue graduate studies as well as research collaborations in the university where I was a faculty member. The same scenario was repeated in nearly every university across North America.

Across the U.S., there was indeed a deep sense of anticipation in the air, people were all wondering what this "new beginning" between the U.S. and China would mean in the decades to come.

This was my preparation for entering China for the first time.

To end this section, I should point out that some professional schools, such as law, have not been developing with the same degree of robustness, as in, say, science and technology, in the history of Chinese higher education. In its most fundamental level, a nation is of course a collection of people interacting with each other. The definition of a civilized society is to have dynamically changing but clear, transparent, well understood and well accepted rules and regulations which citizens can follow and improve. To this end, the impact of not having a strong and robust legal community in China is clear. Prior to the Communist reign of China, only a handful of universities, such as Suzhou University, had law programs. Even today, legal education is still a small part of the higher education landscape, although I understand that its influence is growing. This is a good sign.

Challenges of Higher Education in the Decade of the 90s and Beyond

I am a firm believer that universities must be relevant to the society they "serve."

Perhaps few people in China, or for that matter even in the world, would argue against the observation that there was enormous and rapid societal transformation for China in the decade of the 90s. The most spectacular of these transformations, for whatever reason or reasons, was a lift-off of China's economy. Not being a social scientist, nor an economist, and not even a philosopher, I could only speculate about the reason or reasons as to why this occurred. Many would say that this was due to clear directives from China's leadership for accelerating the open-door policy. There is also speculation that this was due to the rapid ease and rise of communications between people at the grass-roots level, such as the rapid growth of usage of the internet in China. Still there are those who say that provincial leaders were given more responsibilities to make economic and other decisions.

The outcome is clear. There is wealth generation in China.

From my personal, albeit limited observation, I did notice that the residence of my friends in China seemed to "increase in size" every time I visited them. In fact, not only did their apartments increase in size, but the apartments were better equipped with luxury items such as wood paneling or even carpeted floors. I also noticed that while in U.S. dollars, faculty salaries are still low, faculty salaries towards the end of the 90s was significantly higher than at the beginning of the 90s. All this increase in wealth implies that "life *is* getting better," as one of my friends would say.

China of the 90s and the 21st century is fundamentally a different country from the days when the Communists first took power in 1949. China of the 50s gave the perception of fear. Indeed, when I was growing up in Singapore, what we were constantly reminded about was the "Red Menace" from China. Today, the perception of China around the globe is a nation profoundly interested in becoming economically strong and intellectually robust. Indeed, today, all across Southeast Asia, there is palpable recognition that it is quite inconceivable to have a robust regional economy without an equally robust, forward-looking and out-reaching Chinese economy.

As I see it, China in the 21st century has at least the following challenges which did not exist in the 50s.

First, there are unquestionably vast increases in international commercial activities. While there were none in the 50s (at least not from the West) and considerably less before the 90s, the amount ballooned significantly in the 90s and beyond. With a large internal market and large and reasonably well-trained workforce in the hundreds of millions, one would expect that there will be no slow-down of this trend any time soon.

Second, while the percentage is still small, but because Chinese population is so large, *in absolute number* there is now a sizable middle-class, and it is growing rapidly. For example, even if the middle class makes up as little as 10 percent of the population (which I am sure could be an underestimation), in absolute number it is around 130 million, which is a third to a half of the U.S. population. It is well known that the middle class will demand a better environment, better health care, better education for their children, and a higher standard of living. All of these demands will place significant pressure on China's soft and hard infrastructure. There is no doubt in my mind that this sector of the population will significantly impact China.

Third, there is a growing private sector and it is undeniable that the wealth in the nation is slowly flowing into the hands of that sector. In fact, in my interactions with China in the past decade, I find that the percentage of friends who work for and/or started private businesses are increasing quite rapidly. For example, I was told that as high as 80 percent to 85 percent of the wealth generated in Zhejiang Province now arises from the private sector. This to me is a welcome sign not just for China but for the world as a whole.

Fourth, fast and at times uncontrolled and unstructured economic growth can bring undesirable elements to the society, such as degradation of the environment and shortage of the necessary resources to propel the growth. The former can significantly lower the quality of life and the latter could lead to conflicts, national or international.

Fifth, as in all modern nations in the 21st century, one should not rely on the inherent human instincts to be ethical. Confucius said that *"Ren Zhi Chu, Xing Ben Shan"*, or 人之初，性本善" meaning "Human at Birth is Ethical." Whether this is true or not, I argue that we should not take this chance and see how each of us may turn out in real life. To this end, modern nations must be nations of law. Some recent spectacular examples in the corporate and academic worlds clearly indicate to us "ethical indoctrination" should never be left to each individual.

I am sure that if you give yourself a few minutes of thought, you can come up with additional features confronting modern-day China. Clearly, all these challenges place enormous pressure on all levels of Chinese society. Since education, from K to infinity, is an inalienable component of Chinese society, how to respond to these pressures will and should be high on the agenda for those who have responsibilities to be the architects of Chinese higher education.

Chinese Academy of Sciences

I should point out also that there was another interesting development after the communists came into power in 1949 which I believe impacted profoundly the development of research landscapes of Chinese universities. That development was the creation of the Chinese Academy of Sciences (CAS). Without a doubt, CAS is omnipresent in the Chinese research and development landscape.

Although not entirely parallel in nature, the CAS certainly had and continues to have the flavor of the powerful Soviet (and now Russian) Academy of Sciences. CAS has research institutes in nearly all disciplines of science and technology dotting the entire country. Besides CAS, there are also academies in social as well as medical sciences. These academies also had (and continue to have) impact on the higher education landscape.

In my humble opinion, the separation of two basic and massive human organizations, universities and CAS, where both have research as part of their missions, will surely profoundly impact universities' research landscapes. Quite recently, I had the pleasure of visiting Oak Ridge National Laboratory (ORNL) in Tennessee. Perhaps the most important recent development of ORNL is that it has constructed one of the most sophisticated new generations of "Spallation Neutron Source". The price tag of this facility is in the multi-hundreds of million of dollars. With SNS, scientists in US and worldwide universities can study problems with a facility which their respective universities have no hope of ever constructing. In an analogous manner, I suspect that it is probably not possible for individual universities in China to set up a new generation of synchrotron radiation facilities. I see that there is one now under construction in CAS's Shanghai Institute of Applied Physics. Perhaps this will be the new *modus operandi* of interactions between national laboratories or CAS with universities.

I suspect that the juxtaposition of these two massive human institutions, even to this date, remains intriguing, exciting and perhaps problematic. I think that there are quite a number of such studies carried out in China that it would not be prudent of me to speculate here what that would be.

Some Observations

In this short discussion, I have only touched on the tip of the iceberg of the vast Chinese higher education. China has approximately 2,000 higher education institutions. Since the nation has a population of 1.3 billion, this is still a relatively small number. For example, if one were to go by the percentage of higher education institutions vs. population in the U.S. (around 3,500 for 300 million in population) as the norm, then China may need as many as 10,000 higher education institutions. I dare say that no country in the history of mankind has ever attempted to reach this number (nor has there been a nation on the surface of the earth with so many people). I am not sure that even with China's enormous economic expansion, this lofty goal can be attained any day soon, if ever.

However, one thing is for sure, this number almost certainly will increase with increased demands. As long as the Chinese economy continues to expand, with more and more population entering middle-class status, the number of students who intend to receive more advanced education is bound to increase. In addition, for China to become not just a nation of cheap laborers but also knowledge workers, this increase is a must. Thus, how to pay for these thousands of new institutions will be a critical issue. Also, what percentage of these institutions should become "world class universities?" What percentage of the institutions should have a specific mission, such as community colleges in the U.S.? These are all important and fundamental issues facing Chinese educators in the 21st century.

Finally, there is a trend in the U.S. which is the decrease of public support of higher education. Many state universities, even truly well-known ones, are experiencing a decrease of support of recurrent funding from the respective States. This becomes a real challenge for university administrators in the U.S.

In China, at this moment, nearly all universities (and nearly all are public) are supported close to 100 percent by the public sector (whether it be by the Ministry of Education from the Central Government, or Provincial Government or even City government and so on). In her recent visit to University of Texas at Dallas, China's Vice Minister of Education, Dr. Qidi Wu (吴启迪), gave a succinct discussion about the ambitious national funding programs known as 985 and 211 to significantly uplift the qualities of Chinese research universities. If, as I mentioned earlier, the number of institutions in China were to increase by just a factor of 2 to 3 (4,000 or 6,000), my suspicion is that these programs would be difficult to sustain. Indeed, how the public sector can or will have the financial resources to support the institutions at the current level will be a serious challenge. Does that mean that it is inevitable that the support will drop, and that it may drop quite precipitously?

Confronted by this possible eventuality, it may not be too soon to seek ways where there will be public and private partnerships. This is especially suggestive because of the increase wealth of the private sector (as I have mentioned earlier.) However, the challenge here is that the private sector in China in particular, and Asia in general, unlike its counterparts in the Western world, does not have a tradition of giving to higher education.

There is no doubt in my mind that sometime in the 21st century, China will be one of the major global economic powers. As such, China must shoulder far greater responsibilities to tackle if not solve the ills of humanity. To this end, Chinese universities, just as their counterparts in the U.S. and India, must be havens for producing global thought leaders, who could find ways to motivate their fellow human beings to seek ways to mitigate ills, right wrongs and create a better world for all mankind. Universities must be havens where all people can come and learn to work together.

Undoubtedly, in the 21st century, Chinese universities must be human organizations that will serve not just China, but the world.

(2006)

34

"Ladies and Gentlemen, there is an Eight Hundred-Pound Gorilla in the Room!"

This was a speech delivered to the River of Trade Corridor Coalition (ROTCC) National Quarterly Meeting, on March 2, 2007, at the Port of Los Angeles Board Room, St. Pedro, Los Angeles, California. The author was Special Assistant to the President for Global Strategies and International Relations and Professor of Physics, The University of Texas at Dallas.

Chairman of ROTCC the Honorary Bill Blaydes, Councilman of Dallas, the Honorable "Buddy" Villines, County Judge of Pulaski County of Arkansas, the Honorable Augustine Garcia, Director of Puerto Nuevo of Tucson, Arizona, the Honorable Steve Salazar, Councilman of Dallas, distinguished participants and elected officials from California, New Mexico, Arizona, Texas and friends from the Republic of Mexico.

I am truly honored and deeply humbled to be here today to give my personal impressions about trade between the U.S. and China in the 21st century. It is very exciting to see so many movers and shakers in the nine States, California, Arizona, New Mexico, Texas, Arkansas, Tennessee, Kentucky, Ohio, Michigan, together with our friends in Canada and the Republic of Mexico, who formed this great consortium to tackle one of the grandest opportunities North America faces: the trade between Asia Pacific and North America.

I noticed that the next great gathering of ROTCC will be in the coming June in Windsor, Canada and the host is the Honorable Eddie Francis, the Mayor. In the past two days, the members attending this meeting were given the grandest of grand tours (I might add with supreme professionalism from our hosts) of Los Angeles and Long Beach Ports. We saw for our own eyes the massive scale of these ports, the incredibly sophisticated logistics of loading, unloading and distribution of the goods to U.S., Canada and Mexico. Annually some **14 million containers (2006)** come into these two ports. These containers bring in dry and liquid bulk, automobiles and whatever.

I am sure I speak for all my colleagues that in the past two days, we felt like we all took an entire series of "Port management" courses, from 101 to 909. The best image I could form in my mind about our two days experiences is "a fire hose on a mouse!"

My friends, when we came into this magnificent building which houses the offices of the LA Port, the first thing which hit us was the large and colorful display at the entrance hall, depicting a map of North America and Asia Pacific. On the map it lists the amount of business (in dollars) coming into LA Port from top five countries in Asia. Even for the most casual observer, it cannot escape his/her notice that in 2005, after the $68.8 billion business from China, the other four countries are way down, somewhere between $10 billion to $20 billion. I learned also that the situation in LB Port is similar. So that means that the business from China alone coming into the two ports in Southern California is around $150 billion in 2006.

Indeed, if there were no China business coming to LA and LB ports, there would not be no need to have such massive ports!

This, my friends, tells me that China is unquestionably an "eight hundred pound gorilla" among the nations doing business with the U.S. Hence the title of this talk!

A Little History of China Since the "Open Door" Policy

In the last two days, I heard from various sources, from our gracious host Anthony Santich, Marketing Manager of LA Port, from Gene Pentimonti, Senior Vice President of Maersk Inc, one of the biggest shipping companies in the world, who also is responsible of Maersk Pier 400 in LA Port, and just a couple of hours ago, from the excellent presentation of Gill Hicks, CEO of Gill V. Hicks and Associates at this same podium, that it is "predicted" by 2020, the number of containers coming into the LA/LB ports will be around 40 million.

The great American baseball icon Yogi Berra once said that "**prediction is very hard, especially about the future**." That is so true! It is my humble opinion that this "prediction" of the future of LA/LB ports should be more accurately called an "extrapolation." It is based on current trends and certain assumptions, one of them must be that in Asia Pacific in general and China in particular there will be no significant social and economic changes or upheavals in the coming fifteen to twenty years.

In fact, it is very interesting to note that in his talk, Gene already underscored that in the past, there was a prediction in the 90's about the number of containers coming into LA/LB ports in 2006. Depending on who was doing the prediction, it was WRONG, an underestimation, by a factor of 2 to 3. This could serve as a warning about the possibility that the "prediction" of 2020 may/could also suffer the same fate.

All the experts agreed that if by 2020, the predicted 40 million containers became a reality, it would put enormous strain not only on LA/LB ports, but will also be nightmarish for the system to distribute them. Now imagine that if the "prediction" is wrong by a factor of 2 or 3, namely instead of 40 million containers coming to LA/LB ports, it is really 80 million to 120 million, the consequence of that could be truly frightening.

Now, if you think that is frightening, consider the following:, if the prediction is wrong in the other direction, namely by 2020, only 5 million containers come in, then the economic consequence for the U.S. in particular, the world in general, would be simply unthinkable!

Two Case Studies

Yesterday, in touring the LA/LB ports, we saw containership after containership parked along the docks. Some of these ships could accommodate up to 7,000 containers. Quite mind boggling indeed! As I mentioned earlier, what is inside the containers could be dry bulk, and when I asked what constitutes the majority shipments in the dry bulk, I was told that at the low-tech end, it could be textiles and at the high tech end, it could be all sorts of electronic gadgets.

So, "armed" with this information, allow me to give you two case studies of Chinese companies: one a textile company called **Guangyu Textile** in Wujiang, which is near Suzhou and the other an electronic company called **Huawei Technologies Inc**. in Shenzhen, which is just north of Hong Kong. Just as most Chinese companies which have every intention of breaking into the global market, Guangyu's website has both English and Chinese versions. I thought that this was indeed an excellent global business practice because this makes communications, which is the first step in any business transaction, infinitely easier.

Case Study 1: Guangyu Textile

Guangyu Textile began by two individuals, who happened to be siblings. On its website, http://www.guangyutex.com, it states the following:

> "Founded in 1995, Guangyu Enterprise still bursts with youthful spirit. We are a foreign company with self-import and export rights. To promote solidarity within Guangyu, production, processing, development, and sales are integrated into one collaborative process. Throughout the years, the Guangyu people have fully devoted themselves to the development and manufacture of novel fabrics. It is this dedication that gives the company sound repute among domestic and overseas clientele."

You can certainly tell from the tone of the language, Guangyu intends to take on the world. Indeed, in the past five years, the company's revenue has grown by at least two orders of magnitude. Today, its annual revenue is around 200 Million RMB ($1 is approximately 8 RMB). In fact, just this past year, Guangyu Textile has established a North American component headquartered in Dallas.

I should point out that the region around Suzhou, using a modern economic terminology, is unquestionably the "textile cluster industry" of China. There are probably of the order of a thousand textile companies in an area of about several hundred square miles, and the corporate size of Guangyu Textile is just about at the average.

There is no doubt in my mind that Guangyu Textile will see significant growth in the coming years.

Case Study 2: Huawei Technologies, Inc

Huawei Technologies, Inc (whose name is a short form of the Chinese phrase *Zhong Hua Ke Wei* 中华可为, or "China can do") is now a global company. Its duo-language website is http://www.huawei.com. The company began in 1985 by a group of several individuals, all very poor and one of them was a recent graduate of one of the many engineering schools in central China. Huawei Technologies, Inc also has a North American subsidiary and the headquarters is also in Dallas (in fact, to be more precise, in Plano).

Today, Huawei Technologies is without question China's largest manufacturer of telecommunications equipment with an annual revenue of $11 Billion and 44,000 employees worldwide. The company makes a broad range of products, including core voice and data switching platforms for communications service providers. Huawei also makes optical networking systems, wireless products, corporate networking equipment, and network management and messaging software. The company primarily serves such Asian carriers as China Telecom, China Unicom, and SingTel; other customers include Hutchison Telecom and Telecom Egypt. Huawei has product joint ventures with 3Com as well as manufacturers in Russia and Japan; it also has a distribution deal with IBM.

In addition, it has significantly penetrated European, South American, Middle Eastern, formerly Soviet Union as well as African (especially South Africa, Zimbabwe and Nigeria) markets. There was also a major presence of about 3000 employees of Huawei in Bangalore, but recently it was downsized and many Indian employees have moved to Shenzhen.

Lessons learned from the two Case Studies

Allow me to summarize what are some of the lessons learned from these two case studies.

First, I believe that these two companies are the tip of the iceberg of Chinese privately owned companies. There is more and more wealth in China flowing from public sectors to private sectors. Just recently, on a visit to Ningbo (which is the hometown of many Hong Kong billionaires), which is a city of a province called Zhejiang, I found out that for this province, which has a population of around 50 million people (France has 60 million) 80 percent of its wealth is now in the hands of private sectors. This tells us that to certain extend, Chinese private entrepreneurial spirit is alive, well and proliferating.

I think one should expect in the coming years, there will be a significant increase in the number of companies at the low-end of technologies, such as Guangyu Textile. Interestingly, with more and stronger internal competition, I would expect that the quality produced by these companies will also increase while the price will decrease. I do not see that there is a steadystate quality/price in the horizon in China in the foreseeable future. For Chinese entrepreneurs in this arean, the landscape is quite volatile.

I think one also should expect in China that there will be a mushrooming of more highend technology companies, such as Huawei. Since 1980, Chinese universities have increased both in numbers and quality. This is merely a result of internal stability. This means that these universities will pump out more and more well educated and globally connected students. Some of these students will be starting their own high-tech companies, which means that a certain percentage of them will become Huawei-like of the 21st century. This also means that newer and more competitive high-tech gadgets will be produced by China in the coming years!. It is interesting to ask at this point whether China will follow the Korean model, and that is some of these companies, such as Huawei, may become supergiants such as Samsung or LG. Since China is so much larger in population, speculation about this is truly intriguing, and the implications of which way China will proceed will have deep economic impact both for China and the U.S.

Thus, unless the world suffers a truly man-made catastrophic event in the coming decade, I do not see that the commercial traffic between China and the U.S. will slow down. This means that the LA and LB ports must be mentally and technologically ready for the onslaught! Jokingly, maybe we need not only LA and LB ports, but also LC, LD, LE....ports? However, there is no obvious way to tell what would be the magnitude of the business between China and the U.S. in 2020. Only time will tell. Let me paraphrase Yogi: *"Prediction of the future is accurate only if it is already the past!"*

China Foreign Reserves

Finally, I like to bring out one additional economic dimension for all to think about and that is the astronomical amount of foreign reserves China now possesses. According to the recent visit to Dallas by the former Vice Minister of Foreign Trade of China, now director of China Foreign Trade Center, the Honorable Zhang Zegang, he mentioned that the foreign reserves of China has reached $1.07 trillion. Most of the reserves, according to Mr. Zhang, are U.S. dollar-based. However, since the U.S. is only about 35 percent of global GDP, and Europe and Japan are around 20 percent and 12 percent respectively, this could imply that China could diversify its foreign reserves to be less U.S. dollar-based. What is the percentage of the reserves will be Euro and Yen based is still unknown, but the direction is quite clear.

Even not as an economist I can tell that such a move may have significant impact on U.S. economy (and business). What impact it will have on LA/LB ports, and thus the ROTCC, is also something that one should not ignore.

Summary

Ever since our nation was created in 1776, Atlantic and Pacific oceans were the moat of our castle. It protected us from enemies and allowed our nation to grow uninhibited. However, the world has now been flattened and the protection of the moat has vanished.

My friends, I hope that I have given you some of my personal and probably naïve views of what the "eight hundred pound gorilla in the room" may affect your business here in LA, LB, and the livelihood of the U.S. in particular and North America in general. What is clear is that this is truly an exciting time for all. In the coming years, there will be challenges and many will be quite severe. However, I am happy to tell you that the Chinese refer to severe challenges as "*weiji* (危机)" or "dangerous opportunities". With this in mind, this is a great time for us in the U.S. to seek all possible and innovative ways to integrate with the rest of the world and leverage such opportunities!

Thank you very much for your attention.

(2007)

35

Stealing Books is not Stealing

This was a testimony delivered in Chinese to the Chinese Academy of Sciences Academicians Round Table Forum (院士圆桌论坛) on "Constructing Innovative Nation and Workforce" (建立创新国家与人才), hosted by Shanghai Association of Science and Technology (SAST) and Municipal Government of Shanghai, on November 15, 2006, at the Conference Center of SAST, Shanghai, People's Republic of China. The author was Special Assistant to the President for Global Strategies and International Relations and Professor of Physics, The University of Texas at Dallas.

Thank you very much, Academician Shen Wenqin (沈文庆院士), for your very kind introduction. I wish my late-mother would be here to hear what you said about me.

The Honorable Vice Mayor Yan Junqi (严隽琪副市长), my distinguished colleagues on this panel, ladies and gentlemen, and through the internet participants throughout China, I am indeed honored to be invited today to participate in this important panel to discuss about innovation. In the so-called knowledge economy of the 21st century, the theme of this year's panel discussion is unquestionably a fundamental concept. Indeed, innovation is critical whether you are trying to solve the world's most profound and difficult problem, such as sustainable energy, or enhancing the economy and thus the quality-of life of as large an entity as China, or define the mission and enhance the quality of as small an entity (as compared to China) as a research university.

In all cases, innovation is the common denominator.

Today, I will discuss the issue of seeking talents for a research university with innovation.

I just had the great pleasure to hear two fabulous testimonies on the subject, delivered by two remarkable individuals.

The first was by Academician Yongfu Sun (孙永福院士), who is formerly Vice Minister of Chinese Ministry of Railways, and whose most recent notable achievement was to serve as the chief engineer responsible for the spectacularly successful construction of the arduous Qinghai-Tibet railway. I understand that the project was completed on-time and on-budget.

The second was Academician Fu-Jia Yang (杨福家院士), who is undoubtedly one of China's most notable modern higher education architects. He is a world renowned atomic and nuclear scientist, the former President of one of China's great universities, Fudan University and now the first Chinese ever in the thousand years of British higher education history (Oxford University began in the 11th century) to be appointed as the Chancellor of a UK research university, University of Nottingham.

I wonder whether it is sheer coincidence or is it preordained for China that these two great builders both have "luck" or "Fu" (福) in their names. Is China that lucky? I am not in the least surprised that these two individuals were invited to give testimonies in this panel. While the former requires *tour-de-force* innovative engineering, and the latter requires extraordinarily innovative management technologies, neither could accomplish their grand mission without "innovation," especially without significant "innovative manpower."

In the 21st century, many aspiring nations are all singing the "innovation" tune, from as large a nation as China to as small a nation as Singapore. If one looked at the economy of the world in the last several centuries, 19th century was dominated by "agriculture", 20th century "silicon" and 21st century "knowledge." In these two hundred years, one sees that global economy made the corresponding transition from "labor intensive" to "knowledge intensive". In fact, in just the last few decades, the transition was significantly accelerated due to the now ubiquitous internet! No doubt that in the 21st century, developing "innovative manpower" is more critical then ever for any entity, albeit a nation or a university.

Although research universities by no means have the stranglehold on innovations, especially producing innovative individuals (counter-examples such as Michael Dell and Bill Gates, both college dropouts, come to mind,) they are human institutions where a significant proportions of such individuals do emerge from. I dare say that no economically and intellectually aspiring nation can have higher education program that is not spectacular. Indeed, building quality research universities is de facto the first step to produce building blocks for innovations.

Building a quality research university is both easy and hard. Easy because all you have to do is to find first rate people. Hard because all you have to do is to find first rate people.

In this short time, I would like to tell you an interesting story of how my university, the University of Texas at Dallas, or UT Dallas, developed a nanotechnology program. I should say that I am not advocating nanotechnology here, but merely use this to illustrate the bigger issue of finding innovative individuals for a university. My example is merely a microcosm of the overall picture of building strengths of a research university, but it does illustrates the bigger picture.

The program I mentioned was literally developed in a very short time from scratch to having an international impact, about five to six years. Recently I told a friend that "if we could do the same 20 to 30 times, UTDallas will be the best in the world." To which my friend replied "if it can be done that easily, then all the universities in the U.S. will be Caltech!"

It should also be underscored that rapidity is in part due to the fact that we are in the "post-internet" era, an era which my good friend Jack Pellicci, former Group Vice President of Oracle corporation referred to time as "internet years (IU)," that is what can be accomplished in one IU will take at least five real years. Therefore, if developing UTDallas' nanotechnology program took five IU, in real years, it would have taken 25.

Since you all have enormous professional responsibilities, I am sure your management style will follow some general guidelines. I am no exception. The following are some of the statements uttered by well known people which I adhere to.

- **"Do more than is required of you." — General George C. Patton**
- **"First rate people invariably look for first rate people. Second rate people invariably look for third rate people." — the late Marcel**

Bardon, NSF Physics Division director (my boss when I was the Theoretical Physics Program Director of NSF in the mid-eighties. Marcel was known as a visionary science leader in the U.S.)
- "Science is People" — Alan MacDiarmid, 2000 Nobel Laureate in Chemistry (Alan is my colleague at UTDallas and a member of this Panel)
- "There are always opportunities passing through. Grab them or they are not opportunities!" T. D. Lee, 1957 Nobel Laureate in Physics
- "If I have to the opportunity to select between brilliant and lucky, I will select lucky every time!" — Author unknown.
- "Vision without funding is hallucination!" — Author unknown.

Let's see how these "mottos" work in this case.

- "Do more than is required of you." — General George C. Patton.
- "Science is People" — Alan MacDiarmid, 2000 Nobel Laureate in Chemistry (Alan is my colleague at UTDallas and a member of this Panel)
- "First rate people invariably look for first rate people. Second rate people invariably look for third rate people." — the late Marcel Bardon, NSF Physics Division director (my boss when I was the Theoretical Physics Program Director of NSF in the mid-eighties. Marcel was known as a visionary science leader in the U.S.)

To me, these are remarkable statements. What Patton implied was that to be a successful manager (or leader), you need to go well beyond what you are supposed to do, and you must do so with a passion. One must not be afraid to get his/her hands dirty, and be willing to do (far) more and the unexpected. What MacDiarmid said is that without talented people, you will not have scientific discoveries and successes. Finally, what Bardon said is that once you have world class people, they will find world class people as team members.

If one looks at any successful leaders, and certainly I put Academician Sun and Academician Yang as people who would not just do their jobs according to "job description," but innovatively and far more.

To begin my story telling, I like to first tell you a famous phrase written by one of my most favorite and great Chinese authors/philosophers of the 20th century, Lu Xun (鲁迅). Among many of the great books Lu Xun wrote, one of them was entitled Kung I-Chi, or Kong Yi-Ji (孔乙己). In the book, Kong is a down-trotted scholar, but a scholar nevertheless. Since he loves books but cannot afford to buy them, he does the next best thing, he steals it. Of course, inevitably, he is caught, and that is when to his accusers Lu Xun wrote the famous statement:

"*Taking a book can't be considered stealing [**Tou Shu Bu Suan Tou** (偷书不算偷)], . . . Taking a book, the affair of a scholar, can't be considered stealing!*"

In merely five Chinese characters, Lu Xun in his usual genius manner depicted, albeit it a little on the comical, dark and extreme side, the Chinese profound and utter love of the intellect. Well, for my story, I would like to paraphrase this wonderful statement to:

偷人才不算偷

or "stealing talents is not stealing!" A softer way to restate this would be "Attracting talents from elsewhere is an acceptable academic practice!"

I think the global scientific world today already know that the nanotechnologists of UTDallas have made profound contributions in the past several years. In fact, in December of this year, Scientific American, a globally respected science magazine has elected Ray and two of his junior scientists, Drs. Mei Zhang and Shaoli Fang, as one of the top 50 scientific groups (in all fields) in 2006. This is just one of the many accolades Ray and his team have received after they have produced some truly amazing scientific results in the past several years.

Since I am in China at the moment, I would be remiss if I did not mention that Mei and Shaoli are both originally from this country. They did their undergraduate physics studies in two of China's best universities, Nanjing University and China University of Science and Technology, respectively. Having such outstanding young scientists surrounding Ray is a clear manifestation that he is so confident in his own ability that the only people he wanted around him are people, like Mei and Shaoli who are first rate. So, how did this happen? In the year 2000, UTDallas decided to find some outstanding individual to jump start our program from zero. The candidate we identified was Ray Baughman of Honeywell International Corporation. Even though Ray was an "industrial scientist," a significant part of his research in developing new materials was funded by the Federal Government, such as DARPA, and therefore he published extensively. In recruiting this talent, I as a Vice President for Research was supposed to work, and had, hand-in-hand with the Provost, the Dean and Department Heads (in this case in physics and chemistry) and through the Department Head his faculty members to Ray. Well, as in life in general, it is never that easy. To attract Ray to Texas, we need to convince his lovely wife Karen, and also his extremely talented collaborator Anvar Zakhidov, and of course his lovely wife Nadira, and of course their lovely children. That means that many of us have to make numerous trips, almost ten, to Honeywell International Corporations, which is in Morristown, New Jersey, a long way from Texas.

So, had we not "do more than is required," not been as aggressive, well above the normal wait for him and his team to apply for the positions in UTDallas, I am confident that UTDallas would not have such a brilliant team of nanotechnologists.

- "If I have the opportunity to select between brilliant and lucky, I will select lucky every time!" — Author unknown.
- "There are always opportunities passing through. Grab them or they are not opportunities!" T. D. Lee, 1957 Nobel Laureate in Physics

You probably want to know how we zeroed in on Ray and his team?

When I accepted the position at UTDallas in late 2000, one of my given tasks was to find a way to establish a nanotechnology center, since this was, and still is, an area where all research intensive universities in the world were interested to pursue. The problem was that not being a nanotechnologist myself, I did not know anyone who had the credentials which we could "steal" (偷) to assist us to build a robust program.

Well, sheer (or dumb) luck and opportunity were at play here. The success of our story was intimately tied to two individuals: James Von

Ehr, a philanthropist and UTDallas alumnus, who had and still has great interest in developing nanotechnology in the university and Alan MacDiarmid, the 2000 Nobel laureate in chemistry, who is also a member of this distinguished panel. In the later 90's, Mr. Von Ehr had agreed to put some of his own money in assisting the university to build the program.

This is roughly how it went. Alan and I were both in Philadelphia before 2000. He was a University of Pennsylvania chemist and I was a Drexel University physicist and later a Vice President of a public company called Science Applications International Corporation. The only reason why I knew Alan was because his daughter's family is close friends of my family. In fact, Robin McConnell, his son-in-law, was the mathematics and science supervisor where my children went to secondary schools.

On a cold morning in late October of 2000, a few days after I accepted the position in UTDallas, I heard on my car radio while driving to work that Alan, MY FRIEND, had won the Nobel Prize in Chemistry! This of course led me to congratulate him immediately and also took the opportunity to invite him to give a public lecture at UTDallas. Alan graciously accepted and said that he would like to give two talks in Dallas: his Nobel acceptance speech and a technical talk on a subject which he has been devoting a great deal of his research in the past several years, **nanoelectronics!** You can imagine how awe struck I was when I learned that Alan, my friend, is a nanotechnologist of the highest caliber, and he was always "under my nose" without me knowing it!

This is what the Chinese would refer to as "as close as the eyebrow!" (近在眼前)

I immediately took the opportunity to ask Alan to help me to identify a person whom UTDallas could steal (偷). He then told me that since Honeywell and General Electric at the end of the 20th century were seriously negotiating a merger, he believed that his good friend Ray Baughman may be available. Alan then further informed Ray about UTDallas' intention.

To move forward, a team of administrators in UTDallas worked seamlessly together. This includes the Provost, the former Dean of Science, Dr. Richard Caldwell and Head of the Chemistry Department, Dr. John Ferraris and Head of the Physics Department, Dr. Rod Heelis.

In fact, unbeknownst to me, for several years already, Ray was one of the scientists which Dr. Ferraris had interest in recruiting him to be the prestigious Robert A. Welch Chair Professor of Chemistry.

Since Alan will be speaking soon, let me not say more about him, other than to say that a year after Ray and his team moved to UTDallas, Alan decided to come as well. In this case, Mr. Von Ehr agreed to put additional money to set up the James Von Ehr Distinguished Chair in Science and Technology and Alan is the first recipient of this position.

The rest, as the old saying goes, is history.

"Vision without funding is hallucination!" — Author unknown.

I should say that building a world class program in nanotechnology with outstanding people is expensive. In order not to "hallucinate", besides the important assistance from James Von Ehr, the University also put into the program significant resources to, for example, convert some dilapidated space into modern research laboratories, and to buy some of the up-to-date facilities.

However, even that is not sufficient. Therefore, working with one of the most visionary political leaders in Texas, the senior Senator from Texas, Senator Kay Bailey Hutchison, UTDallas formed a consortium with powerful research universities in Texas, first the University of Texas at Austin, Rice University and Air Force Material Research Laboratories in Dayton, Ohio, and later with the University of Texas at Arlington and University of Houston. Also, to a lesser extent, we also included the University of Texas at Brownsville and University of Texas at PanAm. We call it Strategic Partnership for Research in Nanotechnology (SPRING). Between 2002–2006, nearly $40 million was generated for these universities in nanotechnology.

I think that the scientific discoveries emerging from these universities, and the accolades scientists from the collaborations received nationally and internationally tell us that this is indeed good science that money can *buy*!

Hence, this was not a hallucination!

Summary

So, ladies and gentlemen, let me make a few comments.

I think you have to agree that the process I described in UTDallas developing a nanotechnology program did follow very closely the mottos I outlined. Indeed, there were many seemingly unrelated dots at play here. If we were unable to connect them, it would simply be unrelated dots! So, connecting these dots was the fundamental of our success. I am sure that this is a general principle.

Also, I have described for you is that building a world class research program can be deeply satisfying. I would say that as a university administration, there is nothing more satisfying is to see something great like this happening during one's watch! Finally, I am sure you have noticed that I have peppered the word "steal" throughout this discussion. Quite recently, there is a great deal of discussion about China making an effort to "recruit" outstanding individuals from abroad to come to China. The most spectacular example for me is Professor Andrew Yao, the distinguished computer scientist from Princeton who is now with Tsinghua University in Beijing. I should add a word of caution here. "Stealing" or "recruiting" can certainly go both ways. I can assure you that soon, if not already, universities outside of China will be raiding outstanding individuals in China! This is the nature of the business.

Thank you very much for your attention.

(2006)

36

China's "The Great Accelerator": A Decision of Science and Politics?

The author was inspired to write this piece after having attended the "Conference on 60 Years of Yang-Mills Gauge Field Theories: C N Yang Contributions to Physics" held from 25th to 28th May 2015 in Singapore, when he was Director of Global Affairs and Special Advisor to the Rector of the University of Macau.

Ever since I arrived at National Tsing Hua University in March of 2011, I began to hear rumors that Chinese scientists were contemplating constructing the next generation CERN (*Organisation européenne pour la recherche nucléaire*) facility, known as "the Great Accelerator". This idea surfaced into the open on February 23rd of 2015 when a group of top mathematicians and physicists from around the world came to Beijing and brainstormed on "new physics beyond the Higgs!"

As reported by the Chinese Academy of Sciences, perhaps the most important outcome of this meeting (http://english.ihep.cas.cn/prs/ns/201402/t20140224_116826.html) was that "the main physics objectives of the future high energy circular accelerator are the precise measurement of Higgs properties as well as exploring the more elementary physics laws beyond the Standard Model." Such an exploration would need a facility significantly more powerful than what CERN could provide. To do so, David Gross, the 2004 Nobel Laureate in Physics mentioned at the meeting that "the Great Accelerator" could be compared to the Great Wall of China. If China built the collider, scientists from around the world would join and work together. New breakthroughs and discoveries could be achieved in the future.

In another meeting at Singapore's Nanyang Technological University, from May 25th-28th the same year celebrating "60 Years of Yang-Mills

Gauge Field Theories", a meeting at which I was honored to be one of the International Organizers, I had the pleasure of hearing some of the major proponents of China's "the Great Accelerator" — the Director of the Institute of High Energy Physics, Academician Wang Yifang (王贻芳), and Professor David Gross — reiterate their strong support of the possibility of China building such a machine.

Having read about the Beijing meeting in detail and then listening to Wang and Gross in Singapore, I could not help but have some thoughts about this effort.

To explore and understand our universe is surely one of the quests of humanity. Such a quest existed not just in ancient Western times, but also in ancient Eastern times. To this end, there is no doubt that as one of the major countries in the world today, rich in intellectual achievements and now financially becoming stronger and stronger by the day, China should shoulder significant responsibilities in trying to understanding the fundamental mechanism of our universe.

In this area of Physics, it is natural that for the construction of "the Great Accelerator", there are two facilities that the decision makers in China could consider. One is a successful effort, namely CERN of Europe, and the other is a failed effort, namely the SUPERCONDUCTING SUPER COLLIDER (SSC) of the U.S.

Perhaps because no single nation in Europe was powerful enough to "nationally" construct the CERN facility, it became a multi-national European effort. The U.S., in the 80s and especially 90s, was the sole "superpower" of the world. It was probably beyond the leaders of the U.S., political and scientific, to conceptually think "internationally". After all, if the U.S. could reach the moon by itself, why would it construct the largest Physics machine in collaboration with other nations? This was especially so because its neighbors in North America are in no way to play a significant role. It was interesting to note that by the time political support behind the SSC vanished, all it took was one vote from the U.S. Congress to close it. In my opinion, while there was a multitude of reasons why the SSC failed, I am convinced that not being an international effort certainly contributed to its demise!

With these two examples as underpinnings, how should China view the construction of "the Great Accelerator"? Several interesting questions come to mind. First, should "the Great Accelerator" be a national or international effort? Second, what should the venue be?

Asia Pacific in many ways resembles both North America and Europe. Asia Pacific has three nations which are similar in economic and technological prowess. They are China, Japan and Korea. This is similar to Europe, whose so-called EFG, or England, France and Germany, are nearly equal in the same dimensions. However, unlike Europe, in Asia Pacific, population wise, China is the dominant nation. This makes it more like the U.S. in North America. Therefore, in deciding to construct "the Great Accelerator", whether China should consider the CERN model or the SSC model is an undeniably intriguing question.

I think the lesson from CERN implies that having an "international" effort is preferred for "the Great Accelerator". As far as Physics and technological advancements are concerned, CERN's model certainly manifested its strengths. After all, it is not only great Physics that has emerged from the facility, such as the recent discovery of the Higgs boson, but also great technology impacting humanity in general, such as the World Wide Web, which has its genesis there as well. Of course, it would be remiss not to mention that if the SSC had been constructed, similar great results probably would have been achieved.

Constructing the next-generation CERN machine, "the Great Accelerator", is a colossal intellectual and technological endeavor. The funding required for the project is undoubtedly enormous, usually in the many many billions of dollars (U.S.), and the demanding technical components, much of which probably do not exist today, would require many years of research to accomplish. The large amount of funding would inevitably become a political issue as well.

China as a fast rising economic power could probably handle the funding by itself. But here lies the lesson of the SSC for China. If ever, like the U.S., China has internal voices against such a massive undertaking, having only a national flavor could result in the project meeting the same fate as in the U.S. In today's China, which is becoming more and more open, the days when leaders from the top could nearly single-handedly demand the construction of such a facility are over. Hence, the danger of the effort being stopped politically, just like in the U.S., is not an impossibility in today's China!

But to engage in the project internationally, Europe has one element which nations in Asia Pacific does not seem to have naturally. Namely, Europe has an economically and technologically strong but small neutral nation — Switzerland. The nation of Switzerland is so neutral that even during WWII, it remained outside the conflict. I am sure one of the reasons for CERN choosing Geneva as its location and not London, Paris or somewhere in Germany, was precisely because EFG could accept Switzerland.

In Asia Pacific, there is no Switzerland equivalent. When I was in Taiwan, I have given thought to the idea that Taiwan could be such a venue for "the Great Accelerator". I think, in this respect, that Taiwan is as close to Switzerland in Europe as one can find in Asia Pacific. After all, China, Japan and Korea may probably all accept Taiwan as a venue. However, there are two reasons why Taiwan would be a near impossibility. First, I do not think there is land in Taiwan to construct a nearly 100-kilometer circumference for the collider tunnel without the government exercising significant "eminent domain!" In Taiwan, it will take infinite time for such a government effort. Second, the Cross-Straits politics between the Mainland and Taiwan will also make such an endeavor extremely problematic. However, if there is one effort that could change the Cross-Straits impasse, this might just be the one.

Finally, I cannot help but to say that it is somewhat interesting, if not misleading for David Gross, one of the greatest theoretical physicists of our times, to say that constructing "the Great Accelerator" is equivalent to the construction of the Great Wall. While this analogy on the surface may seem heart-throbbing, in reality, the Great Wall of China did not fulfill its original intention, namely it did not stop the northern hordes from invading China. The only thing it did is to become a modern-day tourist attraction bringing China much financial resource today. Ironically, some of those resources could even be leveraged to construct "the Great Accelerator"!

In summary, from the Chinese perspective, construction of "the Great Accelerator" could be viewed as the third phase of the science and technology development of the nation. The first phase was in 1978 when China adopted a new "open door" policy to reconstruct the nation from the devastation it suffered during 10 years of Cultural Revolution. The second phase was in the post-June 4th 1989 era of the 1990s all the way to the modern day where China is reaching new scientific heights. With the construction of "the Great Accelerator", whether it is done nationally or internationally, the Chinese scientific communities could be seen as truly merging into the global landscape. As a whole, this can only be a positive outcome for humanity.

(2015)

On Israel

37

"Because We Have Seven World Class Universities!"

This was the speech made during the visit of the University of Macau delegation to Israeli universities in 2014. The author was Special Assistant to the Rector (President) and Director of Global Affairs, The University of Macau.

Preamble

In 1993, when the former and late Prime Minister of Israel Itzhak Rabin was visiting China, he was awkwardly asked why his nation who is severely resources challenged could become the breadbasket and technology haven of the region. Without the slightest hesitation, he answered **"Because we have seven world class universities!"**

Despite the fact that in the 21st century, for a small country and a small number of universities, research faculty members in these universities were awarded 8 Nobel prizes, Rabin's answer was undoubtedly the true motivation as to why the University of Macau with aspiration launched its new and far-reaching global strategy by making its first "pilgrimage" to the holy-land to visit some of these universities. What Israel has demonstrated to the world that any country or region, large or small, who intends to promote the meaningful national ambiance and be highly competitive in the 21st century, creating and maintaining high quality and relevant educational institutions is a MUST and NOT a luxury.

For the University of Macau which intends to someday stand among the ranks of global great and relevant universities, it must inherently understand how to create and sustain ER (education and research) greatness! With that as preamble, Rector Wei Zhao and his delegation can think of no better country to visit than Israel!

So, from December 26, 2014 through January 2, the University of Macau delegation visited Israel. Besides Rector Wei Zhao (赵伟) and I, the delegation members consist of the Dean of Science and Technology Philip Chen (陈俊龙), the Dean of Social Science Yiufan Hao (郝雨凡), and the Dean and Associate Dean of Health Science, Chuxia Deng (邓初夏) and Wei Ge (葛伟), respectively. Patrick Lou (庐柏廉) from the office of Global Affairs accompanied us and literally took care of all the logistics. Without Patrick's paying meticulous attention to all the details from start to finish, I could imagine that the visit could be a nightmare.

The Campuses of Israeli Universities

Given our planned visit was four days only, we originally intended tovisit two of the seven Israeli universities : Weizmann Institute of Science and Technion-Israel Institute of Technology. In the end, the enormous interest arising from the Israeli end made us readjust our extremely tight schedule to include two others: the University of Tel Aviv and the Hebrew University of Jerusalem. In fact, we even squeezed out a breakfast meeting with the Director of Research Office & Global Engagement of a private university, the Interdisciplinary Center (IDC). So it was absolutely wall-to-wall in our four days in Israel! Except for Tel Aviv University, which unfortunately we arrived after dark, we were able to have a detailed survey of the landscapes of Weizmann Institute of Science, Hebrew University's Mount Scopus campus and Technion. Without the slightest exaggeration, these campuses were simply stunning. They have very well-manicured lawns, stunning architecture buildings and dotted with meaningful statues. In Technion's campus, we were very impressed that every tree had a small water tube attached to it. This way, each tree could get the necessary "refreshment" to grow and yet no water, which is precious in Israel, is wasted. What an amazing way to utilize limited resources for maximum usage! I wonder whether that implies that on each campus there is a person who serves as its "gardener?" If so, this is surely something universities in greater Chinese should take note!

On Mount Scopus campus of Hebrew University there is a spot which overlooks the entire glorious landscape of Jerusalem, with the *Dome of the Rock* shinning right in the center! I cannot think of another campus in the world that can claim to have such a magnificent sight!

A view from Hebrew University Mount Scopus Campus

Except for the ever presence of Hebrew signs, one could easily mistake these campuses as the modern campuses of the University of California. In fact, the drive from Tel Aviv to Haifa and Technion, I could easily be convinced that what I saw were California's coastline and UC Santa Barbara or UC San Diego.

California coastline? No! On our way to Haifa!

Meeting with Presidents and Rectors

In quality and substance, I cannot think of better and higher quality receptions we received from these four universities. At Weizmann Institute and Technion, our primary hosts were President Daniel Zajfman and President Peretz Lavie, respectively. At Tel Aviv University and Hebrew University, our hosts were Rector Aaron Shai and Rector Asher Cohen, respectively. It should be noted, in Israel a Rector is more or less equivalent to the Provost position in a US university. Unquestionably, all were men of great intellectual and administrative distinction.

I must add how happy I was when at dinner in Haifa, I met my good friend Yitzhak Apeloig and his wife. Yitzhak was the predecessor of Peretz Lavie and was the one who assisted me in developing close relationship with Technion.

We were treated to a host of interesting and succinct comments about running university by President Zajfman. For example, when asked what the strategy of Weizmann Institute was, his answer was quick: "*the Weizmann Institute has no specific strategy, other than to promote the best science.*" Perhaps the most stunning and in hindsight transparently obvious comment he made was "*In Weizmann, we do not ask how good the science is, we only ask how good the scientist is!*"

President Zajfman with the delegation

Meeting with President Peretz Lavin was equally enlightening. The most memorable quote he made about how a university could be considered as great is *"how relevant it is to the nation!"* Under his leadership, Technion has established two highly visible global initiatives: Jacobs Technion-Cornell Institute in New York City and the Technion-Guangdong Institute of Technology in Shantou China. Both initiatives require a great deal of intellectual and political skills. More important, both initiatives show that Technion is constantly seeking opportunities and is ready and act swiftly when an opportunity arises!

President Lavie explaining to us Technion's mission

Just like all universities in the world, Israeli universities do engage in "coopetition" with one another. However, I was startled to read from a Technion promotion publication, President Daniel Zajfman said that *"There are few institutions like the Technion that can demonstrate so clearly their profound influence on the development of a country."* To display such eloquent professionalism from one president to another university is something I seldom, if ever, see in higher education landscape, Asian or otherwise!

Technology Transfer

Both Weizmann Institute and Technion have palpable, robust and world renowned technology transfer engines. In Weizmann Institute, the engine is known as YEDA and in Technion it is known as T3. Both are "for profit" companies, operated within the affiliated universities, to carry out technology transfer operations such as patents and commercialization. In examining the surroundings of Weizmann Institute and Technion, we noticed the presence of large number of small and large technology companies. Near Weizmann, they were mostly biotech companies (reminded me of La Jolla, San Diego) and near Technion, they were mostly IT related companies. This implies to us that the liaison between YEDA and T3 with entrepreneurs must be extraordinarily close. Likewise, the companies surrounding the universities must see them as sources of high quality human resources and knowledge!

Last year, at the National Tsing Hua University — Israel conference on biotechnology, I listened to a great presentation by Professor Ruth Arnon, President of the Israel Academy of Sciences and Humanities and Paul Ehrlich Professor of Immunology of the Weizmann on the incredible science of understanding multiple sclerosis. This time, the most stunning thing we learned in Weizmann was how it commercialized the "blockbuster drug" known as Copaxone®, which is based entirely on the discovery of Professor Arnon and is licensed to Teva Pharmaceuticals Ltd. In 2007, Copaxone's® global market share was 34 percent and sales was $US 1.7 Billion. In fact, a significant fraction of the $3 billion endowment of the Weizmann Institute is a result of its commercialization effort. In Asia, commercialization has become a buzz word in academic circles. What is unfortunate is that one hears often from government policy makers that universities, especially public ones, need to "repay" society. One form of repayment is to encourage commercialization, which also means that the kind of research should or must be conducive to commercialization.

You would think that with enormous technology transfer successes in all Israeli universities, the administration will strongly encourage, if not strong-armed researchers to do the kind of research with commercialization as their goal! On the contrary, in our discussions with the leaders, they made it abundantly clear to us that universities need to do the best possible science and let commercialization takes care of itself. As I mentioned before, Zajfman's comment that *"In Weizmann, we do not ask how good the science is, we only ask how good the scientist is!"* shows how deeply these leaders understand that "commercialization" should not be the preamble of "research." It seems to me, to achieve greatness, this is an important lesson we could learn!

Meeting the three Israeli Nobel laureates

In our four intense days of meetings at the four universities, we met a cadre of outstanding researchers. They represented disciplines as disparate as "U.S. Asia polices" to "drug discovery." We are also greatly honored that three of the four Nobel laureates in chemistry were available to have discussions with us. They were:

- **Aaron Ciechanover** of the Technion. Aaron received the 2004 Nobel Prize in chemistry *"for the discovery of ubiquitin-mediated protein degradation."*
- **Daniel Shechtman** of the Technion. Daniel received the 2011 Nobel Prize in chemistry *"for the discovery of quasicrystals."*
- **Ada Yonath** of the Weizmann Institute. Ada received the 2009 Nobel Prize in chemistry *"for studies of the structure and function of the ribosome."*

"Because We Have Seven World Class Universities!" 323

Aaron Ciechanover and the group in his lab!

Dinner with Yitzhak Apeloig, Peretz Lavie of Technion and Nobel Laureate

Daniel Shechtman and their lovely spouses.

Ada Yonath with the delegation!

Since all three are well known to us (especially Aaron and Ada,) our discussion concentrates on their attitude towards science and scientific education. For example, when Ada was asked what recommendation she would give to a fledgling university such as the University of Macau, her answer was quick and swift. "**Concentrate on the basics**!" She reiterated the theme we heard over and over again from everyone, which is if one concentrates on "doing the best science," good things will emerge from it directly or indirectly.

Perhaps what was most obvious to all of us was that despite the fact that they have received the highest scientific accolades, they all treat their colleagues with reverence. This was manifestly obvious when Ada entered the room when another colleague was speaking to us. Without fanfare, she sat down, picked up a piece of fruit on the table and munch it, and wait quietly for the speaker to finish. Likewise, when Aaron could have gone on much longer in his discussion with us, he stopped and said "I should not take time away from my colleagues!" These are small gestures, but they reveal the respectful ambiance of the intellectual community of Israel. Indeed, respect of one another need not be a manifestation of capitulation!

We are all pleased to learn from Dan Shechtman that soon he will be the President of the Guangdong Technion Institute of Technology in Shantou which I mentioned earlier. I jokingly asked Shechtman *"are you ready for China?"* With confidence oozing out, his immediate reply was *"is China ready for me!"* I should add that such confidence was quite pervasive!

Epilogue

As I have mentioned in the beginning of this report that the comment of Itzhak Rabin was the motivation for us to visit Israel. In reflection, I believe every member of the University of Macau was convinced that this was indeed the right motivation.

There is another thing we observed which we did not expect. From our discussions and from the body language, it is quite obvious that the interest in Asia Pacific for the Israeli communities was real. With such interest, I felt that the time is ready for Israel and Asia Pacific intellectual communities to establish long, meaningful and sustainable relationship. Israelis are known as much for its tenacity as they are for their humor. The best line which combines their humor and interest in Asia is the one by President Peretz Lavie. After his discussion about Technion's collaboration with China, he said with a wink that **"together, China and Israel make up one quarter of the world's population!"**

The moment we entered Hebrew U, we encountered a wall with 9 photos of its distinguished alumni and 1 Founder. The Founder was Albert Einstein. All are Nobel Laureates, including our two friends, Aaron Ciechanover, now at Technion and Ada Yonath, now at Weizmann Institute!

(2014)

38

On Aaron Ciechanover

Below are two writings on Aaron Ciechanover, one written in 2007, when the author visited Kaifeng, China with him on April 14–16, and the other in 2014, a speech the author delivered at the Board of Trustees Meeting of Shantou University. The author was Vice President for Research and Graduate Education at The University of Texas at Dallas in 2007, and Senior Vice President, Global Strategy, Planning and Evaluation, National Tsing Hua University, Hsinchu in 2014.

I

In Search of Jewish Heritage in China: A Visit with Aaron Ciechanover of the Technion to Kaifeng (开封)

Nearly 20 years ago, my good friend Professor Joseph Birman of the City University of New York, a prominent theoretical physicist, mentioned to me in passing that "there is a Jewish legacy" in a city called "Kaifeng", which is in Henan Province (河南) of China. Having never heard of it my entire life until then, I thought he was kidding. His comment prompted me to find out more about this unusual legacy (to say the least) and to my surprise, it was indeed true. However, since I have had no connection to Kaifeng, nor to Henan Province, throughout my 102 trips to China, I never thought of visiting the city.

The opportunity came when the following two serendipitous occurrences happened all at once.

First, I was invited to be the Vice Chairman of the Britton Chance Center for Biomedical Photonics of Huazhong University of Science and Technology (华中科技大学) at Wuhan (武汉). Wuhan is the Provincial Capitol of Hubei (湖北) Province, a province which is directly south of Henan Province, and is 400 miles South of Keifang. It was planned since the fall of 2006 that on April 12 and 13 of 2007, the Board would hold its meeting in Wuhan. The proximity of Keifeng to Wuhan spurred my interest in trying to visit the city.

Second, what really tipped me over was that one of the Board members is Professor Aaron Ciechanover, who is not only the 2004 Nobel Laureate in Chemistry, but in this context it is more important that he is a Professor from Technion, Israel Institute of Technology. Aaron is a man who profoundly holds his Jewishness. Apparently he, like me, has heard about the Kaifeng legacy. This legacy was just too much for him to leave unexplored. Thus when trying to set up his trip to Wuhan, he informed me and Professor Qingming Luo (骆清铭), the Director of Britton Chance Center, that despite his unbelievably stressed schedule, he absolutely wanted to spend a few days in Kaifeng in order to explore this Jewish legacy.

Qingming, who is almost a magician when comes to organizational ability, was able to assist us to connect with the leadership of Henan University in Kaifeng. Thus, our visit to Kaifeng was officially hosted by Henan University, one of the best comprehensive universities with 40,000 students in Henan Province. Qingming even asked two of his most able assistances, Hua Shi and Dawson Han, to accompany us to Kaifeng. In fact, Dawson went to Kaifeng two days earlier to make sure that all the logistics were organized perfectly, and indeed it was perfect.

There is another important component in our visit to Kaifeng and that is Professor Xu Xin (徐新), of Nanjing University. Since March of 2004, when I became an Honorary Trustee of Nanjing University, I became very sensitive to the information coming out of that university. About three months ago, when I realized that we were about to go to Kaifeng, I recalled vaguely that about a year ago, one of Nanjing University's (南京大学) faculty members had received an honorary doctorate from Bar-Ilan University in Israel. While I was fascinated by that information then, I did not act on it. Now I still was, and did. Thus, by Googling "Nanjing, Bar Ilan University," I immediately was able to learn that that individual is Xu Xin, a distinguished professor and Director of the Institute of Judaic Studies of Nanjing University. In the past 18 years, Xu had unquestionably become a top authority of Judaic studies in China. His extensive visits to the U.S. had made him many friends, and many of them are truly prominent Jewish leaders, such as Diana and Guilford Glazers of

Los Angeles. In fact the Institute in Nanjing is named after the Glazers. What is even more interesting is that one of his former postdoctoral fellows in this "unusual" area of research in China is Professor Zhang Qianhong (张倩红), who is Dean of the College of History and Culture of Henan University in Kaifeng, and herself now a distinguished researcher on Jewish culture in China.

The author with Professor Zhang Qianhong (张倩红) and Aaron Ciechanover
at the Institute of Jewish Studies, Henan University

According to Xu, there are now 11 Judaic Research Centers scattered among Chinese universities.

On April 14th, Aaron, myself and Hua Shi arrived in Kaifeng after a seven-hour drive from Wuhan. We were met by Professor Xu Xin who took time out from a Conference he was attending in Beijing and came specifically to meet with Aaron and me, and also Dawson.

Thus the stage was set for the visit.

Jewish Legacy

There is absolute certainty from historic relics that via the Silk Route, Jews traveled arduously all the way from the Holy Land to China in the 10th century and settled in Kaifeng. At that time, China was ruled by the all-powerful Sung Dynasty, and the Capital City was Kaifeng. It was a time when great commercial products and technology were developed. In fact, it was this time that gun powder was invented and it was for the first time that paper money was used. Presumably because of the great commercial activities, and Jews being truly outstanding entrepreneurs, they found Kaifeng most pleasing to them and thus stayed.

Aaron enjoying a "kosher" meal in a Jewish Family in Kaifeng

Not only did they stay, but they stayed for a very long time. According to Xu, at their peak, there were more then 5,000 Jews living in Kaifeng. There were synagogues and flourishing Jewish traditions and active cultural life in this city. What is most interesting is that despite the fact that they had very different ways of life from local Chinese, there was no hint, according to Professor Xu, of the slightest sense of anti-Semitism in China. The Chinese completely accepted the Jews, their ways of life and their culture. Thus, for 700 years, until the Qing dynasty shut the door of China to the outside world, Jews from the Middle-East continued to come to China, especially Kaifeng. Indeed, they flourished in China.

Unfortunately, since the closed-door policy was instituted, the number of Jews in China began to dwindle. Coupled with the fact that great turmoil occurred in China in the 19th and 20th centuries, the Jewish community virtually disappeared from Kaifeng. Indeed, if one were to take a nonchalant visit to Kaifeng today, without expert guides like Xu and Zhang, there is no way that one would know that deeply buried in this city, there was once a flourishing Jewish cultural life, community and heritage.

In fact, by now, there is at best only very thin evidence that Jews were here at all at one time. Aaron and I saw a little bit of that when on the evening when we arrived in Kaifeng, we were invited to dinner by a Zhao family (whom Dawson knew) which was one of the 10 or so families with direct Jewish lineage. This family lives a Spartan lifestyle and it is obvious that they are not well-to-do. Yet, Aaron and I, especially Aaron, were so overwhelmed by their hospitality; dinner consisted of 10 courses, with one of them akin to *matzos*. This was simply because they realized that Aaron came from the Holy Land. Interestingly, it was not until we were ready to depart that they found out Aaron was a Nobel Laureate! That apparently was less important to them then the fact that Aaron was a Jew.

By the way, it is interesting that this Jewish family has the family name Zhao. This was because the Sung Dynasty was ruled by the Zhao family (the first emperor of the Sung Dynasty was Zhao Kuan-Yin 赵匡胤). The Jews were allowed seven Chinese family names and one of them is "Zhao"!

Although nowadays the Zhao family does celebrate Jewish holidays, such as Passover, we suspect that they were taught more recently by Jews visiting them from the West in recent times. Still, their desire to identify themselves as "Jewish" was indeed palpable!

Henan University

With Aaron being a Nobel Laureate in Chemistry, Henan University, our host, naturally did not let the opportunity slip by. They organized a public lecture by Aaron. Even though our visit was on a Sunday, the lecture was attended by well over 500 enthusiastic students and faculty. Aaron could have been a rock concert star!

Still, I would say that the highlight of our visit was to the Jewish Research Center of Professor Zhang Qianhong. Both Aaron and I were impressed by the fact that there are 11 graduate students studying for the master degree. As in most Chinese universities, these students were very shy. When Aaron and I were taken to the library of the Center (which has only several thousand books about Judaism), this group of students, who were very interested in meeting Aaron, were quietly standing in the hallway hoping to get a glimpse of this great scientist. Once I noticed them, I invited them in to meet with Aaron. Aaron took the opportunity to ask each and everyone what they were working on. One of them, for example, is working on the "displaced Jews after the holocaust!" However, all were a little on the dismayed side because they do not have access to sufficient literature to carry out their research. For this reason, one of them told us, with sparkle in her eyes, that she had won a scholarship to go to "the Hebrew University" for eight months in the Fall of 2007!

To say that the meeting with Aaron "made their day, or year", would be an understatement!

I took the opportunity to tell them that without knowing it, they could be an extremely important group of intellectuals in China in the 21st century. This is because China and the U.S. will be two of the most important nations in this century. The influence of the Jewish community in the U.S., albeit intellectually, economically or politically, is profound. Therefore understanding the Jewish heritage could be exceedingly important for China in order to appreciate the mood of United States, directly or indirectly, as a nation. Since this group of students, for whatever reason or reasons, have chosen to study in an area that few are studying in China, their appreciation and understanding of the Jewish heritage can and will have profound impact in the relationship between China and the United States.

I could see that they all lit up after my comment.

Our visit to Kaifeng was, as Aaron would say, "unbelievable and unforgettable!"

(2007)

II

"My culture and my people always stand before my professional career!"

Aaron Ciechanover, Technion
2004 Nobel Laureate in Chemistry

The honorable Mr. Li Ka-Sheng (李嘉诚), fellow members of Shantou University Board of Trustees, ladies and gentlemen, good morning.

If I am not mistaken, this is my eighth year attending the Board meeting. Using an old cliché, what I have learned is the year-by-year improvement of the university in its understanding of the inherent meaning of education. Indeed, how lucky it is for students of this exciting university.

In my opinion, 2013/2014 could very well be a watershed moment for Shantou University (汕头大学). I learned that Shantou University and the Technion – Israel Institute of Technology are establishing a most unusual collaboration, which is that through the Li Ka-Shing Foundation's funding of $120 million (U.S.), these two universities are co-sponsoring the establishment of the Guangdong-Technion, Israel Institute of Technology in Shantou.

I have to admit that I was quite startled to learn from Provost Gu Peihua (顾佩华) just now that China is somewhat unfamiliar with the Technion. Since I have had considerable experiences collaborating and dealing with the Technion, please allow me to say a few words here as supplement to your discussion.

When I was still a second year graduate student at the University of Minnesota, I took a course which all graduate students, especially those intending to become theoretical physicists, need to master. The title of the course is "Relativistic Quantum Field Theory." To our surprise, the instructor Professor Jonathan Rosner was not that much older than us students! (Rosner left the University of Minnesota a few years later and is now a world-renowned elementary particle physics professor at the University of Chicago!) I recall in one of the breaks of the class, I had a chance to casually talk to him. I asked him why he had gone to a university which I had not heard of as a Postdoctoral Fellow. His answer was crisp and clear, "I am Jewish, so I went to Israel's Tel Aviv University. Israel has some of the best schools in theoretical physics, and the other one is the Technion!" Dear Mr. Li, it was from that day onwards, that Technion was seared into my cognizance!

Quite by serendipity, in the year before China's Xin-Hai Revolution (辛亥革命 1911), the greatest physicist of the 20th century, Albert Einstein, established in Haifa the Technion, and Technion has been pursuing "excellence" ever since! Compared to China in any dimensions, Israel is a small nation. Yet, Mr. Lee and members of Shantou University's Board of Trustees, as far as education is concerned, it is as large as any nation in the world. When the late Itzhak Rabin, the former Prime Minister of Israel, visited Fudan University (复旦大学) in 1993, the President of Fudan then, who was Academician Fu-Jia Yang who's sitting here as a Board member of Shantou University, asked Mr. Rabin how without a drop of oil underground and with most of the land of Israel being desert, could Israel become the high-tech heaven and bread basket of the Middle East. Without the slightest hesitation, Mr. Rabin said: "Because we have 7 world class universities in Israel!" I think there cannot be a clearer and more succinct comment from a national leader expounding education as the foundation in nation building. We can only hope that Asian political leaders can be just as clear when asked the same question!

Dear Mr. Lee, I think the collaboration between Shantou University and Technion could be considered the third collaboration between Chinese and Jews in this millennium.

The first is during the Southern-Sung Dynasty, where in the capital city Kaifeng there was a large Jewish community. According to history, these Jews came to China via the Silk Road to engage in business enterprise.

The second time was when the Nazis were committing the crime against humanity on the Jews in Europe; China provided safe haven to a significant number of them.

Last but not least, Mr. Lee and members of the Board, the 2004 Nobel Prize winner in Chemistry, Professor Aaron Ciechanover is a very good friend of mine. Aaron is a straight talker. In 2007, he and I went to Kaifeng specifically to "seek his roots." I recall asking him: "Aren't you too busy to do this?"

Without any hesitation Aaron said that "My culture and my people always stand before my professional career!" Mr. Lee and Fellow Board members, these are indeed monumental words.

(2014)

On Russia

39

"If He is the Best, Give it to Him" (Nikita Kruschedov): On Why the Russians are so Good in Science

This was a speech to the Partnerships for International Research and Education, at the "GIREDMET-MISA-UTDallas Alliance: A Precursor to Greater Moscow-Metroplex Intellectual and Economic Alliance in the 21st century?" conference, held on January 18, 2007, at the Moscow State Institute of Steel and Alloys (MISA) and Federal State Research and Design Institute of Rare Metal Industry of Federal State Unitary Enterprise (GIREDMET) Moscow, Russia. The author was Special Assistant to the President on Global Strategies and International Relations, and Professor of Physics, The University of Texas at Dallas.

"If he is the best, give it to him!"

Famous words of Nikita Khrushchev, after he was asked by the Judges of the Tchaikovsky International Piano competition in 1958 whether it was all right to give the award to Van Cliburn, who is, of course, a Texan.

"I hope from now on, MISA and GIREDMET can consider UTD as their window to the Metroplex in particular and Texas and the U.S. in general and UTD can consider our Russian counterparts as its window to Moscow in particular, and Russia and CIS in general."

"Science of Russia became my *scientific soul* ever since I embarked on my career. In fact, few countries in the world I can make such a statement."

Both quotes from the author, Feng Da Hsuan

Preamble

Dr. Yuri Karabasov, Rector of MISA, Dr. Yuri Parkhomenko, Director of GIREDMET, Dr. Vsevilod Ufimtsev, Dr. Evgeny Levashov, Dr. Mikhail Astakhov, scientific and administrative leaders from MISA and GIREDMET, my three distinguished colleagues, Ray Baughman, Austin Cunningham and Anvar Zakhidov from the University of Texas at Dallas, or UTD, ladies and gentlemen and most important of all, students of MISA, my name is Da Hsuan Feng and currently I am the Special Assistant to President David Daniel of UTD on Global Strategies and International Relations. In this capacity, I bring you his best wishes and warmest regards.

Today, I also want to bring you the enthusiasm and excitement in UTD regarding our Alliance with one of Russia's most prominent research universities and research institutes, Moscow State Institute of Steel and Alloys, or MISA and State Research Institute of Materials, or GIREDMET, respectively. Since this speech will also serve as a report of our delegation to UTD and Dallas communities, I want also to take this opportunity to convey to them the delegation's enthusiasm as palpably as I know how and what we have learned in these past four days here in Moscow.

Before I do so, allow me to acknowledge the Herculean efforts in the past several months by Anvar and Vsevilod in bringing our three entities into an Alliance. Without their vision, interest, hard work and understanding of the difference of the cultures of U.S. and Russia, I cannot imagine what is taking place now can happen at all! I hope that from now on, MISA and GIREDMET can consider UTD as its window to the Metroplex and UTD can consider our Russian counterparts as its window to Moscow. More about this later.

I think I speak for all four of us that we were overwhelmed by the truly warm hospitality we received in the last few days. We were excited two nights ago of attending the stunning folk music and dance concert in a venue where a great Texan, Van Cliburn, made his international fame when he won the Tchaikovsky competition four decades ago, at the height of the cold war period.

An interesting story associated with that competition which I believe has some relevance here. After Van Cliburn played, the judges had to ask Nikita Khrushchev whether it was OK to give the award to an American. Khrushchev's only comment to that request was "If he is the best, give it to him!" I believe that this statement underlines the Russian's attitude towards excellence and the modern concept of "globalization." Indeed, it is excellence in research and globalization for our three institutions are what our Alliance is all about!

To prepare my talk, I did the usual preparation: I surf the web of both institutions! In MISA's website, I was immediately struck by the inspirational words of Rector Karabasov. I hope Rector Karabasov would not mind that I quote here his words which I believe outline the essence of my talk:

"......*Today our University is the unique educational and scientific center of training specialists and developing advanced technologies in metallurgy and material science. Programs made by University develop information and marketing activity; metal production and certification; metals and alloys prices monitoring. The University if involved in expertise projects, scientific and technological researches, provides training of experts and auditors. Diversity of the fields the University works in allows students to get high-quality, comprehensive and professional education. Also, it gives to business partners an opportunity to develop mutually beneficial cooperation......"*

This beautiful paragraph encapsulates the essence of the points I want to make today.

In the past three days, my colleagues and I interacted intensely with many individuals in MISA and GIREDMET.

We found that both MISA and GIREDMET have robust and multidimensional research programs. They both have rich and glorious history, and played a critical role in modern Russia's science and technology growth. They must surely be the gold-standards for Russian universities and research institutes. Yet, both obviously do not take what was achieved for granted because what we observed was quiet aggressiveness in both institutions pushing for excellence. MISA and GIREDMET have down-to-earth, practical yet visionary leaders, absolutely first rate faculty members, truly outstanding students, laboratories which are well stocked and well operated logistically and financially with state-of-the-art facilities.

In MISA, it has very large and highly supportive alumni across Russia and the CIS and beyond, in academia, industry and political arenas. Modern research universities are both intellectual centers as well as economic engines. To achieve the latter, reaching out to alumni in industry as well as political arenas is not just a nice thing to do, but an absolute necessity. In other words, you have already found the formula to become a world class research university in a country where the tradition of excellence was well documented.

In 1979, I was a young visiting professor at the Niels Bohr Institute in Copenhagen. There I collaborated with a Russian scientist from Dubna. As a result, he kindly invited me to visit his Institute. Unfortunately the visit was not materialized because of political and military turmoil of that era. What was even more unfortunate was that after we departed from Denmark, because of difficulty in communications, our collaborations ceased.

In 1986, the next opportunity arose when I was invited to present a paper at a conference in Novorsibirsk. That trip also did not materialize because the Soviet Union Embassy in Washington D. C. approved my visa application only *after* the conference was over!

So, after nearly two and a half decades of trying, my first real opportunity to visit this great country came just two years ago. With full anticipation I came, and I was NOT disappointed.

Two years ago, with the help of Anvar and Professor Agranovich, I finally made it to Moscow. The trip was so memorable and exciting. Contrary to perception, I saw hustling and bustling of the scientific and technological communities. In particular I met Vladimir Blanck, whom I noticed his scientific and administrative prominence in Russia continues to grow rapidly! Since then, UTD and Blanck's institute has maintained very strong ties.

The crowning of my first visit to Russia came when I actually had the honor to meet with the great Russian scientific icon and Nobel laureate, Professor Vitaly Ginzburg. I was humbled to have the opportunity to spend an entire afternoon with him and his wife Nina in his summer apartment outside of Moscow. Anvar and Agranovich were also there. Discussions in those three hours ranged from telling each other physics jokes (yes, besides being a world class scientist, Ginzburg is a man of many talents, including telling jokes), his scientific philosophy, and his current activities. I walked away from the visit feeling a little wiser!

I think I am quite typical among physical scientists in the world. Despite my lack of experience being in this country during my scientific formative stage and later on in my professional life, the prowess of Russian science had nevertheless profoundly impacted my personal professional growth. I will discuss more about this later on.

I am here for my second visit to this great country and I must admit that I am even more excited this time then the first. Personally, I am truly honored to have this opportunity to be standing here this morning.

Three days ago in this same room, I was fortunate to witness my two distinguished colleagues from UTD being honored by the Russian Academy of Natural Sciences. Both Ray and Anvar are new laureates of the very prestigious Kapitza Medal award, which I understand is the highest scientific award of this Academy.

They have just joined the scientific elite of Russia. While there is no doubt that these awards are indeed great personal triumphs for Ray and Anvar, they are also tremendous honor for UTD. I will say a bit more about this later on. I am sure that honoring our two distinguished colleagues in this manner will add confidence among your colleagues in general that great things can happen between our two universities.

Last evening, Dr. Cunningham and Dr. Levashov discussed the procedures and logistics, including funding, of students exchange. I have a saying that I am sure resonates well with all administrators and that is:

"Vision without funding is hallucination!"

So the fact that two of them are earnestly working together on these issues, including funding, will guarantee the success of that part of our Alliance. In addition, we know that one of the reasons why our three institutions can even consider such an Alliance is possible because it is a natural next step to the already initiated research collaborations on nanoscience between MISA, GIREDMET and UTD. Indeed, yesterday at GIREDMET, a useful workshop participated by scientists of all three institutions was held. No doubt from now on, more such activities will be held.

There is a very famous Chinese proverb which I sincerely hope will not be operative here. It is **Ren Qu Cha Liang** (人去茶凉) or "After the guests leave, the tea gets cold!" From the enthusiasm we observed this week about the Alliance, and the fact that I know we have on both sides mega-pushers like Anvar and Vsevilod, and now between Austin and Evgeny, there is no possibility that the tea will get cold! If anything, it will only get hotter!

So, the discussions that took place and will take place, and the ongoing collaborations between our nanoscientists, give to both sides utter confidence that this Alliance has all the hallmarks to be successful. The Memorandum of Understanding, or MOU, to be signed later on this afternoon, will definitely not be just be another piece of paper hanging on the wall somewhere in MISA, GIREDMET and UTD, but be a signal of the beginning of a great journey which our three institutions, separated by 12,000 kilometers, will take TOGETHER in years to come.

A Brief Comparison of Knowledge and Technologies in the beginning of the 20th and 21st centuries

We are at the dawn of the 21st century. I therefore find it especially intriguing to compare the landscapes between the beginning of the 20th century and our current era.

UTD is young and aspiring. A couple of days ago, Rector Karabasov told us in no uncertain terms that MISA is in transition. This means that while it has nearly twice UTD's age, it is also an aspiring university. As for all research universities in the world, especially for the aspiring ones, it is obvious that their intellectual growth would take far longer if the growth is carried out in vacuum. If we were in the beginning of the 20th century, this is probably the only way to do so. But in the 21st century, it is no longer an acceptable nor desirable practice.

Knowledge, and especially technologies, in the beginning of the 20th century were just at their "embryonic" stage. For example, human beings barely knew then that the fundamental building block of matter has a central core called the nucleus (in 1908 Rutherford won the Nobel Prize), no one knew that there was a new dynamics lurking in the microscopic world called quantum mechanics, and that speed of light with a limit has some profound implications called relativity. In fact, the realization that the fundamental building block of all life forms is DNA had to wait until the middle of the 20th century, thanks to Watson and Crick. Long distance travel and communications were mostly by boat and mail (not email, the word was invented in the mid-80s). In fact, my brother who went to the U.S. to study in the early 60s had to take a boat from Singapore to Hong Kong to Yokohama to Honolulu and to San Francisco. The trip took 23 days! Why do you think so many students in those days found their spouses during those long trips? What else should you be doing when all you had were horizon and the ocean for 23 days? Furthermore, the rudimentary telephone system which few countries and people have access to made "vacuum" the only choice, almost by necessity.

Today, while we may be as ignorant as ever (for example, I just learned from a good and distinguished colleague that we do not even know the biochemical genesis why a banana is bent!), we are probing the origin of the universe, creating new materials for the betterment of mankind never before imaginable, seeking alternative energy sources, trying to understand the root causes of diseases, both genetic and non-genetic based and we are trying to understand how the human brains work. We are also facing for the first time the possibility of an environmental calamity, maybe even a meltdown, such as Global warming, either within our life time or our children's or grandchildren's life time. Finally we are now in possession of weapons that can simply destroy all of us out in one bang. How do we learn to live in peace and harmony is no longer a philosophical question but an imminent one. Many of these problems are what the late Alan Bromley, Science Advisor to President George H. W. Bush (we call him 41) referred to as "scientific grand challenges!" Indeed, today, many issues and challenges facing mankind no longer can wait for long time solutions. Rather, they require innovative, multi-dimensional, multi-cultural and multi-disciplinary approach **now**! Few universities, if any, in one nation can solve these challenges by themselves and no great ones should avoid the responsibilities in mitigating ills of mankind. Of course, communications in the form of the internet are changing so rapidly that humans are communicating with each other not only faster, but in a manner that can be culturally and behaviorally changing! With the internet, new virtual (scientific) collaborations can take place instantly. Thus, in today's world, globalization is not just a cliché but reality. Therefore for a university at our stage of development, such growth in all likelihood cannot be done within our own boundaries, be it within the definition of a university or a nation.

To this end, it is not surprising that one of the first mandates of UTD president, Dr. David Daniel, is to mobilize the university to seek a small number of truly outstanding institutions around the Globe for us to build a sustainable and of course, win-win, alliance. What is happening here today is a result of that mobilization. These institutions hopefully will be our windows to the world! From our discussions with Rector Karamazov, I believe that he and Dr. Daniel are on the same page!

Something about UTD

Let me say a few things about UTD and the region it is in. UTD, with Dallas in its name, is NOT in Dallas, but in the adjacent northern suburban town call Richardson. Dallas is part of a bigger system called Metropolis, which includes two cites Dallas and Fort Worth and many suburban towns and municipalities are either in between or around them, and Richardson is one of them. The population of Metroplex is five million, which by U.S. standards, is a highly populated region! I will say more about the Metroplex later on. Also details about UTD as a university will be discussed by my colleague Austin Cunningham in the next talk.

Ever since its founding merely forty five years ago, UTD founders, who were the Founders of Texas Instruments, fundamentally believe in welcoming and attracting outstanding talents from all corners of the Globe. In our short 40 years of history, we attracted the service of three Nobel Laureates, the late Polykarp Kusch (Laureate for Physics in 1955), Alan MacDiarmid (Laureate for Chemistry in 2000) and Russell Hulse (Laureate for Physics in 1993).

Actually, the background of the four of us from UTD serves as an excellent microcosm as to why UTD maybe is on its way to become a great university in the 21st century. Of the four of us, only Ray was born and grew up in U.S. Anvar you know well is a physicist who grew up in Uzbekistan and received all his superb education in Moscow. In fact, to this date, he is still a citizen of Uzbekistan! After an exciting scientific career in Tashkant, Japan and Italy, he eventually landed in the U.S. (because of Ray) and five years ago, together with Ray, came to UTD! The third person, who is the next person to speak, is Austin Cunningham. Austin is a physicist who grew up as a Northern Irishman and received all his formal education there. Finally, I am a physicist who was born in India, to Chinese parents, grew up in Singapore, and received all my university education, at least in physics, in the U.S.

This reminded me of one of the fundamental assumptions of quantum mechanics which is the "collapse of wavefunctions"! It is said that before a measurement, a particle's position could have finite probability of being everywhere. After the measurement, it's position is localized. Well, what do you think the probability of four people with such disparate background can be together later? Very very small, you may say. Yet, when we did get together, the probability instantly becomes 100 percent!

For the four of us, our enormous divergence in backgrounds, and convergence of where we are now is a testimony of the strengths of higher education, especially research universities, in the U.S. in general, UTD in particular. In our case, we all contribute differently, but equally importantly, to the growth of this young institution. In fact, the ubiquitous attitude of welcoming people of all nationalities for research universities in the 20th century in the U.S., regardless of their backgrounds, is one of the key factors why many became leading ones in the world, and others could dream and eventually become great ones.

However, with increase ease of communication, with the "flattening" of the globe, merely welcoming people with open arms is no longer sufficient. In the flat world, you can be together "virtually".

The world of the 21st century is telling us, all of us, that as an aspiring university, UTD simply cannot carry out our intellectual growth alone. That is why whenever the opportunities present themselves to us to form alliances with other Global research institutions, we must seize upon them. It is perhaps sheer serendipity that in just the past two weeks we formed strong and sustainable alliances with two truly outstanding institutions: The Technion of Israel last week and MISA of Russia this week!

Russian Scientific and Technological Prowess

I hope that in the past four days, the four of us have demonstrated our utter and palpable excitement to you about this Alliance. Each of us, I am sure, have our own personal reasons for wanting to see this Alliance succeed. So, allow me to expand on my deep personal feelings here.

Russia is a vast and complex country with profound and deep cultures for its highly diverse and talented population. It is the only country which can claim to be as much Asian as it is European. However, one thing which no one can or will dispute, and that is ever since modern science unveils itself to the world, the scientific and technological prowess of Russia, well before the Soviet Union days, became an inalienable part of human existence. So to find a strong partner for alliance for UTD whose primary strengths are in science and technology is what an American youngster would say a "no-brainer!" The only surprising fact is that we did not do it earlier!

I can of course go on and on about the achievements of Russian scientists in the past century, and the great work they are doing today.

However, let me be more personal and give you my own deep feelings about Russian science, from my narrow perspective. However, I do believe that my experiences are not special but very typical, which can easily be extrapolated to a much grander scale.

Russian science became part of my scientific soul ever since I embarked on my career. I could not forget as a student my many late night struggles, some would call it joy, in enriching my knowledge and prepare me for exams to solve problems embedded in the series of books written by two great Russian physicists: Nobel Laureate **Lev Landau** and **Liftshitz**. I learned from Anvar that both of them were in this vicinity when they were still alive. Also, what joy it was for me later on as a research physicist to read beautiful papers on phase transition by **Vitaly Ginzburg** and Landau and the magnificent treaties on group representations by the great Russian group theorist **Gel'fand**. All my colleagues, and I was one for a brief period of my career, who studied one of the toughest quantum systems called the three-body-problem basically revolve around the Faddeev equations, named after the great Russian mathematical physicist **Ludwig Faddeev** of St Petersburg. Anyone working on nonlinear dynamics should and must be aware of the profound contributions of **Ar'nold**, a great Russian mathematician. Just a few days ago in MISA, I also was most pleased to see the picture of **Igor Tamm**, Nobel Laureate of 1958, on the wall of one of the buildings, signaling that this great physicist was once a faculty member of this institution. Again, Tamm-Dancoff Approximation, or TDA, is a standard procure in theoretical physics. I also simply lost count of how many times I discussed with my collaborators about quasi-particles Bogoliubov transformations at or near Fermi surface for nuclear pairing in my nuclear physics research. Many of you know well that this concept of pairing found its genesis in the theory of superconductivity, and one of the great Russian scientists **Kapitza** was unquestionably a towering figure in that field. This is why I am so excited to see that Ray and Anvar have been awarded the Kapitza medal just two days ago!

Last but not least, three years ago, I had the great pleasure of meeting one of MISA's most proud former faculty members in Dallas soon after he became a Nobel Laureate, **Alexei Abrikosov**. Anyone who has been a student in many body problems would have to study the beautiful book by Abrikosov and **Gor'kov**.

Since I am convinced that my narrow experiences are typical, I am confident to say that whatever fields of physical sciences one is in, there is in all likelihood a Russian scientist whose work is seminal in that field. That to me defines the Russian scientific prowess!

In discussing with the Director of GIREDMET, Dr. Yuri Parkhomenko, over dinner a few nights ago, I asked the following question.

I said: "When I was in Taiwan recently, I emailed to my good friend Yitzhak Apeloig, President of Technion, that Taiwan underwent a profound economic transformation from agriculture to silicon in the past three decades. The transformation created enormous wealth for Taiwan. Yitzhak replied to me almost instantly. He said that almost in the same period, so did Israel, and Technion was one of the important drivers of that transformation! Yuri, can you tell me the important position played by MISA and GIREDMET in the transformation of Russia in the past several decades?"

Without hesitation, he replied that "Our institutes are at the forefront of materials science and engineering in Russia. Our aim is not just to react to the progress of the outside world, but to create new form of materials through basic sciences never before conceived by mankind and to find the innovative way to deploy them for intellectual and economic gains. This was our aim, this is our aim and this will be our aim."

I have to admit that this is certainly one of the best statements I have ever heard a leader of research institute made regarding the mission. Succinctly and elegantly, Yuri Parkhomenko said that his institute is basic sciences based and technological applications driven. At another occasion, Rector Yuri Karabosov also said something that is similar. This beautiful answer should leave no doubt in anyone's mind that forming an Alliance with MISA and GIREDMET can only be good for UTD.

The few examples I presented to you here tells you how pervasive and deep the work of Russian scientists have been contributing to the world of knowledge in the 20th century. It is therefore no surprise that with the reinvigorated economy of Russia, science and technology will again flourish in this great country.

Is it not ironic that at least two generations of scientists in the U.S. grew up acquiring many of the knowledge created by Russian scientists even though few ever visited this country because of the Cold War? The fact that I can be here today to talk about it is a testimony that we have progressed so much in the last few decades.

Moscow and the Metroplex

I hope there is no doubt in people's minds that the Alliance of MISA and UTD has all the ingredients for success. There is strong support from above, at the respective president's level, and there is strong support at the grass root levels.

So, besides the obvious collaborations which we have already outlined during this week, which is going on exceedingly well, what other horizons should we be scaling in the coming years? Will we be satisfied with this level of Alliance?

In a recent speech, the President of the National University of Singapore, Dr. Shih Choon-Fong (施春風), proposed an incredibly memorable phrase:

"A good university teaches. A great university transforms!"

These are very powerful words indeed. If we think of great universities such as MIT and Stanford, both certainly satisfy the "transform" criterion. However, this is still a 20th century thinking.

Now that we are in the 21st century, and the world is flat, I hope Dr. Shih would not mind too much if I paraphrase him by saying that

Good international university Alliances teach. Great international university Alliances transform!

This I believe is a step even beyond Dr. Shi's vision. Here allow me to think blue sky a bit.

Moscow is unquestionably the center of gravity of Russian science and technology. The history of Russian scientific developments in the past 100 years made it abundantly clear that such is the case. In Moscow, among its many universities and research centers, MISA and GIREDMET certainly rank among the top. Of course, just next to these two institutions are many research institutes of the powerful Russian Academy of Sciences. Leveraging on the enormous scientific and technology manpower, clustered right around here in Moscow, coupled with the great economic and political changes that are taking place for the country, Moscow is also rapidly becoming one of Europe's entrepreneurial centers as well.

It is very interesting that although the perception that the Metroplex is a center of technology concentration can be improved, in reality Metroplex is one of the top three metropolitan areas in the US with enormous technological and entrepreneurial capital. For sure, it does not have the intellectual prowess of 70 universities, it nevertheless has well over 700 high technology companies. For example, the Metroplex is now one of the two major aerospace centers of the U.S. It is also the home of one of the world's largest semiconductor company, Texas Instruments. Also, many Information Technology companies, such as EDS and Perot Systems, have the corporate headquarters there. It is also interesting that Huawei, which is unquestionably China's largest global telecommunication companies, chose the Metroplex to establish it North America headquarters.

I want to show you, in the next slide made by my colleague Don Hicks. Each dot in the triangle defined by Metroplex, San Antonio and Houston depicts a company which deals with microelectronics. From this diagram, it is obvious that Texas in general and the Metroplex in particular has an abundance in intellectual and economic capital in microelectronic. In fact, from the UTD perspective, it is worth noting that the headquarters and its brand new 12-inch wafer fabrication center (which is a $3 billion investment by TI) of TI are only about one mile and five miles, respectively, from the campus.

So, I hope that with this Alliance, MISA, GIREDMET and UTD can grow and mature together in a global landscape which is very different from a century ago. There are many new unknowns we need to face, new knowledge we need to create and new ignorance we need to mitigate. As an Alliance that is truly global in nature, I am sure we can do this with greater ease together than separately.

Therefore, as three forward-looking institutions, entering into the first Alliance between a great Russian university, a great Russian research institute, and an aspiring university in the Metroplex, at the dawn of a new century, all want to give, as Rector Karabasov said, *".... **business partners an opportunity to develop mutually beneficial cooperation**",* we should leverage all we have to begin thinking and planning a roadmap to create a model of multi-national regional alliance in the 21st century, the Moscow-Metroplex intellectual and economic alliance.

So, our three institutions should not be a tripartite, but a trinity!

Ladies and gentlemen, let the transformation begin!

(2007)

40

An Action-Packed and Intellectually Stimulating Visit to Moscow's Scientific and Technological Communities

This is an account of the visit to Moscow on August 15–21, 2004, when the author was Vice President for Research and Graduate Education, The University of Texas at Dallas.

Why Russia?

During the week of August 15– 21, UTD's Professor Anvar Zakhidov and I visited many of the leading scientific and technological entities in Moscow.

Research is an "international enterprise". In this global village era, to grow one's research enterprise, it is inconceivable not to reach out to the "best-in-anywhere-in-the-world". As Vice President for Research and Graduate Education of the University of Texas at Dallas, it is critical that I be constantly on the lookout to create opportunities, regionally, nationally and internationally, to enhance and deepen UTD's research enterprise through collaborations.

Russia's scientific and technological contributions in the 20th century are well documented. Its vast scientific infrastructure, from St. Petersburg to Vladivostok, which spans eight time zones, has produced many truly outstanding internationally known scientists and technologists. Great Russian scientific minds such as Kapitza, Landau, Ginzburg,

Abrikosov, Migdal, Gel'fand, Mandelshtam and Faddeev are household names in many corners of the scientific world.

In the nineties, with enormous and profound change of government structure, accompanied by economic downturn, there was palpable setback of Russian science and technology. However, since 2000, with increasing government stability and steady economic growth, and the fact that Russian's scientific human infrastructure is strong, deep and — despite personnel migration to other countries — more or less intact, there appears a revival of scientific activities. What I saw in Moscow this week convinces me that this fact is real.

Sustainable UTD's "Russian connection" opportunities arose when Dr. Anvar Zakhidov from Honeywell Corporation in New Jersey was hired in 2001 as the deputy director of the NanoTech Institute and Professor of Physics. Through Anvar, UTD was able to make connection with his mentor, Professor Vladimir Agranovich, an internationally well known scientist of the four decades, and head of the powerful theoretical physics group of the Institute of Spectroscopy of the Russian Academy of Sciences (RAS). The overlap of Russian scientific and technological human-network of Zakhidov and Agranovich in essence gave UTD vast access to the large Russian scientific communities: faculty members in top Russian universities, distinguished members of the RAS, and the fledgling but rapidly growing Russian technological entrepreneurs.

In my mind, this is an opportunity which UTD can ill-afford not to leverage.

What Entities did We Visit and What did We Accomplish?

There were two primary missions of our visit to Moscow. First is to establish strong and sustainable relations with one of Russia's top research university, Moscow State University. The second is to meet with Russia's latest Nobel Laureate, Professor Vitaly Ginzburg, and to invite him to be a member of UTD's Research Advisory Board.

I am pleased to say that both missions were accomplished.

For five days (Monday — Friday), Professor Anvar Zakhidov and I visited eight institutions in greater Moscow. Three of them are RAS institutes:

- P. N. Lebedev Physical Institute, RAS
- Institute of Spectroscopy, RAS
- Photochemistry Center, RAS

One is a top Russian research university:

- Moscow State University

Two from Russian ministries:

- Technological Institute for Superhard and Noval Carbon Materials, Ministry of Industry, Science and Technological of Russian Federation
- Troitsk.Institute for Innovation and Fusion Research of the State Research Center of the Russian Federation

Finally, two private industrial research centers:

- Yukos Research and Development Center
- Optiva Technological Ltd

My Impressions

- Russia's scientific and technological infrastructure is now growing, if not flourishing. Nearly at every stop, I saw senior researchers, young researchers, graduate students and even undergraduates, working closely together with enthusiasm. For example, in the Laboratory of Nonlinear Optics, Nanostructures and Photonic Crystals of Moscow State University, we met the director, Professor Olga A. Aktsipetrov, who is a world renowned scientist, and his two younger colleagues, Professors A. A. Fedyanin and T. V. Murzina. I saw many sophisticated experimental set-ups — some homemade and some purchased, but all state-of-the-art — and was told that they have some 20 students (half of them are Ph.D. students). Unfortunately, since this is vacation time in Russia (and Russians take vacation very seriously, the senior

staff members were around only because we were coming), only a small group of students were present.
- From my discussion with Professor P. K. Kashkarov, the Associate Dean of Research, that of the 35,000 students in Moscow State University, nearly 2000 are very high quality physics undergraduates (chemistry, mathematics, mechanics have about the same number). I know at least one such students (Anvar's son!). I suspect this is true also for other outstanding Russian universities, such as St. Petersburg University. This means that the pipeline for Russian science is now gushing with new blood, which is a critical condition for any society to possess healthy scientific communities. With such a large number of young blood in the pipeline, perhaps a new generation of Kapitza, Landau, Ginzburg, and Abrikosov are in the making? If so, then it is not just good news for Russia, but for the world at large.
- I should mention that Moscow State University's campus imposes on the city. The main building, which is a very tall Soviet style skyscraper, can be seen from many corners of Moscow. I have never seen a university campus anywhere on earth that has equal physical stature as Moscow State University!
- In visiting the Photochemistry Center of RAS, Technological Institute for Superhard and Noval Carbon Materials of the Ministry of Industry, Science and Technological of Russian Federation, Yukos Research and Development Center and Optiva Technological Ltd, I saw significant new and state-of-the-art experimental facilities. I also met a large cadre of scientists, junior and senior, busily working in the labs. For example, we were taken to the Institute for Superhard and Noval Carbon Materials new and not quite finish building. Looking at the architectural drawings, and the building's interior and exterior skeleton structure, one could extrapolate that this will be a state-of-the-art Institute when finished sometime next year (2005). I should say that nearly all experimental equipments we saw were recently purchased and they are NOT CHEAP. Therefore their presence in the laboratories imply that there is now some steady government and private research funding of science and technology, certainly in the best research institutes, in Russia.

- Over a delicious lunch in a German restaurant in Troitsk with Dr. Vladimir Blank, the Director of the Technological Institute for Superhard and Noval Carbon Materials, we learned that his center will be a focal point for nanotechnology research activities in Russia. I also learned that Russia, from the highest government level, is now paying serious attention to and launching a fairly ambitious research program in this field. There are now some 600 research groups throughout Russia devoted to this field. Dr. Blank, who heads the committee to launch the program, said that after the first year of modest funding (around $15 million), subsequent years will see enormous increase. The fact that there is such discussions going on in Russia implies to me that the dark days of Russian science, in the decade of the 90's, may be over. With UTD's growing strength in nanotechnology, micrielectronics and nano-biotechnology, it is very timely that we made contact with Blank at this point in time.
- Meeting the Nobel laureate Vitaly Ginzburg had to be the highlight of our trip to Moscow. I was, accompanied by Zakhidov and Agranovich, indeed humbled to have the opportunity to spend an entire afternoon with him and his wife, Nina. Discussions in those three hours ranged from telling each other physics jokes (yes, besides being a world class scientist, Ginzburg is a man of many talents, including telling jokes), his scientific philosophy, and his current activities. I walked away from the visit feeling a little wiser!
- Meeting Academician Mikhail Alfimov was most interesting. Besides being a global scientific leader in photochemistry, he was for ten years the head of Russian Science Foundation (sort of the equivalent of our National Science Foundation). For this reason, he possesses a global view of Russian science. From our discussion, I would say that his impression of Russian science can be termed as "upbeat" and "hopeful".
- For sure, low salary in government research laboratories is still a challenge to Russian science. However, the fact that scientists now do have salaries, and more important, steady research fundings, are already a significant step forward from a decade ago. In addition, outstanding researchers, which are the ones we met in this week, all receive research fundings either from Russian government agencies, or private

foundations, or abroad. I do not detect that there is an atmosphere of "uncertainty" or "despair". On the contrary, the scientists we met are all anxious to "do something" for science, and by extrapolation, for Russia.

A Few Comments about Moscow

Due to our enormously busy professional schedule, rushing from one research venue to the next in this enormous city, our "sight seeing" schedule was understandably reduced to a minimal. However, this report would be incomplete if I did not at least give some of my superficial impressions of Moscow.

By any standard, Moscow is a massive metropolitan of over 7 million inhabitants. During the week we were there, Moscow had an unusual "heat-wave", with day time temperature reaching as high as 85 degrees. Perhaps it was the fact that the city was basking in magnificent weather that I saw how excellently and colorful Russians were dressed. I was also impressed by how friendly they were in trying to help foreigners to get around the city.

Moscow is a city of history and culture. We had a lunch in an interesting restaurant near Pushkin Square (named after the great Russian poet Pushkin). The restaurant is called — you guessed it — Pushkin restaurant. I was told that the restaurant site was where the poet had romantic liaisons with his many lady friends. No wonder the food and ambiance were simply marvelous and inviting. I was also given a "cultural baptism" by Tchaikovsky's "sleeping beauty" ballet performance. It was by Russia's national ballet group, which is not to be confused with the world renowned Bolshoi ballet. Although the group is second-tier, to an untrained eye, it is already excellent. Even as a "ballet illiterate", I found the performance mesmerizing! Finally, I was invited one evening to an ethnic music and dance performance. There I heard powerful yet beautiful singings, great performance of traditional instruments and highly skillful Kazak's traditional sword dancing. Undoubtedly, Moscow is a city of cultural action!

During the week, except when our visit took us to the science city Troitsk, which is many miles from downtown, travel within the city is essentially by its subway. Moscow's subway system is good, clean, efficient, and can transport you for merely 10 rubles, or 30 cents (US), from anywhere to anywhere in the system's vast network. The stations of the system are well lit, and well decorated with either Soviet era's paintings or imposing sculptures. Along many walking tunnels underground, there were well stocked small shops, one after another, selling practically anything imaginable: lingerie's, books, food and jewelries. I would say that except for the omnipresent Russian language — which is my handicap in effectively using the system by myself — the subway system in Moscow mind as well be New York City's. It certainly has the familiar features of having hundreds of thousands of people rushing about, going up and down the extremely long escalators, walls lined with big commercial advertisements, and last but not least, noisy clanging sound of traveling trains.

Then there is Red Square, Kremlin, St. Basil Basilica and Lenin Mausoleum which I visited briefly on a bright and sunny Saturday morning. These are obviously symbols of Russia, past and present, and no visit to Russia is complete without a visit to this area. Under deep blue sky, the Square and the surrounding structures simply appeared absolutely spectacular. No wonder I saw couple after couple in their wedding gowns taking pictures. At the shopping mall opposite the Kremlin, I saw two men dressed as Czar Nicholas and Lenin. Tourists could take pictures with them, for a fee, of course! Intriguingly, I saw a group of about 20 elderlys carrying the old bright red sickle-and-hammer Soviet flags, singing the "international" and parading around Red Square. Even among hundreds of thousands of visitors on the Square, they stood out due to their oddities.

One thing for sure, Moscow is not for the "financially challenged". The price of everything is nearly "world class". Except for the subway, all prices are tourist-motivated. I would suggest that one should, whenever possible, have the luxury of having a "native" to accompany him/her.

Epilogue

In 1979, while I was a visiting professor at Niels Bohr Institute in Copenhagen, I was scheduled to visit several collaborators at the Joint

Institute of Nuclear Research in Dubna to complete a review article. Just as I was about to leave for Moscow, Soviet Union invaded Afghanistan. My trip was cancelled. In 1986, I was invited to attend a conference in Novisibirsk. My Russian visa was issued several weeks after the conference was concluded.

A quarter of a century after 1979, I was fortunate enough to visit Moscow. I always regretted that I did not visit Russia (or Soviet Union) in a different era. I would have loved to compare the Russia then and now.

No doubt, Russia I saw in this trip is very different from its Soviet past. I see that there is a serious effort in building a scientific infrastructure, and there is indeed the practice of good to excellent science. I am convinced that by properly nurturing this relationship with our Russian scientific and technological partners, it will be another important step for UTD to build its sustainable research atmosphere.

Annex: Names of people we met

1. **Academician Vitaly L. Ginzburg**, Nobel Laureate, P. N. Lebedev Physical Institute, Russian Academy of Sciences
2. **Professor O. A. Aktsipetrov**, Moscow State University, Laboratory of Nonlinear Optics, Nanostructures and Photonic Crystals
3. **Assistant Professor of Physics A. A. Fedyanin**, Moscow State University, Laboratory of Nonlinear Optics, Nanostructures and Photonic Crystals
4. **Associate Professor T. V. Murzina**, Moscow State University, Laboratory of Nonlinear Optics, Nanostructures and Photonic Crystals
5. **Professor P. K. Kashkarov**, Professor of Physics and Associate Dean of Research of Moscow State University.
6. **Professor Vladimir Blank**, Director, Technological Institute for Superhard and Noval Carbon Materials, Ministry of Industry, Science and Technological of Russian Federation
7. **Dr. Victor N. Denisov**, Senior Researcher, Technological Institute for Superhard and Noval Carbon Materials, Ministry of Industry, Science and Technological of Russian Federation

8. **Professor Vladimir M. Borisov**, Deputy Director of Pulsed Processes Department, Head of Pulsed Laser System Laboratory, Troitsk.Institute for Innovation and Fusion Research
9. **Professor Vladimir Agranovich**, Head of the Theoretical Physics Department, Institute of Spectroscopy, Russian Academy of Sciences
10. **Academician Mikhail V. Alfimov**, Photochemistry Center, Russian Academy of Sciences
11. **Professor Andrey N. Petrov**, Director, Photochemistry Center, Russian Academy of Sciences
12. **Dr. Nikolai K. Petrov**, Senior Researcher, Photochemistry Center, Russian Academy of Sciences
13. **Dr. Dimitri Y. Likhachev**, Laboratory Head, Yukos Research and Development Center
14. **Dr. Pavel Lazarev**, President, Optiva Technological Ltd
15. **Dr. Elena Sidorenko**, Certified Chemist, Optiva Technological Ltd
16. **Dr. Olga Kuchenkova**, Senior Researcher, Optiva Technological Ltd
17. **Dr. Alexander Grodsky**, Senior Researcher, Optiva Technological Ltd
18. **Dr. Alexy Mikhailov**, Senior Researcher, Optiva Technological Ltd
19. **Dr. Pavel Protsenko**, Researcher, Optiva Technological Ltd

(2004)

Noteworthy People

41

The Two Nobel Laureates Overlapped in the McDermott Suite of UTD

This piece was written in 2005 on the meet organized by The University of Texas at Dallas (UTD) on April 6, 2004. The author was Vice President for Research and Graduate Education at the university.

Alan MacDiarmid (Nobel Laureate in Chemistry, 2000)

Russell Hulse (Nobel Laureate in Physics 1993) speaking to a bunch of IIT Roorkee summer students in UTD

Unquestionably — fair or not — universities with Nobel laureates as faculty tend to receive glittering visibility. This is because not just the academic and industrial worlds attach incredible mystique of "superhuman" to these laureates, but the world at large,

It is therefore not surprising that in the past three years, the entire cadre of UTD senior administrators, together with the Dean of the School of Natural Science and Mathematics, past and the present, and many faculty members from different Schools, worked hand-in-hand, to recruit two such individuals.

They are

Alan MacDiarmid, co-winner of the 2000 Nobel Prize in Chemistry for his **"discovery and development of conductive polymers"**

and

Russell Hulse, co-winner of the 1993 Nobel Prize in Physics for his **"discovery of a new type of pulsar, a discovery that has opened up new possibilities for the study of gravitation"**

Therefore, it is not surprising since their arrival in the Metroplex, even though it is still a relatively short time — MacDiarmid for two years and Hulse for less than one year — they already have profoundly affected the many people's lives in the Metroplex, from researchers in universities and industries, to warm hearted philanthropists with deep interest in building a great workforce for the Metroplex, to bright-eye-bushy-tail high school students.

One thing for sure is that if you are a Nobel laureate, you bound to lead a very very busy lives. These two individuals are no exception. For example, quite recently, Alan MacDiarmid was invited by the Asia Pacific Economic Cooperation to deliver a keynote speech in his hometown of Christchurch, New Zealand and Russell Husle was participating in some panel discussions in Washington D.C. Indeed, the chances of finding them in UTD at the same time is quite rare.

For this reason, once we realized that both are in town on the 6th of April, we decided to organize a reception in the elegant McDermott Suite of UTD. We want to give the greater Metroplex family an opportunity to meet these two truly great individuals up close.

And it was a great success. Nearly a hundred people came to the reception. The atmosphere of the event was oozing with human warmth.

People literally came from all walks of life: from those in the neighborhood, to high school students, to faculty members from nearly every School in UTD, to many of the area high school students who worked in MacDiarmid's laboratories.

One highlight of the event was when two highschool 10th graders, who spent their past summer in MacDiarmid's laboratory, gave their thanks to MacDiarmid. It made everyone in the room remember what is the real and ultimate purpose of a research university!

In my brief opening statement, I said that

"Not many universities in the world would have the privilege and honor of having just ONE Nobel laureate. That number of such universities drops considerably if there were two. Today, UTD is amongst this small

group of privileged universities. It is for this reason, that the community in and surrounding UTD need and should feel proud to see that two truly outstanding individuals — they are great human beings even if they do not have Nobel prizes — are in our midst to contribute to the world their knowledge and humanity!"

It was indeed a most memorable event!

(2005)

42

On Nobel Laureate Vitaly Ginzburg

This was written when Ginzburg accepted The University of Texas at Dallas's invitation to be a member of its prestigious Research Advisory Board in 2004. The author was Vice President for Research and Graduate Education.

Vitaly Ginzburg is a new member of UTD's RAB!

UTD's Research Advisory Board (RAB) (http://www.utdallas.edu/research) consists of global movers and shakers. In the past two years, this Board had made profound contributions to the growth of the University.

On August 17th, 2003, around 2:30 pm (Moscow time, which is 9 hours ahead of Dallas), **Vitaly Lazarevich Ginzburg** of P. N. Lebedev Physical Institute of Moscow, the 2003 Nobel laureate in physics, and also an academician of the extremely prestigious Russian Academy of Science and a Foreign Member of the US National Academy of Sciences, accepted UTD's invitation to serve on its RAB!

According to the Nobel website (http://www.nobel.se), the Nobel committee awarded the Nobel prize to Ginzburg for his "pioneering contributions to the theory of superconductors and superfluids".

In the 20th century, Russian scientific geniuses played a pivotal role in understanding the structure of matter, which eventually led to a technological revolution for the world. Names such as Kapitza, Landau, Gel'fand and Ginzburg would readily come to mind. Thus, to be able to able to tap into the tremendous wisdom and broad and wealth of knowledge of someone such as Ginzburg could only be considered as another RAB's major milestone.

How this came about: Thanks to Agranovich and Zakhidov

Among many fundamental contributions, which included his deep contributions to low temperature (near absolute zero degree Kelvin) phenomena, one that is known by nearly all physicists (and even other scientists such as chemists and biologists) is the theory he developed with the late and legendary Lev Landau on physical systems transition from one phase (such as liquid) to another (such as gaseous). The work is so well known as Ginzburg-Landau phase transition, that when other scientists mention it in their scientific publications, the reference is no longer a necessity (just as no one would refer to the original paper of Sir Isaac Newton when one talks about classical mechanics).

The opportunity for me to meet with Professor Ginzburg came when UTD hired an outstanding Russian scientist, Anvar Zakhidov, to be the deputy director of the NanoTech Institute. Anvar's teacher, Vladimir Agranovich, a world renowned scientist and director of the theoretical physics group of the Institute of Spectroscopy of the Russian Academy of Science, and who is now a member of UTD's prestigious "Pioneers in Nanotechnology", is a lifelong friend of Ginzburg's. When Vladimir learned of my desire to meet with Ginzburg and to invite him to be a member of UTD's Research Advisory Board, he was gracious enough to arrange for me to meet with Ginzburg.

There was only ONE catch: Unless there is absolute necessity, such as going to Sweden to receive the Nobel prize, Ginzburg does not travel much. So, if I wanted to meet and extend the invitation to him, I needed to go to Moscow. Moscow is of course some 8000 miles from Dallas!

Me, Anvar, Ginzburg and Agranovich outside Ginzburg's summer apartment outside of Moscow

A relaxed moment with Ginzburg and Agranovich on Ginzburg's apartment balcony

Well, considering what UTD could leverage from the profound wisdom of one of the greatest scientists of the 20th century, I decided to go to Moscow on the week of 15th of August, 2004, to meet with Ginzburg, and also to sign an Memorandum of Understanding (MOU) for collaboration with one of Russia's most prestigious universities: Moscow State University.

So, on the sunny afternoon of the 17th of August, 2004, accompanied by Anvar Zakhidov and Vladimir Agranovich, I met Vitaly Ginzburg and his charming wife, Nina (who is also a physicist). The venue was their rented apartment in a beautiful resort some 76 kilometers outside of Moscow. At around 2:30 pm, I told Ginzburg that one of the reasons I came to Moscow is to invite him to be a member of UTD's RAB.

Having already been told by Agranovich about my proposal weeks before, and understanding that all communications from him and the RAB will be in Russian (and therefore Zakhidov would play a tremendous role here), HE ACCEPTED!

As my Jewish friends would say, MAZEL TOV!

(2004)

43

On Paul Barbara

Below are two writings on Paul Barbara, one on November 2, 2006, when the author introduced him as the presenter of a talk to the public in Austin on "Nanotechnology: Solutions for Societies Greatest Technological Challenges" after the inauguration of the new $36 Million Nanotechnology Science and Technology building, and the other on November 9, 2010, after learning the demise of Barbara. The author was Vice President for Research and Graduate Education at The University of Texas at Dallas in 2006, and Senior Executive Vice President of National Cheng Kung University in 2010.

I

Paul was standing next to me

I am not sure why or how I was given this enormous honor to introduce Paul Barbara, but I will not refuse it.

Ever since I came to Texas six years ago, I met many outstanding individuals all across the State. Many became truly good personal friends, and Paul is certainly one of them. Paul and his family are genuine people. You get what you see in them. He is just a very good human being.

After I met Paul, I soon found out that he and I had one thing in common: We both spent time in the University of Minnesota. I spent four years as a graduate student and he was for eighteen years a distinguished professor in the chemistry department. I guess after eighteen years, Paul wanted to find a place that is a little warmer (or a lot warmer.) So please take heart at Austin: the truly outstanding quality of the research atmosphere of UT Austin was only a partial reason why Paul was attracted to your university.

There is no question that UT Austin benefited enormously by "luring" Paul from Minnesota. What we experienced earlier today, where we cut the ribbon of the new and magnificent building known as Nano Science and Technology (NST) building, is but one of the benefits of UT Austin received in getting Paul. This $36 million building, where I am sure some of the most spectacular research and development will be carried out in Texas in years to come, was the brainchild of Paul. In the past several years, I have seen Paul eat, sleep and dream NST. His vision, coupled with tenacity to carry out details of the project, was unbelievable.

Second, Texas' nanotechnology program has made incredible strides in the past six years. No doubt, Senator Hutchison is the champion of SPRING (Strategic Partnership for Research in Nanotechnology), and now CONTACT (Consortium for Nanomaterials for Aerospace Commerce and Technology). SPRING and CONTACT have and will continue to make an international name for Texas. At the grass-root level, there are of course many people who can claim and should receive credit. Among them, I think I am not exaggerating to say that Paul absolutely stands out. I am sure I speak for all the SPRING and CONTACT folks that we thank him from the bottom of our heart for his enormous contributions.

Finally, for a scientist, doing research and seeing great results are the ultimate rewards. To this end, Paul is of course already infinitely rewarded.

However, in the U.S., there are two accolades which I am sure will make one feel very rewarded. One is to be inducted to be a member of the National Academy of Sciences. Paul received this accolade just this Spring (no pun intended). The other I am sure will be forthcoming! Let me also take this opportunity to present to Paul a present which my two colleagues, Ray Baughman (who cannot be here) and Anvar Zakhidov, wanted me to present to Paul. This is a cartoon drawn by a Russian scientist during a conference in UTD a few years ago. The cartoon depicted a lamb (perhaps a graduate student) frighteningly presenting a talk, facing the blackboard, and many hungry looking wolves (faculty) staring at the lamb. On the floor, was a pile of bones. People who signed the cartoon were Alan MacDiarmid (Nobel in chemistry in 2000), Alan Heeger (Nobel in chemistry in 2000), Alexi Abrikosov (Nobel in physics in 2003) and Vitali Ginzburg (Nobel in physics in 2003).

Someday, hopefully, Paul will sign this cartoon as well.

May I present to you, Paul Barbara.

(2006)

II

November 9, 2010

Friends:

I learned with great sadness the sudden demise of my dear friend Paul Barbara.

Almost exactly four years ago, I had the great honor of introducing him in UTAustin's inauguration of the massive center of nanotechnology. It was a moment of great exhilaration for Paul and his team, which I could tell by his demeanor. His palpable energy to bring science as he knew it to the next level was simply oozing out of him. I have not followed what he did since, but knowing him, he surely had trail-blazed many new intellectual avenues in the last four years.

In my speech, I mentioned about him signing a special picture. The missing signature in that picture would have to await his virtual signing in the new place he is now in. The world will remember the knowledge he had created with great reverence.

We will sorely miss him, not only in Texas or the U.S., but globally.
Da Hsuan Feng

(2010)

44
Impressions of NCKU and Zheng Cheng-Gong (郑成功)

This is a sharing by the author when he was Senior Executive Vice President of National Cheng Kung University in Tainan, Taiwan. The Annex is the departure message sent to his friends and associates when he was leaving the university.

President Lai and Colleagues:

Ever since I came to NCKU, I have been fascinated by the genesis of our university's name "成功". I learned from Professor H. S. Yan, our museum director and chair professor of mechanical engineering that there is NO DOUBT that it was derived from 郑成功, the magnificent historical figure of Taiwan and Fujian (and maybe China in general.)

My curiosity about 郑成功 has driven me to the point that whenever I visited a historical site in Tainan, or Taiwan in general (including Jinmen or Quemoy,) I was always looking for his symbol, a bust, a portrait, or a statue. I was always very disappointed that I could not find one which I thought could be commensurate with what his stature was (is,) and what he symbolizes to the nearly 50 million (which I was told is a conservative estimation) people with Min-Nan (闽南) heritage.

On this past Thursday, I made a trip which I thought I would not be able to make in my lifetime, and that was to take a boat trip from Jinmen (Quemoy) to Xiamen (Amoy.) I was heartened that I made it!

Then, as we were entering the harbor of Xiamen, I was struck by the most impressive statue of 郑成功. The following is the picture a friend took of this structure. The structure stands tall and proud on the island of 鼓浪屿.

It was positioned that people visiting Xiamen will not be able to miss seeing this statue, there upon immediately will be able to conjure up its historical significance. At that moment, I thought that NCKU meant even more to me than the university I have the pleasure to serve.

In many ways, my experience reminded me of another statue, the Statue of Liberty (which I also include here for comparison.) Both would have profound meanings for people who knew the history. Indeed, anyone entering the port of NY City from Europe could not escape seeing it. So, I thought I would share them with you and my thoughts.

Da Hsuan

(2010)

Annex: My Departure from NCKU

To: World wide friends

Re: With great joy and sense of fulfillment, just as Academician Michael M. C. Lai (赖明昭院士), I am completing my term as Senior Executive Vice President on January 31, 2011, in National Cheng Kung University.

Three and a half years ago, I was invited by Michael, a world renowned virologist, a man of few words and global vision and the then new president of National Cheng Kung University to be the Senior Executive Vice President of the university. Besides knowing NCKU is one of the premier universities in Asia Pacific, with powerful alumni worldwide, I thought it was also a marvelous opportunity to contribute as a bridge, however meager it was, to the region which is the roots of my inherent cultural heritage, Asia Pacific, and my new national affiliation, U.S.

In three and half years, I saw not just enormous and profound transformation of National Cheng Kung University under the "open-minded" and "hands-off" style of Michael, but I also witnessed a robust and exciting intellectual and economic growth of nearly all (North Korea has still a little ways to go) nations in Asia Pacific.

As an "outsider," I often told my friends in Taiwan that I am like a paratrooper (空降部队), who almost without warning to the "locals," was suddenly dropped into Tainan (台南). Somehow, I managed to leverage my southeast Asia background, coupled it with my deep Chinese and American brackgrounds, and the fact that travel from one Asian country to the next needs almost no time change, to witness first hand an Asia Pacific new era: to discover about NCKU as an unusual and remarkable institution in particular, Taiwan and China (and of course Hong Kong and Macau,) as an incredible combination in general and how they are able to connect intellectually and economically with Northeast Asia, Southeast Asia and South Asia. After three and a half years, I also now am in possession of a new and dangerous "firearm": I can give a full presentation in Chinese almost without aid of any English! Indeed, I climbed the steepest learning curve in my life about people, psychology, and political realities, for sure not since I travelled to North America as a young student some 40 years ago. This experience has bestowed me with a deeper (and probably deep) understanding of the ways and means of Asia Pacific.

In my capacity as the Senior Executive Vice President, I see the grandest part of my portfolio is to promote with all my energy and vigor Michael's vision, which is to propel NCKU along the path to become a university where "ideas count." I have often said that Cambridge University and University of Chicago are not great because they have Newton or Darwin or Friedman. They are great because they gave humanity Newtonian view of mechanics, Darwinian view of evolution and Friedmanian view of economics. Likewise, Peking University is not great because it had the likes of Hu Shi (胡适.) It is great because of May Fourth Movement (五四运动) and Modern Chinese movement (白话运动). Such movements affected quarter humanity for an entire century and beyond.

I would be remiss if I did not unabashedly state that I was completely smitten by Min-Nan culture (闽南文化) ever since I came to Tainan and realized to my utter astonishment that NCKU is named after the great Min-Nan icon Zheng Cheng-Gong or Cheng Cheng-Kung (郑成功.) This recognition allows me to realize that NCKU stands in the core of this massive, omnipotent and millennium long Asia Pacific culture. I cannot believe that NCKU has this fabulous fortune as one of the intellectual (and in spin off economic) epic centers where this culture roams: Taiwan, Quemoy (金门,) Fujian (福建) and of course the entire Southeast Asia. To me, this brought new meaning to the existence of NCKU as a university. This recognition made me aware with exhilaration that NCKU is not simply "just another" university in Taiwan or Asia Pacific, but a unique one, one with unparallel heritage. Subconsciously, this excitement moved me with all my might and energy to promote this concept within university and throughout Taiwan, Quemoy, Mainland China and Southeast Asia. I have no doubt that while many intellectual disciplines may come and go, Min-Nan Culture as the underpinning will be here for millenniums!

Michael's push towards globalization, and the fact that NCKU is the epic center of Min-Nan culture, gives the university an added solemn responsibility: the responsibility to leverage the culture's deep presence in Southeast Asia to understand, appreciate and grow the vast, rich and robust multi-cultural aspects of the entire region. If NCKU were to greatly opening its doors to all outstanding intellects in the region, it could conceivably be the necessary spark to create a prairie fire of a new era of Asia Pacific landscape. If indeed NCKU could meet this Asia Pacific grand challenge in the 21st century, it will truly become world-class!

Last but not least, I also see that my portfolio includes promoting with all my might Michael's courageous vision to seek fundamental transformation of higher education in general and NCKU in particular. Like Michael and many truly outstanding colleagues all across campus, all across the Republic of China and beyond, I have full confidence that a possible transformation into an autonomous structure for NCKU will have deepest and ubiquitous impact for Republic of China in its quest to become a higher education haven. It could be the incentive to alter Asians mindset in the long run by impacting all higher education institutions in Asia Pacific. Indeed, I fully believe that such an effort will ultimately influence the world. In this respect, I am equally confident that having the *"can do attitude"* of Americans, what my Jewish friends would refer to as *"chutzpah,"* and by becoming an Asia Pacific *"insider,"* not just an *"often travelled to"* Asia Pacific visitor, was I able to acquire necessary skill-sets, whatever little wisdom, and *"Asian style finesse"* to initiate this arduous but incredibly rewarding march towards excellence.

My friends, I am but a minute drop of color ink fallen into a glass of pure water. It is my earnest hope that small I may be, the glass of water has altered ever so slightly its complexion.

On February 1, 2011, NCKU will have a new president, Dr. H. H. Hwung (黃煌輝.) I have no doubt, and have full confidence, that this new leadership of the university will continue to uphold the sacred and heavy responsibility of being one of the flagship universities of the Republic of China, that is to immerse the university in Asia Pacific culture and shine on the global higher education radar screen. It will continue the momentous push towards excellence, a momentum which is derived from eighty years of preparation since its founding. I am sure that the new team will have even greater, broader and deeper visions to educate next generations of leaders. Indeed, this university deserves no less! I am confident that by wave after wave of marching towards excellence, NCKU will ultimately become an icon of a world renowned university to stand shoulder to shoulder with the world's best in the 21st century.

In the last three and a half years, my wife Evelyn (蔣懿雯) and I have bonded with literally thousands upon thousands of truly remarkable and highly talented individuals all across Asia Pacific. Our lives were simply profoundly enriched. These people made and continue to evolve Asia into what it is and will be in the 21st century. Galvanizing these individuals into a cohesive force, 21st century will undoubtedly be Asia's. However, I would be remiss if we did not say that we will forever remember the warm and deep friendships we received from all walks of life in beautiful and deeply Confucius-centric Tainan, the cultural heritage of the Republic of China.

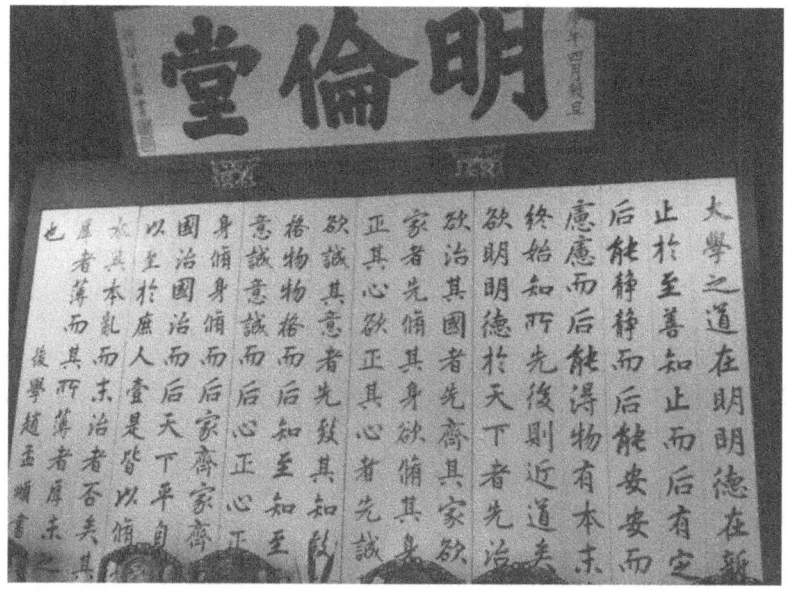

Photo taken inside the Confucius Temple of Tainan by a good friend Olivia Cheng, CEO of Aurora Technologies

For me, it is now permanently seared into my memory the genuine greetings I received without fail each morning from the campus police at the university gate as I rode to work on my bicycle and smile of a particular student who told me that I have made a difference in his life.

As the old saying goes,

"you can take us out of Tainan, you cannot take Tainan out of us!"

(2011)

45

A Global Intentional Effort: The Lifetime Contribution to Tsing Hua by Mei Yiqi (梅贻琦)

This was a speech delivered by the author at National Tsing Hua University on October 27, 2012 in a conference in memory of Mr. Mei Yiqi. The author was the Senior Vice President of Global Strategy, Planning and Evaluation at the University.

The author delivering his speech

Good morning, President Lih J. Chen, distinguished guests, alumni, colleagues and fellow students. As a new comer to this great institution, the National Tsing Hua University (NTHU), I am probably the least qualified at this gathering to say something or anything about our beloved late President, Mr. Mei Yiqi. Indeed, when President Chen asked me to give this talk, I accepted it with great trepidation. Then I began to think about Mr. Mei and what he meant to me, and not just since I came to NTHU. I then realized that I may be able to say something about him from my perspective, which may be unusual. So here goes.

In my talk today, I will have two parts.

1. I will share with everyone my unexpected relationships with the people of Tsing Hua.
2. The essence of Mr. Mei's lifetime work can be characterized by the attitude of "letting no stone unturned".

By historical serendipity, there are today two 'Tsing Hua's. The one in Beijing is known as Tsinghua University and the one in Hsinchu is known as National Tsing Hua University. Throughout my talk, whenever I mean the one at Beijing, I shall refer to it as Tsinghua, and the Hsinchu one as Tsing Hua. In Chinese, they are the same!

I should point out that throughout my professional career as a physicist, I have had deep working relationships with many folks from Tsinghua and Tsing Hua. In fact, as far back as 1979, when I was spending a year as a visiting professor at the Niels Bohr Institute of the University of Copenhagen, I met an outstanding theoretical physicist from Tsinghua. His name was Xu Zhan (徐湛). Later, two outstanding theoretical physicists from Tsinghua, Hong Zhou Sun (孙洪洲) and Mei Zhang (张玫), came to work in my research group in Philadelphia. Also, in the 80s and 90s, I had some collaborations with a number of nuclear physicists in Tsing Hua, namely S. T. Hsieh (谢世哲) and H. C. Chiang (蒋享进).

Although the above individuals had a profound impact on my career, the fact that they came from Tsing Hua or Tsinghua was not the real reason why I was deeply impressed with Tsing Hua or Tsinghua *per se*. Indeed, through them, I knew nothing about the late President Mei Yiqi.

I learned about President Mei Yiqi soon after I arrived in Drexel University in 1976. I met a senior colleague in the Business School. His name was Anmin Chung (钟安民). I later learned from Anmin that he was a student at the famed National Southwest Union University in Kunming during WWII. Even more importantly, he told me that his wife, Mei Zushan (梅祖杉), was the daughter of Mei Yiqi! (It is with deep sadness that soon after I arrived in Tsing Hua, I learned of the demise of Anmin and Zushan!) In my nearly 20 years as a colleague of Anmin, I became thoroughly aware of Mei Yiqi and his life and his contributions to National Tsing Hua University, before and after 1949!

As I have mentioned, Mei Yiqi's lifetime's work can be characterized by the attitude of "letting no stone unturned". According to Anmin, Mei Yiqi was not a man of "many words". Yet when he uttered something, usually it was profound. On more than one occasion, Anmin told me the famous quotation of Mei Yiqi, namely, "A university is not measured by its grand buildings. It is measured by its intellectual maestros!" (大学者, 非谓有大楼之谓也, 有大师之谓也。)

By the way, besides the meaning of this phrase being profound, the way it was expressed was equally impressive. This is especially incredible considering that Mei went to the U.S. as an undergraduate, which means that his Chinese training could only have reached secondary school level. I do not know how many people in greater China today with only secondary school education can write Chinese with such elegance!

Also, I should underscore that Mei's concept of prioritizing intellectual excellence as supreme for a university is true for Tsing Hua, before or after 1949, in Beijing or Hsinchu!

Although he was trained as an electrical engineer/physicist, one of Mei Yiqi's greatest contributions to Tsing Hua was rendering it the center for Chinese Classics (国学) research. During his presidency in Beijing before 1949, he recruited the so-called "Four Maestros of Chinese Classics" to the university. They are Wang Guowei (王国维), Zhao Yuanren (赵元任), Liang Qichao (梁启超) and Chen Yinque (陈寅恪). According to experts, these are *de facto* the Einstein, Schroedinger, Dirac and Niels Bohr of Chinese classics!

I am sure that if Mei Yiqi were alive today, he would not claim that this was all to his credit. But I am equally certain no one would dispute that deep in Mei's heart, he truly believed that a great Chinese university cannot be disassociated from the culture it was erected on!

I am sure that when Mei became the President of NTHU in 1931, even in his wildest dreams would he not have realized that there would be a bloody war of resistance with the Japanese and that he would *de facto* be operational president of the tri-universities known as National Southwest Union University in Kunming. As I have mentioned in Chapter 28, under his leadership, the National Southwest Union University was one of the greatest intellectual achievements of China in the 20th century. Again, although Mei if alive would dispute that this is entirely to his credit, I would reiterate that its success is entirely in line with the higher education vision of Mei!

After I came to NTHU a year ago, I made contact with Anmin. Let me quote for you here what he said about Mei in an email he sent to me before he passed away:

> *"Mrs. Mei was a tough yet dignified lady. I want to just say a few words about her role as the wife of a university president during WWII. I illustrate the private side of her character. The wartime salary of even a university president is not enough to maintain a household. From time to time, Mrs. Mei had to find a way to cover her extra household expenses. The most expeditious way to achieve this was by means of* "摆地铺"*, which means selling one's possessions on the street. And on a few occasions she had to do just that in spite of her social status. The income was meager, but it helped in the hard times during the War, and I admired her courage to do so.*
>
> *Please do what you think is proper with the little story above. To me it reflects the strength of her character, and that's why I offer it to you.*
>
> *Good night,*
> *Anmin."*

I have also said that to this day, with nearly four thousand universities in greater China (Taiwan, Mainland, Hong Kong and Macau,) the short-lived National Southwest Union University under the leadership of Mei was the only university where two of its students, Chen Ning Yang (杨振宁) and Tsung-Dao Lee (李政道), were able to receive the highest scientific accolade of the world, the Nobel Prize in Physics.

Then of course, in 1955, President Chiang Kai-Shek (蔣介石) invited Mei to establish the National Tsing Hua University here in Hsinchu. Although his tenure here lasted until 1962, there is no question in my mind that his style of building a university is as much palpable here today as it was during his presidency in Beijing and Kunming. For example, the great push by President Lih J. Chen of Hsinchu's NTHU to become the platform for China and India to understand each another is very much in line with the legacy of Mei.

Mei's presidency in Tsing Hua (before and after 1949) and by extension, Tsinghua, left a deep legacy on both shores. I do not know what was the real reason why both institutions today have the same motto: 自強不息, 厚德載物, meaning *"The enlight'ned exert themselves constantly. The virtuous bear duties onerous."* Or why they have the same school anthem. But I am quite certain that having Mei Yiqi regarded by both as the "eternal president" was one of the reasons, if not the only reason why the two institutions could be "joined at the hips" and why both are two outstanding institutions serving as two intellectual pillars on both shores!

When Mei Yiqi was president of Tsing Hua before 1949 in Peking (Beijing), he devoted his entire professional effort to building as good a university as he possibly could. Afterwards in Hsinchu, he again devoted his entire professional effort the same way. It is very interesting to note that in the 21st century, Asia Pacific is the fastest growth region in the world. In this regard, Mainland China and Taiwan are experiencing spectacular transformation, from cold war to peaceful existence. In a sense, the lifetime contributions of Mei Yiqi, exemplified by Tsing Hua and Tsinghua, are a miniature of this transformation.

I think any university president in the world would agree when I say that building a single great university in one's lifetime is already an arduous task. In history, one saw Charles Eliot of Harvard University and Cai Yuan-Pei (蔡元培) of Peking University doing just that. But entirely through "unintended consequences", Mei Yiqi had direct or indirect contributions to the building of two great institutions. Indeed, through Tsinghua and Tsing Hua, and their importance not only for cross-straits relations but world peace in general, Mei Yiqi made contributions to humanity *ad infinitum.*

In 1962, Mei Yiqi completed his life and was buried in NTHU in Hsinchu.

The two presidents of Tsinghua and Tsing Hua, Chen Jiling (陈吉宁) and Chen Lih J. respectively, paying respects to Mei Yiqi at his Mausoleum on the Tsing Hua campus.

Rest in peace, Mr. Mei!

(2012)

46
On S. S. Chern (陈省身)

The first piece of writing was penned on December 3, 2004, titled "The Passing of a World Class Mathematician and Great Human Being: S S Chern". The second is a speech for the "Convergence of US, Mexico and China: S S Chern Legacy Conference in CIMAT Mexico", held on November 17–19, 2005. The author was Vice President for Research and Economic Development, The University of Texas at Dallas, when he wrote both articles.

I

I woke up early this morning (December 5th, 2004) to get ready to go on a 10-day trip to India as a member of UTD's delegation to visit India. I engaged in my normal habit: I checked my email first.

As soon as I got onto the Internet, I was immediately stunned to learn that the world had lost one of the greatest mathematicians, Professor S. S. Chern.

Chern's contributions to mathematics are at the level of some of the iconic mathematicians the world has seen, such as Newton, Laplace, Lie and Cartan. He was undoubtedly a 20th century mathematician, just as Newton was for the 16th/17th century, Laplace was for the 18th century, Sophus Lie for the 19th century and Elie Cartan for the early part of the 20th century.

I met Chern for the first time in 1989, May 21st, in Philadelphia. I invited him to deliver a University-wide lecture entitled "The Meaning of Geometry". It was a memorable lecture. I was especially impressed by his ability to explain the extremely complicated and technical subjects such as "Chern Classes" to the entire audience, which included undergraduates NOT majoring in mathematics. I was even more impressed to see that he was willing, in fact anxious, to talk to the students after the lecture.

Between 1991–1993, I organized every summer a summer school in nuclear astrophysics in Nankai University, the alma mater of Chern. Nankai University (南开大学) is in Tianjin, China, about two hours from Beijing. On the campus of the University, Chern has constructed a very comfortable and spacious bungalow which he appropriately named "the Home of Geometry" (几何之家). Since he was not in residence when my school was conducted, Chern was very gracious in allowing me to house some of the speakers there. It was an experience I will never forget.

Chern's son-in-law is Professor Paul C. W. Chu (朱经武), a world-class physicist who discovered high temperature superconductivity. Paul is also a member of the Research Advisory Board of the University of Texas at Dallas. In this capacity, I indirectly learned from him about what Chern was "up to" in the past few years. Apparently, after leaving Berkeley in 2000, he moved to Nankai University. Presumably, he took up residence in "the Home of Geometry". Though at an advanced age, Chern's mind was still racing at a high speed, tackling some of the hardest problems in mathematics and inviting many of the world's best mathematicians to come to Nankai to work on them.

I sent the following email to Paul after I learned of Chern's passing:

Paul

I just read the news that the great S. S. Chern has passed on.

Please accept my deep sympathy. Your wife lost a great father. You lost a great father-in-law. China lost a great Chinese, U.S. lost a great Chinese American, and the world lost one of the greatest mathematicians of all times.

Da Hsuan

II

I was asked by the organizers to say a few words at the end of this great conference organized by Centro de Investigacion en Matematicas, or CIMAT, Clay Institute and the University of Texas at Dallas, in honor of the deep contributions of one of the world's greatest mathematicians, S. S. Chern.

First, I must congratulate everyone in CIMAT, from the Director General to all the enthusiastic students. Your warm hospitality is palpable.

I am not a mathematician. During my professional career, I marveled and am deeply impressed that for a mathematician, a sphere is a coset space called SU(2)/U(1) and a plane is a coset space of H(4)/U(1). Such characterizations, and indeed their generalizations, have unlocked the doors for mathematicians to travel into the deepest areas of human thoughts. I knew then that a mathematician I will never be.

However, I have always enjoyed listening to great mathematicians speak. In fact, I was privileged that I heard Chern talk on "What is Geometry" on May 23rd, 1989, in Philadelphia. I should mention that I also heard another great mathematician, Eugenio Calabi, not speaking about mathematics, but playing the violin! Actually, to me, that is not too regrettable. After all, for me, listening to a mathematician talk is like listening to an Italian opera: *It's beautiful and I don't understand a word of it*. Indeed, for the past two and a half days, I have sat through a lot of operas, delivered by some of the best mathematicians Latin America has to offer the world!

Nevertheless, "armed" with that small and dangerous (and I am sure you would call insignificant) knowledge of mathematics, it has given me a profound belief as a university administrator that an institution of higher learning must be accompanied by outstanding mathematics if it were to reach the highest level of intellectual achievement. It is for this reason that I am so enthusiastic about my university's collaboration with CIMAT, and to co-sponsor this great conference in honor of a great mathematician and human being of the 20th century: S. S. Chern.

However, having heard the truly emotional discussion of Chern by his son-in-law Paul Chu, I realize that this conference is more than just mathematics. As you know, Paul is a great scientist, a distinguished professor of the University of Houston and the President of Hong Kong University of Science and Technology. He is also an individual who spans two continents: North America and Asia. In fact, while he was here two days ago, by now, he is already back in Hong Kong.

Ever since I came to Texas five years ago, I became intimately aware of the importance of Mexico. U.S. and Mexico not only share two thousand miles of border, they are also economically and intellectually linked. What is happening at this conference is a manifestation, albeit small, of this linkage. I am convinced that the future of the United States and Mexico will depend on how these two nations can co-exist in a mutually beneficial manner.

Chern, on the other hand, was a man deeply ingrained in China and the United States. Of the many speakers of this conference, a majority came from Latin America, and it is clear that Chern's influence in Latin America is just as deep.

Therefore, to conclude, please allow me to conjecture (using your language) that this conference is not just for mathematics, but a convergence, albeit still a microcosm, of China, the U.S. and Latin America. I hope that CIMAT and the University of Texas at Dallas, leveraging the spirit of Chern as a human being and as our guiding light, can continue to play a role, however minor, in promoting this convergence for world peace for years to come.

(2005)

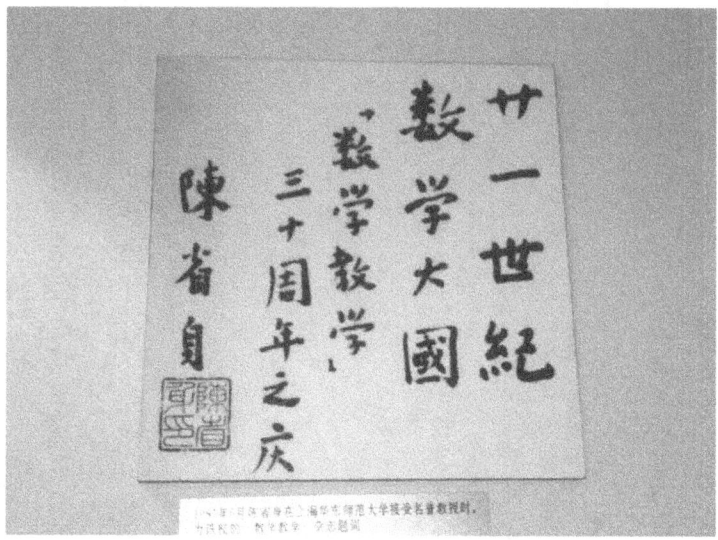

Great Nation of Mathematics in the 21st Century 30th Anniversary Celebration of *Shuxue Jiaoxue (Mathematical Teaching)* by S. S. Chern

(2013)

47
On Chen Ning Yang (杨振宁)

Below are three accounts on Nobel Laureate C. N. Yang, the first two written in 2013, when the author was Senior Vice President, Global Strategy, Planning and Evaluation, National Tsing Hua University. The last was the banquet comment at the "Conference on 60 Years of Yang-Mills Gauge Field Theories: C. N. Yang's Contributions to Physics", held on 26 May 2015 in Singapore, when the author was Director of Global Affairs and Special Advisor of the Rector of the fledgling University of Macau.

I

Cliff Swartz, "Heroes," *The Physics Teachers*, December, 1991

In 1991, *The Physics Teachers* selected 18 physicists whose contributions are considered the most profound. Independent as to whether other physicists should be selected or not, the selection of these 18 are indisputable.

In the past three days in Hsinchu Tsing Hua University, one of the only remaining 18, who is also the only Asian, Professor Chen Ning Yang came to visit and lectured in Hsinchu Tsing Hua University. What is especially exciting for all communities in Hsinchu Tsing Hua is that Professor Yang is an "old boy" of National Tsing Hua University (NTHU). He received his B.Sc. from Southwest Union University, in which NTHU is a component, and his M.Sc. from NTHU. He is also the first recipient of a doctor of science, *honoris causa* from Hsinchu Tsing Hua University and currently is a faculty member at Beijing Tsinghua University.

For this reason, in my introductory comment in the Physics Department of Professor Yang, I unabashedly declared that "Professor Yang is unquestionably the pride of both Beijing Tsinghua and Hsinchu Tsing Hua, and the pride of humanity!"

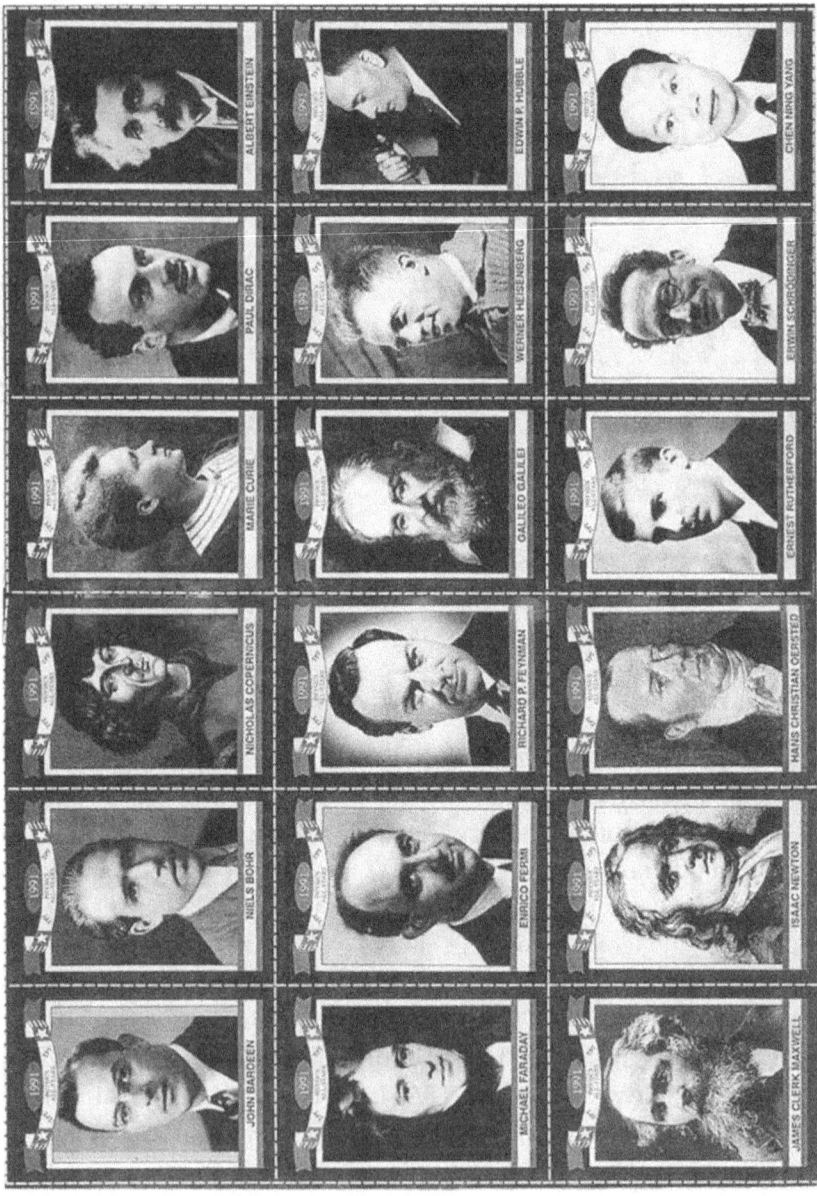

(2013)

II

Chen Ning Yang's elder son Franklin and Albert Einstein

On December 19, 2013, Chen Ning Yang spoke to an audience of 1,000 in National Tsing Hua University. The title of his talk was "My Learning and Research Experiences." In that one hour of speech, there was one slide which I found to be particularly intriguing, and that was the photo taken in the early 50's where his elder son Franklin is with Albert Einstein at the Institute of Advanced Studies in Princeton. If my memory is not faulty, Yang said that: "Professor Einstein was a man of great order. Therefore, everyone at the Institute knew when he would call it a day, and what route he would take to walk home. Therefore, many of us would wait at that time and place, hoping to catch him and have a few exchanges of Physics with him. This picture was one such occasion when I brought Franklin along to take a photo with him!"

In China, Yang received a rigorous training from some of the best China had then, such as Ta-You Wu and Zhu-Xi Wang. When he came to the U.S., giants such as Enrico Fermi, Edward Teller, Oppenheimer, and of course, last but not least, Albert Einstein expanded and deepened his appreciation and understanding of nature.

In his talk, Yang mentioned that in China, he mastered the skill of deduction, which is to go from theory to phenomena. When he came to the U.S., he acquired the skill of induction, which is to establish a theoretical understanding from phenomena. I presume the work of Lee and Yang on "Parity Non-Conservation" is an excellent example of the latter, while the immortal work of Yang and Mills on "Gauge Invariance" or Yang-Mills Field is perhaps a shining example of the former.

(2013)

III

A Thank You Note to Professor Chen Ning Yang

Professor and Mrs. Yang, colleagues at this conference, I am not sure why I was asked to say a few words at such a distinguished gathering. I think the only reason I can think of is that Dr. K. K. Phua and I go back a long way. He and my elder brother were schoolmates in elementary school here in Singapore, and so he has always been a big brother to me. I am sure you all know that in the Chinese tradition, when big brother says "jump," you say "how high!"

I have one confession to make here. Unlike anyone here at this conference, my life did not and does not revolve around "Yang-Mills!" Actually, I am "Yang-Mills free!" I know that is hard to believe, but believe me, it is true. In fact, I think it is also true that if you pick anyone off the street anywhere in the world and ask him or her what he or she thinks of the impact of Yang-Mills, the answer will inevitably be, "say what?"

Although my life is not affected by Yang-Mills, my life is affected by Yang! On the day when the Nobel Committee announced that Tsung-Dao Lee and Chen Ning Yang had won the Nobel Prize in Physics, that memorable day in October of 1957, not only Lee and Yang's lives were changed forever, so was mine in my own diminutive way.

As a young Chinese 5th-grade student living in Singapore at that time, we were informed that something remarkable had happened. I was told, "Those two Chinese, Lee and Yang, just like 'you and me,' have done something so fantastic that the highest accolade of the world has been bestowed on them." (Now that I think back, that phrase "you and me" is the greatest stretch of the imagination.)

To my generation of Chinese everywhere in the world, perhaps a generation before me and for sure several generations after me, whether the person is a physicist or not (and believe me, contrary to common belief, most Chinese are not particle physicists), the name "Chen Ning Yang" simply means "a shot of inherent self-confidence."

In this conference, I have heard talk after talk about the deep impact of Yang-Mills on our understanding of the universe. Indeed, Yang-Mills' gifts to the world of science are innumerable. But my friends, I can assure you that Yang-Mills' gift to the world of science pales in comparison to Professor Yang's gift to the Chinese civilization. With sheer intellectual prowess and with profound dignity, Professor Yang lifted the spirit, the sense of belonging and the deep inherent self-confidence of all Chinese at an era when that was in great need. For me, before Yang was cognizant to all, the end was nowhere in sight. After Yang, there was bright light.

My friends, for the past 58 years, I have often wondered what I would say to Professor Yang face to face if I ever got a chance to thank him, without sounding contrived. I now realize that this is the moment and while I am indeed seizing the moment, it is incredible that all I can muster my energy and determination to say is: "Thank you Professor Yang, from the bottom of my heart!"

(2015)

48

"What Physics Have You Done Lately?": On Sam C. C. Ting (丁肇中)

This is the welcome note by the author at the National Tsing Hua University 2014 Nobel Laureates Lectures. Prof Sam Ting delivered a lecture on "Alpha Magnetic Spectrometer Experiment on the International Space Station". The author was Senior Vice President, Global Strategy, Planning and Evaluation, National Tsing Hua University.

Academician Ting, dear students, colleagues, good morning.

In 1957, two Chinese, Chen Ning Yang (杨振宁) and Tsung-Dao Lee (李政道) won the highest scientific accolade, the Nobel Prize in Physics. An interesting but less known fact, as told to me by Professor Yang, is that

Professor Yang was still holding the passport of the Republic of China at that time! 19 years later, in 1976, the third Chinese won the Nobel Prize, again in physics. That person is our speaker today at the National Tsing Hua University, Academician Samuel C. C. Ting.

I am sure no one would doubt that these three gentlemen are the pride of Chinese globally. My fellow students, what I would like to talk about today is something even more important than their winning the Nobel Prize. Please don't get me wrong, winning the Nobel Prize is a very big deal! However, what I would like to impress upon you, especially the youngsters in the audience, is that these individuals were, and still are, able to leverage their enormous wisdom and the resources at their disposal to carry out earth-shaking and world-renowned activities others either had not thought of, could not think of, or both!

When I was asked to introduce and say a few words about Academician Ting here today, it caused me a moment of anxiety. After all, Academician Ting's scientific contributions are absolutely well-known. Even if you are so ignorant about who he is, all you have to do is to Google him, and you can literally obtain mountains of believable or unbelievable information about him!

So after much self-debate, I decided to share with you two rather small but not inconsequential stories about Academician Ting.

The first story occurred in 1979. That year, Singapore's Professor K. K. Phua organized an international physics conference. That was my first encounter with Academician Ting in flesh and blood! In one of the many tea-breaks of the conference, a group of physicists, mostly theoreticians, were arguing vehemently about a particular physics problem. I must say that I cannot recall what they were arguing about so passionately (but that probably it is irrelevant in my present discussion). When passion was running high, someone noticed that Academician Ting was standing next to the group in absolute silence. So one of the persons turned to him and said: "Sam, what is your opinion?" I remember distinctly Academician Ting without the slightest hesitation and with a crystal-clear voice said: "what does the experiment say?"

In five words, it summarizes in totality and profoundly the physics research attitude of Academician Ting!

The second story also occurred in 1979, but it does not link directly to Academician Ting. As we all know, Academician Ting is a faculty member of the famed physics department of MIT. One of his colleagues, whom I know since we were both spending time at the Niels Bohr Institute of the University of Copenhagen that year, is John Negele. If my memory does not fail me, John was the director of MIT's Institute of Theoretical Physics. In one of my casual conversations with John I asked him: "How good is MIT's physics department?" Without any hesitation, John answered me: "I often meet Sam in the elevator. Almost every time I meet him, he would inevitably and solemnly ask me: 'What physics have you done lately?'"

"Among us colleagues at MIT," John said, "it is known that this is not a casual question from Sam!"

In a truly great physics department, or any department within an outstanding university, the relationship among colleagues must be built on professional ambiance. Furthermore, having constant official and unofficial professional self and mutual evaluation should be the norm and not the exception!

My fellow students, I sincerely hope that when you walk away from hearing Academician Ting's talk today, you have gained the understanding on how to push forth and realize transformational visions, and how to accumulate world class people together to create the future!

Thank you!

(2014)

49

The Supreme Courage of a Chinese Intellectual: Preface to a Memorial Volume Dedicated to Prof Jin-Quan Chen (陈金全)

This is the Preface to a Memorial Volume Dedicated to Professor Jin-Quan Chen, Professor of Physics, Nanjing University, published by World Scientific Publishing Co in 2003. The author was Vice President for Research and Graduate Education and Professor of Physics at The University of Texas at Dallas. The main title of this article was added by the Editor.

My friend Professor Jin-Quan Chen, a world renowned mathematical physicist, departed from this earth, sadly, in 1999. This scientific volume, contributed by many of his friends and colleagues, is published in his memory. Professor Chen's life mirrors a generation of Chinese intellectuals. It was profoundly sad, yet exhilarating.

1976 was a defining year for modern China. Chairman Mao died on Sept. 9 that year, followed immediately by the spectacular collapse of the so-called "Gang of Four", thus bringing closure to ten painful years of "Cultural Revolutions", and ushered China into a new era. Someday, historians will undoubtedly consider the new era as the "miracle of the world in the 20th century".

In 1976, after a decade of utter devastation, China was at the verge of a complete "meltdown", economically, technologically and intellectually. Having quarter humanity, and a land size spanning nearly half of Asia, such a meltdown would have horrifying global implications!

Yet, no meltdown occurred.

A fundamental reason why there was no meltdown was because of the Herculean contributions of the tens of millions of Chinese intellectuals. In their darkest hours during that era, enduring the hardest of hardships and suffering the deepest personal humiliations, they always maintained palpable hope for themselves, their family, their professions and their nation. Indeed, even without personal liberty, both physically and mentally, they remained important pillars of the nation, holding up its dignity. The successes of China of the 21st century are in no small part due to this group of individuals.

This is the joyous and sad story of one of them, our friend Professor Chen Jin-Quan.

In 1977, as a young Chinese American Assistant Professor of Physics in Philadelphia, I was profoundly curious about the state of China in general and the state of its science in particular. I wanted to initiate scientific relations and collaborations with colleagues in China. Since I knew virtually no one in China, certainly none in my research area, there was no direct and efficient way for me to establish the necessary connection.

Serendipitously, that Fall, I invited one of the most well respected Chinese American physicists and Nobel Laureates, Chen Ning Yang, to deliver a "Distinguished Lecture" in Philadelphia. Yang delivered a beautiful lecture, understandable even by lay people, on some of the deepest issues of unifying forces in nature. As a habit, a colleague and I transcribed the lecture. Knowing that Yang was, and still is, a household name in China, I thought the best way to cast a wide net to make contact with colleagues in China was to send this transcription to the libraries of major universities, hoping someone would notice it and respond to me. Nanjing University was one of the universities I sent the document.

Months went by. There was no response. Finally one (and only one) came, and it was from Professor Chen Jin-Quan. In a style that I became deeply familiar with in the next twenty years, Jin-Quan wrote to me in perfect English, and profound reverence. From the few words I added in the transcription about myself, he was able to extrapolate, albeit roughly, my research interest. With great dignity and in no uncertain terms, he expressed a strong desire to communicate with me on scientific matters. This was the beginning of our long association.

In hindsight, this letter from Professor Chen to me was written with great courage.

Why was courage necessary? Well, if one considers for a moment China's predicament at the time, it was understandable. After all, China just emerged from a period of extreme political turmoil and control. For ten years, intellectuals were brutalized. Therefore, even though there was an official declaration of the ending of the era, the nation was still in a state of "*xin you yu ji*" (心有余悸 the heart still fills with legacy fear!) And fear there was! Indeed, there was no guarantee that China would not reverse back to its dark age any time soon. With that as background, it is not difficult to imagine that supreme courage was necessary for Chen to write to me.

Chinese intellectuals never allowed their minds to cease functioning during those ten terrible years. Nearly everyone one of the thousands I came to know had an extremely interesting and heart-warming story to tell about the way he/she remained intellectually alert. Chen was no exception. I think the following story about Chen was worth telling.

Chen had a great capacity for memorization. He used it effectively during those ten years. When he was sent to the countryside, to be "re-educated" as a peasant, he brought with him two books: an English-Chinese dictionary, and an English translation of Leo Tolstoy's "War and Peace". During those years, every night, he studied and memorized several words from the dictionary, and read the novel over and over, until he virtually memorized it. This was how he became perfect in the usage of the English language, and how he possessed an inexhaustible vocabulary.

In a sense, writing to me was perhaps Chen's way to "cast his net" to the outside world. In hindsight, this response marked a watershed in my contacts and friendship with literally thousands of individuals in China for the next quarter of a century. In a style which I became quite familiar within the next quarter of a century, I was consumed by his letter and responded quickly and positively to Chen, thus initiating a scientific collaboration which lasted nearly two decades. I guess you might say that it was indeed, in modern terms, a win-win situation!

As I have indicated earlier, Chen's courage was not in the least unusual. In fact, tens of thousands of Chinese intellectuals did something similar, and within a decade, the world outside of China was filled with Chinese intellectuals as visiting scholars, bettering themselves in all areas of intellectual pursues. And within the next twenty years, a large percentage of this group made their way back to China.

Many are now the pillars of modern China.

With China's rapidly growing importance on the global landscape, and thus must be a major factor in world peace, one cannot underscore the important contributions of this group of intellectuals in the 21st century!

(2003)

50

A "Thank You" Note to Iris Chang (张纯如)

Iris Chang, author of the international bestseller The Rape of Nanking, died on November 9, 2004. When the author learnt of her untimely death, he wrote the following message to his friends: "On April Fools day of this year, I met Iris for the second time. When I said goodbye to her that evening, where she and I had exchanged a few heartfelt words to each other, I did not know that those were forever goodbye words."

Below is an introduction of Chang by the author during her lecture in Richardson, Texas, held on April 1, 2004, when the author was Vice President for Research and Graduate Education at The University of Texas at Dallas.

Good evening, ladies and gentlemen.

Iris Chang, an author with Global impact, needs NO introduction

Since she needs NO introduction, I thought the best I could do here is to use this opportunity to say a profound "thank you" to her.

About 35 years ago, when I was still an undergraduate in New Jersey, and was a struggling "foreign student", a friend of mine, who was Jewish, invited me to go to a lecture on campus. My roommate told me that the lecture was by a "Holocaust" survivor. Until then, I have never heard of the phrase "The Holocaust".

The lecture, and the photos she showed, which were so haunting and so profoundly lacking in humanity, left a deep impression — probably more correctly, a deep scar — in my mind. I remember to this date the final phrase of the lecture: "NEVER AGAIN!"

When I returned to my room after the lecture, I began wondering about the meaning of the phrase THE HOLOCAUST. Did it apply only to the deep sufferings, in mind, soul and bodies, of the Jews in Europe?

Well, in fact, it wasn't until last night, when I was preparing for this introduction, I looked up Cambridge Dictionary and found that it defined the phrase "The Holocaust" as

The systematic murder of many people, esp. Jews, by the Nazis during World War II.

Yes, any systematic murder of "many people", is a Holocaust!

I learned from my mother as a child in Singapore, who was a professor of music in Jinling Woman's University in Nanjing (or Nanking) after WWII, about the "Nanking Massacre". I am sure because it was so painful for her to remember the Nanking Massacre that she was only willing to tell me bits and pieces of this horrible event in China during WWII. I remember that I was deeply angered by what I learned, but was frustrated because I could not learn more. There were no books I could find on the subject, at least none readily available!

Soon, life went on for me and the issue of the Nanking Massacre was put on the back burner. It was not until I read Iris' book a few years ago, entitled the RAPE OF NANKING, that rekindled that deep feeling of rage in me. Her writing was not just great, it was haunting. For the first time in my life, I could profoundly appreciate why anyone possessing a sense of justice — whether you are Chinese ethnically or not — could say NEVER AGAIN!

The book articulated for me, for the first time, why not being Jewish, I could be so deeply angered by THE HOLOCAUST in Europe. It succinctly stated for me that I am their fellow human being.

I am sure that any one reading Iris' book, whether he/she be ethnically Chinese or not, can feel the deep pain and profound anger as a fellow human being.

It was the first book which brought some justice to the deep sufferings of the hundreds of thousands in Nanking in WWII.

So, thank you Iris, for being so brave, for me, and for all humanity!

51

Lee Kuan Yew (李光耀) and Education

Lee Kuan Yew, the founding Prime Minister of Singapore, passed on March 23, 2015. Having grown up in Singapore, the author wrote a personal note to commemorate this major statesman, focusing on the relevance to education, keeping close to the theme of this book.

On March 23rd of this year (2015), Lee Kuan Yew departed. On that day, I was literally in a daze.

For as long as I can remember, Lee Kuan Yew was with me figuratively. In my youth, I remember his palpable presence, from listening to the radio, from seeing the ubiquitous political posters during elections, and in person in a distance in political rallies. As I grew older, I began to understand his political philosophy and practice. And in the past three to four decades, I saw him as a major global political statesman and how he and his political party, the People's Action Party (PAP) transformed Singapore from a third world country to a first world country.

Also for as long as I can remember, Nanyang University (南洋大学 the original one and not the current Nanyang Technological University) was also with me, first in real terms and later figuratively.

In my youth, my mother, a prominent piano teacher in Singapore, had an outstanding student whose father was a professor of chemistry of Nanyang University. I remember the mother of this student was a fantastic cook and the student's family were very kind to my mother, and thus by extension, to me as well. On many occasions, my mother would take the family to visit them, and usually the visit would end with a fantastic dinner. These visits, and thus Nanyang University, were etched into my memory. In fact, I remember vividly the magnificent gate of Nanyang

University which our car had to pass through every time we visited it. I did wonder every now and then whether someday I could study in this university.

While I was a graduate student in the U.S., a postdoctoral fellow in the same group who is an Indonesian Chinese actually completed his undergraduate studies in Nanyang University. From our many conversations, I learned about the importance of the university for many wandering Chinese educated students in Southeast Asia.

After I received my doctorate in physics, some colleagues in the physics department of Nanyang University and I discussed about the possibility of my joining the department. While that did not happen, it made me even more cognizant of the importance of this university.

Then the sky dropped for me. In 1980, Nanyang University merged with University of Singapore and *de facto* ceased to exist. One can find all sorts of discussions in the literature and in the internet about how and who made the decision to close Nanyang University. There are many articles one could read by authors who spent far more hours and are more knowledgeable on this issue than I. For example, the article "Nanyang University and the Dilemmas of Overseas Chinese Education" by Justus M. Van Der Kroef in the *China Quarterly*, No. 20 (Oct.–Dec., 1964), pp. 96–127 depicted the situation at that time in a very comprehensive manner. Another article by Ta-Shi Gong-Sun (太史公孙) published in Nanyang Alumni Website discussed about who made the final decision to "close" Nanyang University.

To me, after so many years, and however complex the issues were involving the closing, and remembering the famous motto of President Harry Truman: "The Buck Stops Here," the ultimate decision must had been Lee Kuan Yew's. He was then the Prime Minister of the Republic of Singapore and therefore, if nothing else, had to node his head to execute this decision.

A quarter of a century has passed since Nanyang University is no longer. And now Lee Kuan Yew was no longer. Therefore, in writing a book on higher education in Asia, I would be remiss if I do not say a few words about my personal feelings regarding this convoluted chapter of Asian higher education.

Let me just give a few of my personal feelings about all this.

Even though I have travelled widely in many continents, experienced deeply a large number of cultures, and I think I am a reasonably open-minded and tolerant individual, I cannot deflect the fact that in Singapore I was "Chinese educated" and my Chinese heritage is profoundly important for me. Therefore seeing the demise of Nanyang University, which was erected with Chinese cultural heritage, and had developed during my youth some warm and longing feelings toward it, I could not help but to have a touch of sadness.

Of course, I must recognise that I left Singapore even before it became a country. In a few days of this year, 2015, the nation will celebrate its 50th anniversary. So much water has passed under the bridge. In the past 50 years, on numerous occasion I visited Singapore, and saw its transformation from a third world country to the first. In the past seven years, I saw many Asian nations with weak, indecisive, even timid, leadership. Hence, I often wondered out loud what Singapore would become had it not had someone like Lee Kuan Yew who unquestionably provided strong, some even called it brutal, leadership when the country departed from Malaysia to be an independent nation. Absolutely lacking in natural resources, Singapore today is the best example of economic success of an Asian country. Surely one cannot discuss Nanyang University in the absence of Singapore's emergence into the world stage. After all, on that stage, the presence of Lee Kuan Yew, even after he had departed, was still palpable!

Finally I think to discuss about Nanyang University and not discuss Nanyang Technological University (NTU) is at best incomplete. Without a doubt, it is fair to say that NTU today is a highly visible outstanding university in Asia, if not beyond. Although NTU has greatly expanded its campus, the central core of the university is the original Nanyang University. In fact, every time I came to its Chinese Heritage Center, which was the former library of Nanyang University, I felt I was "time transported back in time!" In this sense, I suspect for many Singaporeans, for sure those 50 and above, especially if the person is like me Chinese educated, separating Nanyang University and NTU is very difficult, if not an impossibility.

But do not fooled by appearance. If a Martian were dropped into NTU away from those few historical buildings, it would sense a completely different ambiance. As this alien walked around the well-constructed and well-manicured campus of NTU today, it could easily imagine that it is in any Western university. Indeed, the "westernization" of NTU is nearly, if not totally, complete.

I have no doubt that the education NTU provides for its students are high quality. However, it is also true that NTU today aims to educate the leaders of Asia of tomorrow. If these leaders do not inherently understand Asians, Asian cultures and Asian values, how are they able to connect to Asians not just in Singapore, but all around Singapore. Even as far as north and western Asia?

Recently, Shantou University (汕头大学) and Technion, Israel Institute of Technology, initiated a joint campus. As a member of Shantou University's Board of Trustees, I made the following comment.

"I think anyone who had visited Israeli universities can feel that, whether it be in software or hardware, they resemble some of the most outstanding American-like universities outside of U.S.. But there is one aspect that Israeli universities do not compromise, nor will they forgo and that is the dignity and self-confidence of being Israeli high education institutions. The moment I step onto the campus of Technion in Haifa, I can inherently feel the palpable "Israeliness!" To me, this is the ultimate form of inherent self-confidence."

Recently, I attended a conference in NTU. A good friend told me that the gate of the original Nanyang University which is etched in my mind is no longer part of the campus. It now sits quietly and without any sense of its history or significance near a big shopping mall. When my friend drove me to see the gate, I was simply overwhelmed by emotions and had to hold back my tears.

(2015)

Appendix
Where it all Begins...

The author started his non-technical writing in 1995, as mentioned in his Preface. In two decades, he eventually shifted his focus to education, higher education in particular. He was M. Russell Wehr Professor of Physics and Atmospheric Science at Drexel University when he started writing. However, it is a pity that he could not locate the original article, so what you will be reading below is the enriched version, written two years later.

Congressional Delegation (CODEL) Weldon and Asia:
A Personal Account

I. Preliminary

From January 21st to 31st of 1997, Congressman Curt Weldon organized a bi-partisan congressional delegation (Codel) to China, Hong Kong and Taiwan. The original plan of the trip was to go to four cities: Shanghai (where Congressman Weldon was to deliver the Lincoln Lecture at Fudan University), Beijing, Hong Kong and Taipei. However, due to aircraft trouble, in which we had to spend about 15 hours in Anchorage, the Shanghai part of the visit had to be cancelled. This was of course a real disappointment for the Codel, especially Congressman Weldon and me.

As is well known, Shanghai, since 1989, is undergoing an unimaginable economic transformation. Having it as the first stop would have given the Codel an exciting first impression of the new Orient. Fortunately, it turns out that President Yang of Fudan University, who has an invitation from President Clinton, will be in Washington D.C. this coming week. So Congressman Weldon and I have arranged to meet him in Washington D.C. then to reschedule the lecture.

In addition, because of the heavy demands on the schedule, the Codel was not able to have all possible meetings, in China, Hong Kong and Taiwan. As it is, the Codel had 27 meetings, each lasting at least as long as an hour, and often much longer.

CODEL-Weldon, the formal name for the delegation, consisted of the following members:

Congressman Curt Weldon (R-Pennsylvania), Chairman of the delegation
Congressman Solomon Ortiz (D-Texas)
Congressman Jon Fox (R-Pennsylvania)
Congressman John McHugh (R-New York)
Congressman Matt Salmon (R-Arizona).

In Beijing, Codel-Weldon was joined by Congressman Gary Ackerman (D-New York) and in Taipei, by Congressman Michael R. McNulty (D-New York). (R=Republican and D=Democratic).

There were also a number of professional staff members from the House National Security Committee in the Codel. They are Steve Ansley, who handled much of the schedule logistics for the Codel, and David Trachtenberg, an expert on China and Russia affairs, who also prepared a many hundred pages notes for the Codel on aspects ranging from cultural to military of that region (within two weeks). It was, to say the least, an impressive document! The Chief-of-Staff of Congressman Salmon, Robert U. Glazier, was also with the Codel until Hong Kong.

There were also five members of the military who accompanied the Codel. Colonel Daniel E. Fleming and Lieutenant Colonel Mark Wise were both army escorts. They were there to handle the travel logistics as well as other military matters. Colonel (Dr.) Al Nagia from the air force was the Codel medical doctor. Judging from what I saw he was carrying, I think Dr. Nagia must have sufficient medicine and equipment to handle the most complicated medical problem if it were to arise! Finally, two other army escorts, Sargent First Class Gary Hardy and Staff Sargent Edward LaRosa, were there throughout the trip to handle all other needs of the Codel. It was interesting for me to learn that both Sergeants belong to the elite honor guards of the Army, and just two weeks ago, they performed their duties during the inauguration ceremony of President Clinton!

Finally, there were also two "civilians" on this trip: Dr. Gerrit W. Gong, who is the Freeman Chair in China Studies and Director of Asian Studies Program of a well known think-tank in Washington D.C. known as the Center for Strategic and International Studies. From what I was told, and from what I observed, Gerrit was obviously an intellectual of significant proportion in this important field of study. He had, I was told, testified repeatedly in the Congressional hearings on East Asia policies. I was the other civilian, unofficially representing the academic world. My presence was of course supported by the President of Drexel University, President Constantine Papadakis. Both Dr. Gong and I were invited by Congressman Weldon to be a part of this Codel.

II. Why the trip?

Every event and every meeting will be reported by David Trachtenberg, the professional staff member of the House National Security Committee. The report he is currently preparing will be part of the Congressional records and therefore part of the report is available to the public. David promised me that when it is available, he will let me know when and where one can get a copy.

I would like to take a few paragraphs here to recapture my own feelings and impressions of this trip.

Let me say from the outset that we have often heard from the media that many of the trips taken by congressmen are "junkets", namely they are more (or all) sight-seeing and partying and less (or no) work. Undoubtedly, junkets do occur from time to time. However, I must confess that if Codel-Weldon was a junket, than I certainly would pity those who would be going to one which is not a junket!

The purpose of Codel-Weldon is very surgical. East Asia, especially China — Hong Kong - Taiwan, are becoming increasingly important for the U.S., since the U.S. is now the ONLY "western" Pacific power, technologically, industrially, business-wise and last but not least, militarily in the region. Increasingly our business and industrial activities are linked to that region, there is a great deal of technology transfer back and forth between the two regions, our industry is setting up joint-ventures there. Politically, there are several potential flash-points in the Orient, such as the Taiwan Straits, which if hostility is initiated, will surely involve the U.S. in one way or another. For example, a year ago, events at Taiwan Straits caused President Clinton to direct the presence of two aircraft carriers to the region, a command which very few recent US presidents had to do. Personally I could not recall any since the days of the Quemoy-Matsu incident in the late 50's!

It is my opinion that once a person is elected to be the Congressional representation from a region, he/she is one of the 430 members of our national leadership. To carry out his/her job effectively, he/she must not only be fully aware of the parameters of the regional concerns, but national as well as international ones as well. In this vain, if all our elected congressmen are as hard working and as astute as those on this Codel about regional, national and international affairs, and how serious they approach such problems, then we as citizens are in good hands! For example, in whatever manner a congressman would vote on the issue of MFN for China, we as citizens would certainly want him/her to have the best interest of the U.S. at heart, and to do so could only come from a complete understanding of all aspects of the MFN issue.

When I was a young boy in Singapore, I read a book entitled "the Ugly American" which depicted the incompetence of the U.S. diplomats in the world. Again, if the US foreign service personnel are anything like those we met on this Codel, then what was described in the book was probably something of the past, if it ever was true! Indeed, the diplomats we met on this trip, from our Ambassador or military attaché in Beijing to the General Affairs Officer in Taipei, they are all highly trained, exceedingly hard-working and usually bilingual professionals. The briefings in the Embassies, Consulate and the American Institute in Taiwan (since US and Taiwan have no formal relationships, a non-profit institute was set up to run the day-to-day business between the two countries) were succinct and concise! They certainly demonstrated that the personnels do know the local situation and people well.

From what I can surmise, Codel-Weldon had the following purposes:

1. Bring to the table a proposal for the Chinese People's Congress a direct mechanism to contact with the U.S. Congress. It turns out that virtually all substantial contacts between China and the U.S. were through the Administrative branch of the Government, and inadequate contacts between the respective legislative branches. However, increasingly the U.S. Congress has to deal with many Chinese issues, such as the "annual" MFN votes or to vote on providing Lee Teng-Hui's a private citizen visa to visit his alma mater Cornell University. In addition, there are trade, military and other issues relating to bi-lateral relationship which require in-depth understanding of the situation by the Congress in order to protect U.S. interests. Although the Chinese People's Congress is not parallel in stature and power as the US Congress, it is gaining in importance in recent years.
2. To initiate a dialogue with the Chinese on how to transfer "cold war" hardwares for non-military purposes, especially in the realm of environmental protection (which for China, this is a very serious concern).
3. To see first hand what is happening in Hong Kong five months prior to the transfer of power (from United Kingdom to China).
4. To understand the concerns and aspirations of the Government in Taiwan.

III. What did we do there?

The following is a complete listing of all the meetings we had on this trip. Most meetings were two hours long!
Meetings in Beijing

1. Briefing by the U.S. Embassy (Ambassador Sasser chaired)
2. Meeting with the Host: China People's Institute of Foreign Affairs (PIFA)
3. Working lunch with CPIFA
4. Meeting with the National Environmental Protection Agency

5. Meeting and Dinner with the National People's Congress Foreign Affairs Committee (Chairman Zhu Liang chaired)
6. Meeting with the Ministry of Defense (Lt. General Xiong Guangkai chaired)
7. Meeting with National Defense University (Major General Pan Zhengqiang)
8. State Dinner with State Council Foreign Affairs Director Liu Huaqiu
9. Dinner with US business leaders (IBM, Boeing, Motorola etc)
10. Working breakfast with the American Chamber of Commerce in Beijing.
11. Working lunch at Ambassador Sasser's residence with the Think Tankers Scholars in Beijing regarding strategic matters.
12. Meeting with the Foreign Trade and Economic Cooperation Minister.
13. Meeting with the Staff Members of the Institute of Coal Mining Research.
14. Meeting with State Science and Technology Commission (Chaired by international cooperation bureau deputy director Sun Wanhu)
15. Meeting with China Center for Adoption Affairs (meeting chaired by Director Guo Sijian)
16. An hour meeting with the Prime Minister, Li Peng Meetings in Hong Kong
17. Briefing by Consulate General Richard Boucher
18. Meeting with the Vision 2047
19. Meeting with American Chamber of Commerce in Hong Kong (Due to our delayed arrival, meetings with the Chief executive-designate Tung Chee-Hwa and governor Patten were cancelled)

Meetings in Taipei

20. Briefing at the American Institute in Taiwan (Chaired by Chrisopher Lafleur, Deputy Director of AIT)
21. Meeting with Taipei's city council
22. Meeting with the New Party members of the Taiwan City Council
23. Working dinner with Taiwan's Business people
24. Briefing by the Ministry of Defense (General Tang chaired)
25. Meeting with the Joint Chiefs of Staff

26. Meeting with the Defense Minister
27. Meeting with President Lee Teng-Hui
28. Meeting with Prime Minister Lien Chen
29. Working dinner with Acting Minister of Foreign Affairs.

Epilogue

There is an old Chinese saying: Gan-Kai-Wan-Qian (having a thousand to ten thousand feelings)! I certainly felt that way when I got home and saw my family, after such a whirlwind trip. The best way for me to summarize this report is to give the final anecdote:

Our plane landed in Andrews Airforce base near Washington D.C. As Congressman Weldon and his wife Mary drove home to Philadelphia (they were kind enough to give me a ride home), a bit of "reality" sets in for me since Congressman Weldon's primary concern in that two hour drive was to be able to get to his son's hockey game in West Chester. When we arrived at the game at half time, he was visibly relief! This in itself had some built in humor. After all, some 18 hours earlier, Codel Weldon were driven to the airport by a police escort in Taipei, and was given a high honor sent off by the Ministry of Foreign Affairs in Taiwan. Along the way back, there was a special briefing at Yokuda Airforce Base (near Tokyo), and the Codel was met by all the top brass there. Then at Elmendorf Airforce Base in Alaska, there was a change of crew. During that short stop over, at 4:30 am and –15 degrees below zero (F), we met the Base commander there as well. Therefore it was good to know that when the Congressman got home, attending his son's hockey game was his top priority!

Useful URLs for this report

http://www.ccri.ac.cn/
http://www.redfish.com/USEmbassy-China/frames.htm
http://www.usia.gov/posts/hong_kong.html
http://www.amcham.org.hk/home.html
http://china-window.com/edu/ccmr.html
http://ait.org.tw/

(1997)

www.ingramcontent.com/pod-product-compliance
Lightning Source LLC
Chambersburg PA
CBHW051107230426
43667CB00014B/2470